IMMIGRATION IN THE 21ST CENTURY:
POLITICAL, SOCIAL AND ECONOMIC ISSUES

IMMIGRATION

BORDER SECURITY, CONTROL EFFORTS AND ENFORCEMENT POLICY

IMMIGRATION IN THE 21ST CENTURY: POLITICAL, SOCIAL AND ECONOMIC ISSUES

Additional books and e-books in this series can be found on Nova's website under the Series tab.

IMMIGRATION IN THE 21ST CENTURY:
POLITICAL, SOCIAL AND ECONOMIC ISSUES

IMMIGRATION

BORDER SECURITY, CONTROL EFFORTS AND ENFORCEMENT POLICY

ABEL THOMPSON
EDITOR

snova
New York

Library of Congress Cataloging-in-Publication Data

ISBN: 978-1-53616-187-8

Published by Nova Science Publishers, Inc. † New York

CONTENTS

PREFACE

In January and March 2017, the President issued a series of executive orders related to border security and immigration. The orders direct federal agencies to take a broad range of actions with potential resource implications. For example, Executive Order 13767 instructs DHS to construct a wall or other physical barriers along the U.S. southern border and to hire an additional 5,000 U.S. Border Patrol agents. Executive Order 13768 instructs federal agencies, including DHS and DOJ, to ensure that U.S immigration law is enforced against all removable individuals and directs ICE to hire an additional 10,000 immigration officers.

Executive Order 13780 directs agencies to develop a uniform baseline for screening and vetting standards and procedures; and established nationality-based entry restrictions with respect to visa travelers for a 90-day period, and refugees for 120 days. For the last several years, Central American migrant families have arrived at the U.S.-Mexico border in relatively large numbers, many seeking asylum. Federal immigration laws set forth procedures governing the exclusion and removal of non-U.S. nationals (aliens) who do not meet specified criteria regarding their entry or presence within the United States. Typically, aliens within the United States may not be removed without due process

Chapter 1 - In January and March 2017, the President issued a series of executive orders related to border security and immigration. The orders direct federal agencies to take a broad range of actions with potential resource implications. For example, Executive Order 13767 instructs DHS to construct a wall or other physical barriers along the U.S. southern border and to hire an additional 5,000 U.S. Border Patrol agents. Executive Order 13768 instructs federal agencies, including DHS and DOJ, to ensure that U.S immigration law is enforced against all removable individuals and directs ICE to hire an additional 10,000 immigration officers. Executive Order 13780 directs agencies to develop a uniform baseline for screening and vetting standards and procedures; and established nationality-based entry restrictions with respect to visa travelers for a 90-day period, and refugees for 120 days. GAO was asked to review agencies' implementation of the executive orders and related spending. This chapter addresses (1) actions DHS, DOJ, and State have taken, or plan to take, to implement provisions of the executive orders; and (2) resources to implement provisions of the executive orders, particularly funds DHS, DOJ, and State have obligated, expended, or shifted. GAO reviewed agency planning, tracking, and guidance documents related to the orders, as well as budget requests, appropriations acts, and internal budget information. GAO also interviewed agency officials regarding actions and budgetary costs associated with implementing the orders.

Chapter 2 - In 2014, the United States and Mexico experienced a surge in unauthorized migration from Central America, a region that has overtaken Mexico as the primary source for immigrants apprehended at the U.S.-Mexican border. With U.S. support, Mexico has since increased its immigration control efforts. From 2015 to 2017, Mexico apprehended more than 450,000 migrants and asylum seekers from the "northern triangle" countries (El Salvador, Guatemala, and Honduras; see Figure 1). As at the U.S. southwest border, Mexico's apprehensions of migrants from the northern triangle fell in 2017 but increased by 57% in the first half of 2018 as compared to that period last year. Mexico has received U.S. assistance for its immigration control efforts through the Mérida Initiative, a bilateral partnership launched in 2007 for which Congress has appropriated nearly $2.9 billion. Mexico also has received support for its humanitarian protection program through U.S. Migration and Refugee

Assistance (MRA), implemented by the U.N. High Commissioner for Refugees (UNHCR) and others. Some U.S. policymakers have praised Mexico's immigration control efforts. Others have questioned Mexico's ability to protect migrants from abuse and to provide asylum to those in need of protection. Concerns about Mexico's asylum system have increased as the Trump Administration reportedly has sought to have Mexico absorb U.S.-bound asylum seekers who transit its territory. Negotiations and migration cooperation may shift after Mexico's president-elect, Andrés Manuel López Obrador, takes office on December 1, 2018. López Obrador has pledged to work with the United States on migration issues but has suggested a focus on addressing root causes of illegal migration from southern Mexico and Central America through development programs.

Chapter 3 - In recent years, the migrant population arriving at the U.S.-Mexico (Southern) border without legal immigration status has shifted from being comprised predominantly of Mexican adult economic migrants to being comprised primarily of Central American adults, family units (adults with at least one child under age 18), and unaccompanied children, many of whom seek asylum in the United States. How they are processed and what options they have for legal admission and residing lawfully in the United States depend on how they attempt to enter the United States, whether they are children and/or arrive in families, what country they originate from, and if they request asylum. Aliens (foreign nationals) who wish to enter the United States may request admission legally at a U.S. port of entry or may attempt to enter the United States illegally between ports of entry. The Department of Homeland Security (DHS) has broad discretion to detain aliens, including asylum seekers, during the pendency of removal proceedings that determine whether they are admissible or have other grounds to remain in the United States. Removal proceedings involve either a formal hearing before an immigration judge or a streamlined removal procedure (i.e., *expedited removal*) without hearings or significant review. Arriving foreign nationals who seek asylum (described below) may request it at a U.S. port of entry before an admissions officer with the DHS Customs and Border Protection (CBP) Office of Field Operations, or upon apprehension between U.S. ports of entry before an agent with CBP's U.S. Border Patrol. All aliens requesting asylum are entitled to an interview with an asylum officer to assess the credibility of their asylum claims.

Chapter 4 - The federal government has broad authority over the admission of non-U.S. nationals (aliens) seeking to enter the United States. The Supreme Court has repeatedly held that the government may exclude such aliens without affording them the due process protections that traditionally apply to persons physically present in the United States. Instead, aliens seeking entry are entitled only to those procedural protections that Congress has expressly authorized. Consistent with this broad authority, Congress established an expedited removal process for certain aliens who have arrived in the United States without permission. In general, aliens whom immigration authorities seek to remove from the United States may challenge that determination in administrative proceedings with attendant statutory rights to counsel, evidentiary requirements, and appeal. Under the streamlined expedited removal process created by the Illegal Immigration Reform and Immigrant Responsibility Act of 1996 and codified in Section 235(b)(1) of the Immigration and Nationality Act (INA), however, certain aliens deemed inadmissible by an immigration officer may be removed from the United States without further administrative hearings or review. INA Section 235(b)(1) applies only to certain aliens who are inadmissible into the United States because they either lack valid entry documents or have attempted to procure their admission through fraud or misrepresentation. The statute generally permits the government to summarily remove those aliens if they are arriving in the United States. The statute also authorizes, but does not require, the government to apply this procedure to aliens who are inadmissible on the same grounds if they have been physically present in the country for less than two years. As a matter of practice, however, immigration authorities have applied expedited removal in more limited fashion than potentially authorized by statute—in general, the process is applied strictly to (1) arriving aliens apprehended at a designated port of entry; (2) aliens who arrived in the United States by sea without being admitted or paroled into the country by immigration authorities, and who have been physically present in the United States for less than two years; or (3) aliens who are found in the United States within 100 miles of the border within 14 days of entering the country, who have not been admitted or paroled into the United States by immigration authorities. Nevertheless, expedited removal accounts for a substantial portion of the alien removals each year. And in January 2017, President Trump issued an executive order directing the Department of Homeland Security to expand expedited removal within the broader framework of INA Section 235(b)(1). The agency has yet to promulgate regulations implementing this directive. In some circumstances, however, an alien subject to expedited removal may be entitled to certain procedural protections before he may be removed from the United States. For example, an alien who expresses a fear of persecution may obtain administrative review of his claim, and if his fear is determined credible the alien will be placed in formal removal proceedings where he can pursue asylum and related protections. Additionally, an alien may seek administrative review of a claim that he is a U.S. citizen, lawful permanent resident, admitted refugee, or asylee. Unaccompanied alien children also are statutorily exempted from expedited removal. Given the streamlined nature of expedited removal and the broad discretion afforded to immigration officers to implement that process, challenges have been raised contesting the procedure's constitutionality. In particular, some have argued that the procedure violates aliens' due process rights because aliens placed in expedited removal do not have the opportunity to seek counsel or contest their removal before a judge or other arbiter. Reviewing courts have largely dismissed such challenges for lack of jurisdiction, or, in the alternative, rejected the claims on the grounds that aliens seeking entry into the United States generally do not have constitutional due process protections. But such cases have concerned aliens arriving at the U.S. border or designated ports of entry, and such aliens may be entitled to lesser constitutional protections than aliens located within the United States. Expanding the expedited removal process to aliens located within the interior could compel courts to tackle questions involving the relationship between the federal government's broad power over the entry and removal of aliens and the due process rights of aliens located within the United States.

Chapter 5 - For the last several years, Central American migrant families have arrived at the U.S.-Mexico border in relatively large numbers, many seeking asylum. While some request asylum at U.S. ports of entry, others do so after entering the United States "without inspection" (i.e., illegally) between U.S. ports of entry. On May 7, 2018, the Department of Justice (DOJ) implemented a "zero tolerance" policy toward illegal border crossing both to discourage illegal migration into the United States and to reduce the burden of processing asylum claims that Administration officials contend are often fraudulent. Under the zero tolerance policy, DOJ prosecuted all adult aliens apprehended crossing the border illegally, with no exception for asylum seekers or those with minor children. DOJ's policy represented a change in the level of enforcement of an existing statute rather than a change in statute or regulation. Prior Administrations prosecuted illegal border crossings relatively infrequently. Criminally prosecuting adults for illegal border crossing requires detaining them in federal criminal facilities where children are not permitted. While DOJ and the Department of Homeland Security (DHS) have broad statutory authority to detain adult aliens, children must be detained according to guidelines established in the Flores Settlement Agreement (FSA), the Homeland Security Act of 2002, and the Trafficking Victims Protection Reauthorization Act of 2008. A 2015 judicial ruling held that children remain in family immigration detention for no more than 20 days. If parents cannot be released with them, children are treated as unaccompanied alien children and transferred to the Department of Health and Human Services' (HHS's) Office of Refugee Resettlement (ORR) for care and custody. The widely publicized family separations were a consequence of the Trump Administration's zero tolerance policy, not the result of an explicit family separation policy. Since the zero tolerance policy was implemented, up to 3,000 children may have been separated from their parents. In addition, thousands more were separated prior to the public announcement of the policy change. Following mostly critical public reaction, President Trump issued an executive order on June 20, 2018, mandating that DHS maintain custody of alien families during the pendency of any criminal trial or immigration proceedings. DHS Customs and Border Protection (CBP) subsequently stopped referring most illegal border crossers to DOJ for criminal prosecution. A federal judge then mandated that all separated children be promptly reunited with their families. Another rejected DOJ's request to modify the FSA to extend the 20-day child detention guideline. DHS has since reverted to some prior immigration enforcement policies, and family separations continue to occur based upon DHS enforcement protocols in place prior to the 2018 zero tolerance policy. Administration officials and immigration enforcement advocates argue that measures like the zero tolerance policy are necessary to discourage migrants from coming to the United States and submitting fraudulent asylum requests. They maintain that alien family separation resulting from the prosecution of illegal border crossers mirrors that which occurs regularly under the U.S. criminal justice system policy where adults with custody of minor children are charged with a crime and may be held in jail, effectively separating them from their children. Immigrant advocates contend that migrant families are fleeing legitimate threats from countries with exceptionally high rates of gang violence, and that family separations resulting from the zero tolerance policy are cruel and violate fundamental human rights—such as the ability to request asylum. They maintain that the zero tolerance policy was hastily implemented and lacked planning for family reunification following criminal prosecutions. Some observers question the Trump Administration's capacity to marshal sufficient resources to prosecute all illegal border crossers without additional resources. Others criticize the family separation policy in light of less expensive alternatives to detention. In prior years, most individuals apprehended were single adult males. Family unit apprehensions, which increased from just over 11,000 in FY2012 to 99,901 in the first four months of FY2019, and apprehensions of unaccompanied alien children are occurring within the context of otherwise relatively low historical levels of total alien apprehensions. In addition, the national origin of recently apprehended family units and unaccompanied children has shifted to mostly Central American from long-term trends of mostly Mexican.

Chapter 6 - Congress's power to create rules governing the admission of non-U.S. nationals (aliens) has long been viewed as plenary. In the Immigration and Nationality Act (INA), as amended, Congress has specified grounds for the exclusion or removal of aliens, including on account of criminal activity. Some criminal offenses, when committed by an alien who is present in the United States, may render that alien subject to removal from the country. And certain criminal offenses may preclude an alien outside the United States from being either admitted into the country or permitted to reenter following an initial departure. Further, criminal conduct may disqualify an alien from certain forms of relief from removal or prevent the alien from becoming a U.S. citizen. In some cases, the INA directly identifies particular offenses that carry immigration consequences; in other cases, federal immigration law provides that a general category of crimes, such as "crimes involving moral turpitude" or an offense defined by the INA as an "aggravated felony," may render an alien ineligible for certain benefits and privileges under immigration law. The INA distinguishes between the treatment of aliens who have been lawfully admitted into the United States and those who are either seeking admission into the country or are physically present in the country without having been lawfully admitted. Aliens who have been lawfully admitted into the country may be removed if they engage in conduct that renders them *deportable*, whereas aliens who have not been legally admitted into the United States—including both aliens seeking initial entry into the United States as well as those who are physically present in the country but were never lawfully admitted—may be excluded or removed from the country if they have engaged in conduct rendering them *inadmissible*. Although the INA designates certain criminal activities and categories of criminal activities as grounds for inadmissibility or deportation, the respective grounds are not identical. Moreover, a conviction for a designated crime is not always required for an alien to be disqualified on criminal grounds from admission into the United States. But for nearly all criminal grounds for deportation, a "conviction" (as defined by the INA) for the underlying offense is necessary. Additionally, although certain criminal conduct may disqualify an alien from various immigration-related benefits or forms of relief, the scope of disqualifying conduct varies depending on the particular benefit or form of relief at issue. This chapter identifies the major criminal grounds that may bar an alien from being admitted into the United States or render an alien within the country removable. The chapter also discusses additional immigration consequences of criminal activity, including those that make an alien ineligible for certain relief from removal, including cancellation of removal, voluntary departure, withholding of removal, and asylum. The chapter also addresses the criminal grounds that render an alien ineligible to adjust to lawful permanent resident (LPR) status, as well as those grounds barring LPRs from naturalizing as U.S. citizens. The chapter also discusses the scope of several general criminal categories referenced by the INA, including "crimes involving moral turpitude," "aggravated felonies," and "crimes of violence."

In: Immigration
Editor: Abel Thompson
ISBN: 978-1-53616-187-8

Chapter 1

BORDER SECURITY AND IMMIGRATION: INITIAL EXECUTIVE ORDER ACTIONS AND RESOURCE IMPLICATIONS*

United States Government Accountability Office

ABBREVIATIONS

ADP	Average Daily Population
AUSA	Assistant United States Attorneys
BSFIT	Border Security Fencing, Infrastructure, and Technology
Border Patrol	U.S. Border Patrol
CA	Bureau of Consular Affairs
CAP	Criminal Alien Program
CAPSET	Criminal Alien Program Surge Enforcement Team
CBP	U.S. Customs and Border Protection
DHS	Department of Homeland Security

* This is an edited, reformatted and augmented version of United States Government Accountability Office; Report to Congressional Requesters, Publication No. GAO-18-470, dated June 2018.

DOJ	Department of Justice
EOIR	Executive Office for Immigration Review
EOTF	Executive Order Task Force
EOUSA	Executive Office for United States Attorneys
FDNS	Fraud Detection and National Security
FLETC	Federal Law Enforcement Training Centers
ICE	U.S. Immigration and Customs Enforcement
OHC	Office of Human Capital
PEP	Priority Enforcement Program
PRM	Bureau of Population, Migration, and Refugees
State	Department of State
USCIS	U.S. Citizenship and Immigration Services
USMS	U.S. Marshals Service
USRAP	U.S. Refugee Admissions Program
VOICE	Victims of Immigration Crime Engagement

Why GAO Did This Study

In January and March 2017, the President issued a series of executive orders related to border security and immigration. The orders direct federal agencies to take a broad range of actions with potential resource implications. For example, Executive Order 13767 instructs DHS to construct a wall or other physical barriers along the U.S. southern border and to hire an additional 5,000 U.S. Border Patrol agents. Executive Order 13768 instructs federal agencies, including DHS and DOJ, to ensure that U.S immigration law is enforced against all removable individuals and directs ICE to hire an additional 10,000 immigration officers. Executive Order 13780 directs agencies to develop a uniform baseline for screening and vetting standards and procedures; and established nationality-based entry restrictions with respect to visa travelers for a 90-day period, and refugees for 120 days.

GAO was asked to review agencies' implementation of the executive orders and related spending. This chapter addresses (1) actions DHS, DOJ, and State have taken, or plan to take, to implement provisions of the executive orders; and (2) resources to implement provisions of the executive orders, particularly funds DHS, DOJ, and State have obligated, expended, or shifted. GAO reviewed agency planning, tracking, and guidance documents related to the orders, as well as budget requests, appropriations acts, and internal budget information. GAO also interviewed agency officials regarding actions and budgetary costs associated with implementing the orders.

What GAO Found

The Departments of Homeland Security (DHS), Justice (DOJ), and State issued internal and public reports such as studies and progress updates, developed or revised policies, and took initial planning and programmatic actions to implement Executive Orders 13767, 13768, and 13780. For example:

- DHS's U.S. Customs and Border Protection (CBP) started the acquisition process for a Border Wall System Program and issued task orders to design and construct barrier prototypes. In November 2017, CBP awarded a contract worth up to $297 million to help with hiring 5,000 U.S. Border Patrol agents, 2,000 CBP officers, and 500 Air and Marine Operations agents.
- DOJ issued memoranda providing guidance for federal prosecutors on prioritizing certain immigration-related criminal offenses. Additionally, from March through October 2017, DOJ detailed approximately 40 immigration judge positions to detention centers and to the southern border to conduct removal and other related proceedings, according to DOJ officials.
- State participated in an interagency working group to develop uniform standards related to the adjudication of visa applications, interviews, and system security checks. State also implemented

visa and refugee entry restrictions in accordance with the Supreme Court's June 26, 2017, ruling.

Agency officials anticipate that implementing the executive orders will be a multiyear endeavor comprising additional reporting, planning, and other actions.

DHS, DOJ, and State used existing fiscal year 2017 resources to support initial executive order actions that fit within their established mission areas. GAO found that it was not always possible to disaggregate which fiscal year 2017 funds were used for implementation of the orders versus other agency activities. All three agencies indicated that they used existing personnel to implement the orders and, in some cases, these efforts took substantial time. For example, according to ICE data, personnel spent about 14,000 regular hours (the equivalent of 1,750 8-hour days) and 2,400 overtime hours planning for the ICE hiring surge from January 2017 through January 2018.

In March 2017, the President submitted a budget amendment along with a request for $3 billion in supplemental appropriations for DHS to implement the orders. In May 2017, DHS received an appropriation of just over $1.1 billion, some of which DHS used to fund actions to implement the orders. For example, CBP received $65 million for hiring and, according to CBP officials, used these funds to plan and prepare for the surge in U.S. Border Patrol agents. As of January 2018, CBP had obligated $18.8 million of the $65 million.

Agencies plan to continue to use their base budgets and request additional funds as needed to carry out their missions and implement the orders. For example, for fiscal year 2018, CBP requested approximately $1.6 billion and received (in March 2018) approximately $1.3 billion to build new and replace existing sections of physical barriers along the southern border. For fiscal year 2019, ICE requested $571 million to hire 2,000 immigration officers and DOJ requested approximately $40 million to hire new immigration judges and supporting staff.

June 12, 2018
Congressional Requesters

In 2017, the President issued a series of executive orders related to border security and immigration. The orders direct federal agencies to take a broad range of actions with potential resource implications. Specifically, Executive Order 13767, *Border Security and Immigration Enforcement Improvements*, instructs the Department of Homeland Security (DHS) to immediately plan, design, and construct a wall or other physical barriers along the U.S. southern border and to hire an additional 5,000 U.S. Border Patrol (Border Patrol) agents, among other border security initiatives.[1] Executive Order 13768, *Enhancing Public Safety in the Interior of the United States*, instructs federal agencies, including DHS and the Department of Justice (DOJ), to ensure that U.S immigration law is enforced against all removable individuals; establishes the administration's enforcement priorities; and directs U.S. Immigration and Customs Enforcement (ICE) to hire an additional 10,000 immigration officers, among other things.[2] Finally, Executive Order 13780, *Protecting the Nation from Foreign Terrorist Entry into the United States*, among other things, states that it is U.S. policy to improve the screening and vetting protocols and procedures associated with the visa-issuance process and U.S. Refugee Admissions Program; imposed visa entry restrictions on foreign nationals from certain listed countries for a 90-day period; and suspended all refugee admissions for 120 days.[3]

In light of the number of policy and programmatic requirements in the executive orders, you asked us to review federal agency actions and budgetary costs associated with implementation. This chapter examines (1)

---

[1] Exec. Order No. 13767, §§ 4, 8, 82 Fed. Reg. 8793, 8794-95 (Jan. 30, 2017) (issued Jan. 25). The order defines the southern border as the contiguous land border between the United States and Mexico, including all points of entry. The order also defines "wall" to include a contiguous, physical wall, as well as other similar physical barriers.

[2] Exec. Order No. 13768, §§ 4, 5, 7, 82 Fed. Reg. 8799, 8800 (Jan. 30, 2017) (issued Jan. 25).

[3] Exec. Order No. 13780, §§ 1, 2, 6, 82 Fed. Reg. 13,209, 13,212-,213, 13,215-,216 (Mar. 9, 2017) (issued Mar. 6). Throughout this chapter, we generally use the term "foreign national" in reference to an "alien," defined under U.S. immigration law as any person who is not a citizen or national of the United States. See 8 U.S.C. § 1101(a)(3).

actions DHS, DOJ, and the Department of State (State) have taken, or plan to take, to implement provisions of the executive orders; and (2) resources to implement provisions of the executive orders, particularly funds DHS, DOJ, and State have obligated, expended, or shifted.

For the purposes of this review, we focused our audit work on DHS, DOJ, and State because they are responsible for implementing the majority of the provisions in the three executive orders.[4] To address the first objective, we identified actions planned, completed, or underway at DHS, DOJ, and State as of March 2018 by reviewing and cataloguing specific provisions included in the executive orders and by reviewing available agency-wide planning and tracking documents, such as a DHS inventory of tasks related to the executive orders and their implementation status. We also obtained and reviewed executive order-related memoranda issued by agency leadership to identify actions they directed within their respective departments. We conducted semi-structured interviews with officials at key components, program offices, and bureaus at the three agencies, and utilized a data collection instrument in which we asked agencies to identify actions either planned, completed, or underway to implement the executive orders. We corroborated actions identified with documentation, such as recruiting and hiring plans and statements of work. Additionally, we reviewed strategic and operational policies, guidance, and memoranda that agencies developed or revised in response to executive order provisions.

To address the second objective, we worked to identify any funds DHS, DOJ, and State obligated, expended, or shifted within or between appropriation accounts to implement tangible, measurable, and quantifiable executive order provisions. Specifically, we reviewed the executive orders and placed each provision into one of three categories: (1) *analyses and reports*, (2) *policies,* and (3) *programs*. We defined the *analyses and reports* category as executive order provisions that direct agencies to review and analyze data, policies, processes, and operational mission areas and produce reports. We defined the *policies* category as executive order

[4] Additional agencies tasked with fewer, supporting responsibilities in the executive orders include the Department of Interior, Office of the Director of National Intelligence, and Office of Personnel Management. Given their general supporting roles, these agencies are excluded from the scope of our review.

provisions that establish new or modify existing policies, guidance, or processes related to border security or immigration. We defined the *programs* category as tangible, measurable, and quantifiable executive order provisions that implement policies. We confirmed our categorization with each agency, particularly for the *programs* category, since the extent to which a provision is tangible, measurable, and quantifiable was not always clearly discernable. To confirm the *programs* category for DHS, we conducted a crosswalk between our internal categorization, actions in the DHS inventory of tasks, and provisions that the DHS Office of Budget identified as requiring resources. To confirm the *programs* category for DOJ and State, we corroborated our categorization by asking officials from each agency if actions taken or planned to implement the provisions required resources. In some cases, we moved policy provisions to the *program* category if agency efforts underway to implement the policy were programmatic in nature.

For each agency, we collected available budgetary information—specifically, any funds requested, appropriated, obligated, and expended—from January 2017 through March 2018 for the implementation of executive order provisions that we categorized as *programs*. We reviewed publicly available budget requests, congressional budget justifications, appropriations acts, and budgetary data from agencies' internal data systems.[5] While we were able to identify certain funds requested, provided, or designated for executive order implementation from these documents, it was not always possible to extract funds specifically meant for implementing the executive orders from budget requests, appropriations, or expenditures for more general purposes. To specifically identify funds used for executive order implementation, we reviewed agency documentation, interviewed agency budget and program officials, and submitted written questions as necessary. In instances where there was no explicit distinction between funds for executive order implementation and funds for regular operations, we identified, and made note of, the larger account used for

[5] There is no central intra- or interagency repository for budget information related to the executive orders. Therefore, we collected and aggregated budgetary data from systems used by individual agency components and offices.

executive order implementation. In addition, where agencies identified that they used personnel resources to implement the executive orders, we collected related data as available. We analyzed agency documentation on the policies, procedures, and processes for maintaining internal data and interviewed agency officials about their data collection practices to assess the reliability of these data. We determined that the data were sufficiently reliable for the purposes of our reporting objectives.

To further address our second objective, we identified official reprogramming or transfer requests and approvals specifically for implementation of executive order provisions that we categorized as *programs*.[6] We also interviewed DHS, DOJ, and State budget officials to identify any funds that were re-classified, reallocated, or otherwise shifted for different programs, activities, or purposes at lower thresholds not subject to time and condition limitations for official reprogramming or transfer requests.[7] Additionally, we collected and reviewed documentation related to funds moved from existing programs to implement the executive orders from January 2017 through March 2018. We corroborated this information by interviewing agency budget and program officials to

---

[6] Reprogramming is shifting funds within an appropriation or fund account for purposes other than those contemplated at the time of appropriation; it is the shifting of funds from one object class to another within an appropriation or from one program activity to another. Transfer is the shifting of all or part of the budget authority in one appropriation or fund account to another. Agencies may transfer budget authority only as specifically authorized by law. In certain instances, there are also statutory requirements related to reprogrammings. See, e.g., DHS Appropriations Act, 2017, Pub. L. No. 115-31, div. F, tit. V, § 503, 131 Stat. 135, 424; DHS Appropriations Act, 2018, Pub. L. No. 115-141, div. F, tit. V, § 503 (setting notification thresholds and procedures for the reprogramming of fiscal year 2017 and 2018 funds).

[7] Section 503 of the DHS Appropriations Act, 2017 prohibits, among other things, reprogramming of fiscal year 2017 funds to augment funding for existing efforts by the lesser of more than $5 million or 10 percent, unless the Senate and House Appropriations Committees are notified at least 15 days in advance of any such reprogramming. As to transfers, up to 5 percent of any appropriation made available for fiscal year 2017 may be transferred between such appropriations if the Senate and House Appropriations Committees are notified at least 30 days in advance, provided further that no appropriation is to be increased by more than 10 percent. The aforementioned restrictions on reprogrammings and transfers also apply to the use of prior year deobligated balances. Pub. L. No. 115-31, div. F, tit. V, § 503, 131 Stat. 135, 424-425; see also Pub. L. No. 115- 141, div. F, tit. V, § 503. There are certain exceptions to these general limitations. See e.g., Pub. L. No. 115-31, div. F, tit. II, § 209, 131 Stat. at 412; Pub. L. No. 115-141, div. F, tit. II, § 209 (generally allowing unrestricted reprogramming and transfer within and into ICE's Operations and Support account to detain removable foreign nationals).

determine resource prioritization and what funds, if any, agencies reprogrammed or transferred—or planned to reprogram or transfer—from other existing programs to implement the executive orders.

We conducted this performance audit from October 2017 to June 2018 in accordance with generally accepted government auditing standards. Those standards require that we plan and perform the audit to obtain sufficient, appropriate evidence to provide a reasonable basis for our findings and conclusions based on our audit objectives. We believe that the evidence obtained provides a reasonable basis for our findings and conclusions based on our audit objectives.

BACKGROUND

Executive Order Summaries

The President issued two executive orders addressing border security and immigration enforcement on January 25, 2017.[8] These orders direct executive branch agencies to implement a series of reporting, policy, and programmatic provisions to carry out the administration's border security and immigration policies and priorities.[9]

---

[8] Exec. Order Nos. 13767, 13768, 82 Fed. Reg. 8793 & 8799 (Jan. 30, 2017). An executive order is a signed and written directive from the President of the United States that manages operations of the federal government, and is published in the *Federal Register*. While executive orders are not legislation passed by Congress, they are directives authorized by the President, and therefore have the force of law and are binding within the Executive Branch, except to the extent there is any inconsistency with existing statute.

[9] The administration has taken other border security and immigration enforcement actions related to these executive orders. For example, on April 4, 2018, the President issued a memorandum directing the Department of Defense to support DHS in securing the southern border by requesting the use of National Guard personnel to assist in fulfilling the mission of border security. Further, on April 6, 2018, the President issued a memorandum related to Sections 5, 6, and 11 of Executive Order 13767 and Sections 6 and 12 of Executive Order 13768, which directed federal agencies to take various actions, including submitting a report to the President on, among other things, efforts to establish detention facilities at the southern border, assign asylum officers to such facilities, ensure detention of foreign nationals apprehended for immigration violations, and prevent exploitation of parole and asylum provisions.

- Executive Order 13767 lays out key policies of the executive branch with regard to securing the southern border, preventing further unlawful entry into the United States, and repatriating removable foreign nationals.[10] To support these purposes, the order directs DHS to, among other actions, produce a comprehensive study of the security of the southern border; issue new policy guidance regarding the appropriate and consistent use of detention of foreign nationals for violations of immigration law; plan, design, and construct a wall or other physical barriers along the southern border; and hire and onboard, as soon as practicable, 5,000 additional Border Patrol agents.[11]
- Executive Order 13767 also directs DOJ to assign immigration judges to immigration detention facilities in order to conduct removal and other related proceedings.[12]
- Executive Order 13768 focuses on immigration enforcement within the United States. Among other things, the order lays out the administration's immigration enforcement priorities for removable foreign nationals;[13] directs ICE to hire 10,000 additional immigration officers; states that, as permitted by law, it is the policy of the executive branch to empower state and local law enforcement officials to perform the functions of immigration officers; calls for weekly public reports on criminal actions committed by foreign nationals and any jurisdictions that do not honor ICE detainers with respect to such individuals;[14] and terminates the Priority Enforcement Program while reinstituting

---

[10] Exec. Order No. 13767, § 1, 82 Fed. Reg. at 8793.

[11] See id. §§ 4, 6, 8, 82 Fed. Reg. at 8794-8795.

[12] Id. at § 5(c), 82 Fed. Reg. at 8794.

[13] Under U.S. immigration law, a foreign national is removable if: (1) not admitted to the United States and found inadmissible under section 212 of the Immigration and Nationality Act (INA); or (2) admitted to the United States and deemed deportable under INA § 237. See 8 U.S.C. §§ 1182, 1227, 1229a(c), (e)(2). Those determined to be removable and not eligible for any requested relief or protection are to be removed pursuant to an administratively final order of removal. 8 C.F.R. § 1241.1.

[14] A detainer is a notice of ICE's intent to assume custody of a foreign national who is suspected or determined to be removable by ICE, along with a request that the law enforcement agency maintain custody of the foreign national for up to 48 hours and notify ICE before such removable individual is released.

> Secure Communities.[15] The order also directs DHS and DOJ to ensure that jurisdictions that willfully prohibit or otherwise restrict communication with DHS regarding immigration status information are not eligible to receive federal grants, except as determined necessary for law enforcement purposes.[16]

On March 6, 2017, the President issued Executive Order 13780.[17] This order directed agencies to take various actions to improve the screening and vetting protocols and procedures associated with the visa-issuance process and the U.S. Refugee Admissions Program. Specifically, the order directed agencies to conduct a worldwide review to identify any additional information needed from each foreign country to adjudicate visas and other immigration benefits to ensure that individuals applying for such benefits are not a security or public-safety threat.[18] The order also instituted visa

---

[15] Exec. Order No. 13768, §§ 5, 7, 8, 9, 82 Fed. Reg. at 8800-8801. Under the Priority Enforcement Program, ICE issued a request for detainer (with probable cause of removability), information, or transfer, for a priority removable individual, such as one posing a threat to national security or public safety, including a foreign national convicted of a felony, among others, under DHS's former tiered civil enforcement categories. Under Secure Communities, ICE may issue detainers for removable individuals charged, but not yet convicted, of criminal offenses, in addition to individuals subject to a final order of removal whether or not they have a criminal history.

[16] See id. § 9(a), 82 Fed. Reg. at 8801. Executive Order 13768 refers to jurisdictions that willfully refuse to comply with 8 U.S.C § 1373, and prohibit sending immigration status information to, or receiving such data from, DHS, as "sanctuary jurisdictions."

[17] Executive Order 13780 (82 Fed. Reg. 13,209 (March 9, 2017)) revoked and replaced a prior order, Exec. Order No. 13769, 82 Fed. Reg. 8977 (Feb. 1, 2017) (issued Jan. 27), implementation of which had been largely blocked nationwide shortly after issuance, due to a federal court injunction. See *Washington v. Trump*, 2017 U.S. Dist. LEXIS 16012 (W.D. Wash. 2017), *aff'd*, 847 F.3d 1151 (9th Cir. 2017). On September 24, 2017, pursuant to section 2(e) of Executive Order 13780, the President issued Presidential Proclamation 9645, Enhancing Vetting Capabilities and Processes for Detecting Attempted Entry into the United States by Terrorists or Other Public-Safety Threats, which expanded the scope and duration of nationality-based visa entry restrictions from six to eight countries (removing Sudan, and adding Chad, North Korea and Venezuela), and from a 90-day to an indefinite period for the revised list of countries. After challenges to Executive Order 13780 entry restrictions, as curtailed by the Supreme Court's ruling of June 26, 2017, were rendered moot, litigation continued with respect to Presidential Proclamation 9645. Beginning on December 8, 2017, the Proclamation's visa entry restrictions have been fully implemented pursuant to the Supreme Court's December 4, 2017, orders staying the lower courts' injunctions, while the Supreme Court reviews Hawaii and Maryland federal district court rulings generally upheld by the Ninth and Fourth Circuits, respectively.

[18] Exec. Order No. 13780, § 2, 82 Fed. Reg. at 13,212.

entry restrictions for nationals from certain listed countries for a 90-day period; directed agencies to develop a uniform baseline for screening and vetting standards and procedures; and suspended the U.S. Refugee Admissions Program for 120 days in order to review refugee application and adjudication procedures.[19] The order further directed DHS to expedite the completion and implementation of a biometric entry-exit tracking system for travelers to the United States.[20] Implementation of Executive Order 13780 entry restrictions for visa travelers and refugees commenced on June 29, 2017, subject to a June 26 ruling of the U.S. Supreme Court prohibiting enforcement of such restrictions against foreign nationals with a credible claim of a bona fide relationship to a person or entity in the United States.[21]

Federal Budget Process and Status Since Executive Order Issuance

The federal budget process provides the means for the President and Congress to make informed decisions between competing national needs and policies, allocate resources among federal agencies, and ensure laws are executed according to established priorities. The President generally submits the budget request for the upcoming fiscal year to Congress no later than the first Monday of February (e.g., the fiscal year 2019 budget request was submitted in February 2018). To ensure there is not a lapse in appropriations for one or more federal departments or agencies, regular appropriations bills must be enacted to fund the government before the expiration of the prior appropriations, which would typically be in effect through September 30 in a regular appropriations cycle. If these regular

---

[19] See id. §§ 2, 5, 6, 82 Fed. Reg. at 13,212-,213, 13,215-,216. Specifically, visa entry restrictions applied to foreign nationals from six countries of particular concern—Iran, Libya, Somalia, Sudan, Syria, and Yemen—for a 90-day period. Executive Order 13769, which was revoked and replaced by Executive Order 13780, had temporarily suspended entry of Iraqi nationals as well; however, Executive Order 13780 did not include Iraq in the list of countries whose nationals were subject to visa entry restrictions, citing it as presenting a special case.

[20] Id. at § 8, 82 Fed. Reg. at 13,216.

[21] See *Trump v. Int'l Refugee Assistance Project*, 137 S. Ct. 2080 (2017) (per curiam).

full-year appropriations bills are not enacted by the deadline, Congress must pass a continuing appropriation (or resolution) to temporarily fund government operations into the next fiscal year. For fiscal year 2017, multiple continuing appropriations were enacted to extend funding until the Consolidated Appropriations Act, 2017, was enacted in May 2017.

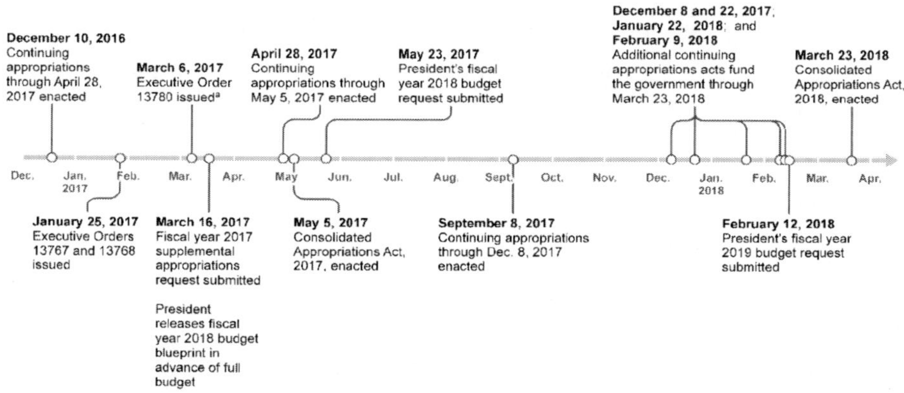

Source: GAO summary of executive order and federal budget information. | GAO-18-470.

[a]Executive Order 13780 revoked and replaced a prior order, Executive Order 13769, implementation of which had been largely enjoined nationwide shortly after issuance due to a federal court injunction.

Figure 1. Timeline of Executive Order Issuance and Federal Budget Milestones, Fiscal Year 2017 through March 2018.

At the time the President issued the executive orders in January and March of 2017, agencies were operating under a continuing appropriation which did not incorporate any funding explicitly for the administration's immigration and border security priorities, such as hiring 5,000 additional Border Patrol agents. The administration sought additional funds to implement the executive orders through an out-of-cycle March 2017 budget amendment and supplemental appropriations request for the remainder of fiscal year 2017.[22] In May 2017, Congress provided funding for selected priorities through the Consolidated Appropriations Act,

[22] This March 2017 request for additional appropriations was made as part of an amendment to the President's fiscal year 2017 budget submitted under the prior administration.

2017.[23] The administration submitted additional funding requests related to the executive orders through the President's fiscal year 2018 and 2019 budget requests. A number of continuing appropriations acts were enacted from September 2017 through February 2018, providing fiscal year 2018 funding at fiscal year 2017 levels through March 23, 2018. The Consolidated Appropriations Act, 2018, was signed into law on March 23, 2018, providing funding for government operations for the remainder of fiscal year 2018.[24] Figure 1 below provides a timeline of executive order issuance and key milestones in the budget process from December 2016 through March 2018.

Agency Roles and Responsibilities

DHS, DOJ, and State each play key roles in enforcing U.S. immigration law and securing U.S. borders. Key components and bureaus at the three agencies, and their general roles and responsibilities with regard to border security and immigration enforcement, are described in Table 1.

DHS, DOJ, and State Took Initial Planning and Programming Actions to Implement Provisions of the Executive Orders

DHS, DOJ, and State issued reports, developed or revised policies, and took initial planning and programmatic actions in response to the executive orders. Each agency took a distinct approach to implementing the orders based on its organizational structure and the scope of its responsibilities.

---

[23] See Pub. L. No. 115-31, 131 Stat. 135, and accompanying Explanatory Statement, 163 Cong. Rec. H3327 (daily ed. May 3, 2017).

[24] Pub. L. No. 115-141, 132 Stat. 348.

Table 1. Selected Department of Homeland Security (DHS), Department of Justice (DOJ), and Department of State (State) Components and Bureaus and Their Roles in Border Security and Immigration Enforcement

DHS Components	Role in border security and immigration enforcement
U.S. Customs and Border Protection (CBP)	Within CBP, the U.S. Border Patrol serves as the office with primary responsibility for securing the border between land ports of entry; Air and Marine Operations interdicts and disrupts threats to the United States in the air and maritime environments at and beyond the border and within the nation's interior; and the Office of Field Operations coordinates CBP enforcement activities at land, air, and sea ports of entry, to include conducting immigration and customs inspections.
U.S. Immigration and Customs Enforcement (ICE)	ICE is responsible for immigration enforcement and investigations within the United States, and also plays a role in preventing terrorism and combatting transnational criminal threats. This includes identifying, apprehending, detaining, litigating charges of removability against, and removing foreign nationals in the United States in violation of U.S. immigration laws; as well as investigating, disrupting, and dismantling terrorist, transnational, and other criminal organizations.
U.S. Citizenship and Immigration Services (USCIS)	USCIS oversees lawful immigration to the United States through adjudicating immigration applications and petitions, verifying immigration status for public benefits, and granting employment authorization, among other duties.
Federal Law Enforcement Training Centers	Federal Law Enforcement Training Centers provides career-long training to law enforcement professionals, including CBP and ICE officers.
DOJ Components	
Executive Office for Immigration Review	Executive Office for Immigration Review conducts immigration court proceedings, appellate reviews, and administrative hearings to administer and interpret U.S. immigration laws.
U.S. Attorneys Offices	U.S. Attorneys serve as the nation's principal federal prosecutors enforcing federal laws in their respective districts throughout the country. They prosecute federal criminal cases in their districts, including those involving criminal immigration offenses.
U.S. Marshals Service (USMS)	USMS provides federal judicial security, apprehends fugitives, and secures and transports pre-trial detainees and federal prisoners from arrest to incarceration, including individuals suspected or determined to be in violation of U.S. immigration laws.
Federal Bureau of Prisons	Federal Bureau of Prisons is responsible for the custody and care of federal inmates, including inmates suspected or determined to be in violation of U.S. immigration laws.

Table 1. (Continued)

State Bureaus	
Bureau of Consular Affairs	Bureau of Consular Affairs provides consular services to, among other things, protect U.S. citizens and their interests abroad, ensure U.S. border security, and facilitate the entry of legitimate travelers. Bureau staff at embassies and consulates overseas adjudicate visa applications and manage the application process in coordination with several departments and agencies.
Bureau of Population, Refugees, and Migration	Bureau of Population, Refugees, and Migration manages the process by which refugees seek to be resettled in the United States, including working with USCIS, which makes refugee admission determinations, and coordinating travel and arrivals of refugees.

Source: GAO summary of DHS, DOJ, and State information. | GAO-18-470.

Each executive order established near-term reporting requirements for agencies, including updates on the status of their efforts, studies to inform planning and implementation, and reports for the public. According to officials, agencies focused part of their initial implementation efforts on meeting these reporting requirements.[25] In addition, agencies developed and revised policies, initiated planning efforts, and made initial program changes (such as expanding or expediting programs) to reflect the administration's priorities.

DHS

DHS established an Executive Order Task Force (EOTF), which was responsible for coordinating and tracking initial component actions to implement the executive orders. The EOTF assembled an operational planning team with representatives from key DHS components, such as U.S. Customs and Border Protection (CBP) and ICE. The EOTF and the planning team inventoried tasks in the orders, assigned component responsibilities for tasks, and monitored the status of the tasks through an online tracking mechanism and weekly coordination meetings. Additionally, the EOTF coordinated and moved reports required by the

[25] Examples of executive order reports are included in the sections below. For a full list of reports agencies completed in response to the orders, see appendix II.

orders through DHS. For example, Section 4 of Executive Order 13767 directed DHS to produce a comprehensive study of the security of the southern border. DHS completed and submitted this chapter to the White House on November 22, 2017, according to EOTF officials. DHS also publicly issued three Declined Detainer Outcome Reports pursuant to Section 9 of Executive Order 13768.[26] Additionally, EOTF officials stated that, in 2017, DHS produced and submitted to the White House 90-day and 180-day reports on the progress of implementing Executive Orders 13767 and 13768.

The Secretary of Homeland Security issued two memoranda establishing policy and providing guidance related to Executive Orders 13767 and 13768 in February 2017. One memorandum implemented Executive Order 13767 by outlining new policies designed to stem illegal entry into the United States and to facilitate the detection, apprehension, detention, and removal of foreign nationals seeking to unlawfully enter or remain in the United States.[27] For example, the memorandum directed U.S. Citizenship and Immigration Services (USCIS), CBP, and ICE to ensure that appropriate guidance and training is provided to agency officials to ensure proper exercise of parole in accordance with existing statue.[28] The other memorandum implemented Executive Order 13768 and provided additional guidance with respect to the enforcement of immigration laws.[29] For example, it terminated the Priority Enforcement Program, under which ICE prioritized the apprehension, detention, and removal of foreign

---

[26] In declining a detainer, a law enforcement agency will release a potentially removable individual upon conclusion of their term of imprisonment, instead of continuing to hold them in custody pursuant to a detainer request. The Declined Detainer Outcome Report is a weekly report that shows jurisdictions with the highest volume of declined detainers and includes a list of examples of crimes associated with those released individuals. ICE issued three reports in January and February 2017. According to ICE officials, ICE subsequently suspended issuance of this chapter to analyze and refine its reporting methodologies.

[27] Department of Homeland Security, *Implementing the President's Border Security and Immigration Enforcement Improvement Policies,* (February 2017).

[28] Parole, granted on a discretionary and case-by-case basis by the Secretary of Homeland Security for urgent humanitarian reasons or significant public benefit, permits a foreign national to enter the United States temporarily, without constituting an admission. 8 U.S.C. § 1182(d)(5).

[29] Department of Homeland Security, *Enforcement of the Immigration Laws to Serve the National Interest*, (February 2017).

nationals who posed threats to national security, public safety, or border security, including convicted felons; and restored the Secure Communities Program, pursuant to which ICE may also target for removal those charged, but not yet convicted, of criminal offenses, among others. Additionally, the memorandum reiterated DHS's general enforcement priorities. ICE, CBP, and USCIS may allocate resources to prioritize enforcement activities as they deem appropriate, such as by prioritizing enforcement against convicted felons or gang members.

DHS components subsequently issued additional guidance further directing efforts to implement the executive orders and apply the guidance from the memoranda. For example, ICE issued guidance to its legal program to review all cases previously administratively closed based on prosecutorial discretion.[30] ICE's new guidance requested its attorneys to determine whether the basis for closure remains appropriate under DHS's new enforcement priorities. USCIS also reviewed its guidance for credible and reasonable fear determinations—the initial step for certain removable individuals to demonstrate they are eligible to be considered for particular forms of relief or protection from removal in immigration court.[31]

---

[30] During removal proceedings, DHS's exercise of prosecutorial discretion has generally referred to requesting that an immigration judge administratively close a case because the respondent does not meet enforcement priorities. On May 17, 2018, the Attorney General determined that, except as specifically provided in regulation or a judicial settlement, immigration judges and the Board of Immigration Appeals lack general authority to administratively close removal proceedings. For cases which were administratively closed without requisite authority, if DHS or the respondent seeks reopening, the case shall be recalendared. See *Matter of CASTRO-TUM*, 27 I. & N. Dec. 271 (AG 2018).

[31] Arriving and other designated foreign nationals subject to expedited removal and deemed inadmissible as a result of seeking entry (or any other immigration benefit) by fraud or willful misrepresentation, falsely claiming U.S. citizenship, or lacking valid immigration documents and who express a fear of persecution or torture, or an intention to apply for asylum, are to be referred by DHS to a USCIS asylum officer for a credible fear interview. See 8 U.S.C. §§ 1182(a)(6)(C), (a)(7), 1225(b) (inspection of applicants for admission, including process for determining, and definition of, "credible fear of persecution"); 8 C.F.R. §§ 1208.30, 208.30. If a foreign national who is subject to administrative removal for conviction of an aggravated felony at any time after admission, or a reinstated order of removal for having illegally reentered the country expresses a fear of persecution or torture if removed, DHS refers that individual to a USCIS asylum officer to determine whether this individual has a reasonable fear of persecution or torture. 8 U.S.C. §§ 1228(b), 1231(a)(5); 8 C.F.R. §§ 208.31, 1208.31, 238.1, 1238.1, 241.8, 1241.8.

Table 2. Examples of Department of Homeland Security (DHS) Planning and Programmatic Actions to Implement Executive Orders 13767, 13768, and 13780

Executive Order Provision	Actions
Physical Security of the Southern Border (Executive Order 13767 Sec. 4)	• U.S. Customs and Border Protection (CBP) started the acquisition process for a Border Wall System Program, which includes the construction of new and replacement physical barriers along the southern border. CBP awarded eight task orders with a total value of over $3 million for the construction and development of barrier prototypes in fall 2017.[a] CBP selected segments of the border in San Diego, California and the Rio Grande Valley in Texas as the first locations for barrier installations. • In order to further obtain operational control of the southern border, U.S. Immigration and Customs Enforcement (ICE) officials stated that they increased personnel and prioritized specific investigations in El Salvador, Guatemala, and Honduras. ICE officials also reported that they expanded Border Enforcement Security Task Forces targeting individuals and organizations that undermine border security. In fiscal year 2017, ICE established 13 new task forces, according to ICE officials.
Hire Additional Border Patrol Agents and Immigration Officers (Executive Order 13767 Sec. 8 and Executive Order 13768 Sec. 7)	• DHS requested and the Office of Personnel Management approved hiring authority changes to assist DHS with implementing the executive orders. These changes include granting CBP and ICE direct hire authority and a special salary rate for polygraphers, among others. • CBP awarded a contract not to exceed $297 million to a contractor to help with hiring 5,000 U.S. Border Patrol agents, 2,000 CBP officers, and 500 Air and Marine Operations agents. • ICE Office of Human Capital officials reported that they took planning steps to ensure policies and procedures are in place to begin hiring additional personnel if funds are appropriated. The office also issued a contract solicitation for help with hiring 10,000 law enforcement agents, including 8,500 deportation officers, 1,500 criminal investigators, and approximately 6,500 additional support personnel positions.[b]
Federal-State Agreements—Immigration and Nationality Act § 287(g)[c] (Executive Order 13767 Sec. 10 and Executive Order 13768 Sec. 8)	• ICE officials reported expediting review of pending 287(g) requests and approved 46 additional state and local jurisdictions for ICE's 287(g) program from February 2017 through March 2018. ICE and CBP officials also stated that they conducted additional outreach with state and local officials and identified potential law enforcement partners with whom to enter into possible future 287(g) agreements. • According to ICE officials, ICE is leveraging a Basic Ordering Agreement, a procurement tool to expedite acquisition of a substantial, but presently unknown, quantity of supplies or services. See 48 C.F.R. § 16.703. A Basic Ordering Agreement is not a contract, but rather, is a written instrument of understanding, negotiated between ICE and state and local jurisdictions, to

Table 2. (Continued)

Executive Order Provision	Actions
	house detainees upon ICE's issuance and their acceptance of an Immigration Detainer and either a Warrant for Arrest of Alien or Warrant of Removal. For any orders placed under the agreement, ICE will reimburse the service provider $50 for up to 48 hours of detention.
Office for Victims of Crimes Committed by Removable Aliens (Executive Order 13768 Sec. 13)	• ICE established the Victims of Immigration Crime Engagement (VOICE) Office in April 2017 to aid victims affected by crimes committed by individuals suspected or determined to be removable under U.S. immigration law. ICE established a support call center, including a toll free number to assist victims, and developed an online presence for the office. • Additionally, DHS tested and launched an automated service that helps victims track the immigration custody status of perpetrators of crime called the DHS Victim Information and Notification Exchange.
Expedited Completion of the Biometric Entry-Exit Tracking System[d] (Executive Order 13780 Sec. 8)	• According to CBP Office of Field Operations officials, the office is working on the same implementation plan for the Biometric Entry Exit Program that existed prior to the executive order. However, officials told us they are focusing on increasing the number of public private partnerships with airlines as a means to expedite implementation of the program. This effort is partly in response to the order, and partly in response to the program's fee-based funding structure, which generated fewer fees than anticipated in fiscal year 2017.[e]

Source: GAO analysis of DHS information. | GAO-18-470.

[a]The Consolidated Appropriations Act, 2018, limited the use of funds provided for primary pedestrian fencing to previously deployed fencing designs. Pub. L. No. 115-141, div. F, tit. II, § 230(b); 164 Cong. Rec. at H2557. Primary fencing is the first layer of fencing encountered when moving north from the southern border and may include both pedestrian and vehicle fencing. The secondary fence, located behind the primary fence, consists solely of pedestrian fencing.

[b]In May 2018, the contract solicitation was cancelled; however, the government anticipates re-soliciting the requirement in fiscal year 2019.

[c]Section 287(g) of the Immigration and Nationality Act, as amended, authorizes the federal government to deputize state and local law enforcement officers to carry out immigration enforcement activities pursuant to agreements with state and local law enforcement agencies including, among other things, certification that officers have received adequate training regarding enforcement of U.S. immigration law. See 8 U.S.C. § 1357(g).

[d]Since 1996, a series of federal statutes has required that the federal government develop and implement an entry and exit data system to match records, including biographic and biometric identifiers, of foreign nationals entering and leaving the country and to identify overstays. The Intelligence Reform and Terrorism Prevention Act of 2004 also required a plan to accelerate full implementation of an automated biometric entry and exit system. The Consolidated Appropriations Act, 2016, provided an appropriation of up to $1 billion dollars for DHS to develop and implement a biometric exit system beginning in fiscal year 2017. See GAO, *Border Security: DHS Has Made Progress in Planning for a Biometric Air Exit System and Reporting Overstays, but Challenges Remain,* GAO-17-170 (Washington, D.C.: Feb. 27, 2017).

[e]See GAO, *U.S. Ports of Entry: CBP Public-Private Partnership Programs Have Benefits, but CBP Could Strengthen Evaluation Efforts,* GAO-18-268 (Washington, D.C.: March 15, 2018).

As a result, USCIS made select modifications pursuant to Executive Order 13767, including adding language related to evaluating an applicant's credibility based on prior statements made to other DHS officials, such as CBP and ICE officers.

DHS also initiated a number of planning and programmatic actions to implement the executive orders. In some cases DHS components expanded or enhanced existing regular, ongoing agency activities and programs in response to the orders. For example, in response to Executive Order 13768, ICE officials reported that they expanded the use of the existing Criminal Alien Program.[32] In other instances, DHS components altered their activities consistent with the administration's immigration priorities. For instance, in response to Executive Order 13768, the Secretary of Homeland Security directed ICE to terminate outreach or advocacy services to potentially removable foreign nationals, and reallocate all resources currently used for such purposes to a new office to assist victims of crimes allegedly perpetrated by removable foreign nationals (the Victims of Immigration Crime Engagement, or VOICE, office, established in April 2017). Additional examples of planning and programmatic actions that DHS took, or officials reported taking, in response to the executive orders are described in Table 2.

DOJ

Within DOJ, the Office of the Deputy Attorney General coordinated and oversaw DOJ's initial implementation of key provisions in the executive orders, according to DOJ officials.[33] Specifically, DOJ officials said that the Office of the Deputy Attorney General coordinated and collected information for executive order reporting requirements and

[32] The Criminal Alien Program provides ICE-wide direction and support in the biometric and biographic identification, arrest, and removal of priority aliens who are incarcerated within federal, state, and local prisons and jails, focusing on those that pose a risk to public safety.

[33] While DOJ does not have any specific responsibilities under Executive Order 13780, officials told us that DOJ served in a consultation role and provided DOJ's perspectives on implementation.

participated in an interagency working group related to Executive Order 13780, and interagency meetings related to Executive Order 13767. However, DOJ components were responsible for implementing the provisions and ensuring that they met executive order requirements. In addition, DOJ assisted in the creation and issuance of various reports. For example, officials told us that DOJ provided data to State for a report on foreign assistance to the Mexican government, as required by Section 9 of Executive Order 13767. DOJ also jointly issued three reports with DHS in response to Executive Order 13768 Section 16, which included information regarding the immigration status of foreign-born individuals incarcerated under the supervision of the Federal Bureau of Prisons and in pre-trial detention in U.S. Marshals Service (USMS) custody.[34]

The Attorney General issued two memoranda providing policy and guidance related to Executive Orders 13767 and 13768 in April and May of 2017. The April 2017 memorandum contains guidance for federal prosecutors on prioritizing certain immigration-related criminal offenses. For example, the memorandum requires that federal prosecutors consider prosecution of foreign nationals who illegally re-enter the United States after prior removal, and prioritize defendants with criminal histories. The May 2017 memorandum addresses Executive Order 13768's provision directing DOJ and DHS to ensure that jurisdictions willfully prohibiting immigration status-related communication with the federal government (referred to as "sanctuary jurisdictions") are not eligible for federal grants. It requires jurisdictions to certify their compliance with 8 U.S.C §1373, under which a federal, state, or local government entity or official may not prohibit, or in any way restrict the exchange of citizenship or immigration status information with DHS.

---

[34] Exec. Order No. 13768, § 16, 82 Fed. Reg. at 8802. Department of Justice, *Pursuant to Executive Order on Public Safety, Department of Justice Releases Data on Incarcerated Aliens* (May 2017); Department of Justice, *Pursuant to Executive Order on Public Safety, Department of Justice Releases Data on Incarcerated Aliens* (August 2017); and Department of Justice and Department of Homeland Security, *Alien Incarceration Report, Fiscal Year 2017, Quarter 4* (December 2017). According to DOJ officials, DOJ provides a daily list of all prisoners to DHS that includes the nationality or citizenship of the prisoner, as self-reported.

Table 3. Examples of Department of Justice (DOJ) Planning and Programmatic Actions to Implement Executive Orders 13767 and 13768

Executive Order Provision	Actions
Prosecution Priorities for Immigration-Related Offenses (Executive Orders 13767 Sec. 13 and 13768 Sec. 11)	• The Executive Office for United States Attorneys detailed 12 Assistant United States Attorneys (AUSAs) to the southern border between June 2017 and January 2018 to aid in prosecutions of foreign nationals entering or reentering the United States illegally, human smugglers, or those committing other immigration-related crimes. • Additionally, all 94 judicial districts in the United States designated one AUSA each to be the district border security coordinator, according to DOJ officials. Border security coordinators are to oversee investigations and prosecutions and ensure that they align with guidance in the Attorney General's April 2017 memorandum.
Detention Centers for Immigration Offenders (Executive Order 13767 Sec. 5)	The Executive Office for Immigration Review detailed approximately 40 immigration judge positions to detention centers and the southern border from March through October 2017 to conduct removal and other related proceedings, according to DOJ officials.
Sanctuary Jurisdictions—Sharing Immigration Status Information (Executive Order 13768 Sec. 9)	The Attorney General issued a May 22, 2017, memorandum clarifying the applicability of Section 9 of the executive order which directs DOJ and the Department of Homeland Security to ensure jurisdictions willfully prohibiting immigration status-related communication with the federal government (referred to as sanctuary jurisdictions) are not eligible for federal grants, and requiring jurisdictions applying for certain DOJ grants to certify their compliance with federal law, including 8 U.S. C. § 1373. On November 20, 2017, enforcement of Executive Order 13768, section 9(a), was permanently enjoined by federal court order. According to DOJ officials, no subsequent action has been taken to implement section 9(a).[a]

Source: GAO analysis of DOJ information. | GAO-18-470.

[a]Executive Order 13768 Section 9(a) was permanently enjoined nationwide by the U.S. District Court for the Northern District of California, thereby prohibiting DOJ from taking actions to deny jurisdictions eligibility for federal grants pursuant to such section. See *Cty. Of Santa Clara v. Trump*, 275 F. Supp. 3d 1196 (N.D. Cal. Nov. 20 2017) (the court granted the plaintiffs' motion for summary judgement regarding section 9(a) of Executive Order 13768, finding that it was unconstitutional on its face as a violation of the separation of powers doctrine and plaintiffs' 10th and 5th amendment rights). Prior to issuance of Executive Order 13768, the DOJ Inspector General conducted a compliance review of certain jurisdictions relative to 8 U.S.C. § 1373, and issued a report in May 2016 finding that 10 jurisdictions raised compliance concerns (*Department of Justice Referral of Allegations of Potential Violations of 8 U.S.C. §1373 by Grant Recipients*). In response, DOJ placed a special condition on certain fiscal year 2016 grant awards, requiring recipients to submit an assessment of their compliance with section 1373. In November 2017, as part of the section 1373 compliance effort predating Executive Order 13768, DOJ sent letters to 29 jurisdictions expressing concern that they may not be in compliance with 8 U.S.C. §1373, and

requesting responses regarding compliance. In January 2018, DOJ sent follow up demand letters to 23 jurisdictions seeking documents to determine whether they are unlawfully restricting information sharing by their law enforcement officers with federal immigration authorities, and stating that failure to respond will result in records being subpoenaed. See *City of Chicago v. Sessions,* 264 F. Supp. 3d 933 (N.D. Ill. 2017), *aff'd*, 2018 U.S. App. LEXIS 9862 (7th Cir. 2018) (While the U.S. District Court for the Northern District of Illinois granted a nationwide preliminary injunction against the Attorney General's imposition of two immigration-related "notice" and "access" conditions on the Byrne Justice Assistance Grants Program awards for fiscal year 2017, the court determined that the Attorney General has statutory authority to require the city to certify compliance with 8 U.S.C. § 1373 as a grant condition, and therefore denied Chicago's motion for a preliminary injunction in that regard).

Additionally, DOJ took a number of initial planning and programmatic steps to implement the executive orders. DOJ officials stated that some provisions outlined in the executive orders represent regular, ongoing agency activities and did not require any major changes to be implemented. For example, DOJ detailed Assistant United States Attorneys (AUSAs) and immigration judges to southern border districts and detention centers to assist in prosecutions and to conduct removal proceedings in response to the executive orders. However, while they expanded their efforts, DOJ officials said that detailing immigration judges and AUSAs to the border districts is a regular practice, and not a new function created by the executive orders. Examples of actions that DOJ took, or officials reported taking, in response to the executive orders are described in Table 3.

State

State's Bureaus of Population, Refugees, and Migration and Consular Affairs led efforts to implement key provisions in Executive Order 13780.[35] Several legal challenges and resulting federal court injunctions affected State's implementation of Executive Order 13780 and at times curtailed specific provisions.[36] Initial State actions included conducting

---

[35] Other than participating in the development of several reports, State generally did not have any responsibilities in Executive Order 13767 or 13768.

[36] See, e.g., *Trump v. Int'l Refugee Assistance Project*, 137 S. Ct. 2080 (2017) (per curiam) (The Court explained that the administration may enforce entry restrictions for visa travelers and refugees except with respect to an individual credibly claiming a bona fide relationship with

reviews and contributing to reports required by the order. For instance, while State generally suspended refugee travel for 120 days, the department, in conjunction with DHS and the Office of the Director of National Intelligence, conducted a review to determine what, if any, additional procedures should be implemented in the U.S. Refugee Admissions Program. According to State officials, the agencies provided a joint memorandum to the President in October 2017 that contained recommendations regarding resumption of the program, specific changes to refugee processing, and further reviews and steps that the interagency group should take. Additionally, State worked with DHS and the Office of the Director of National Intelligence to conduct a worldwide review. This review identified any additional information that the United States may need from each foreign country to adjudicate visas and other immigration benefit applications and ensure that individuals seeking to enter the United States do not pose a threat to public safety or national security. In July 2017, upon completion of this review, DHS, in consultation with State and other interagency partners, issued a report to the President cataloguing information needed from each country and listing countries not providing adequate information.

State also issued a number of policies and guidance in response to the executive orders; however, guidance on how to implement certain provisions often changed due to legal challenges. For example, the Bureau of Population, Refugees, and Migration issued 23 iterations of refugee travel restrictions guidance to overseas refugee processing centers in response to federal litigation and budgetary uncertainties. Similarly, the Secretary of State issued a number of cables to visa-issuing foreign posts on implementing travel restrictions for nationals of selected countries following court orders limiting the implementation of such restrictions.

---

a person or entity in the United States). DHS and DOJ were also involved in implementing Executive Order 13780 provisions and their actions were also affected by federal court rulings.

Table 4. Examples of Department of State (State) Planning and Programmatic Actions to Implement Executive Order 13780

Executive Order Provision	Actions
Enhanced Screening and Vetting (Executive Order 13780 Sec. 5)	State participated in an interagency working group to develop uniform standards related to the adjudication of visa applications, interviews, and system security checks, such as biometric or biographic checks. The working group also identified data elements against which applicants are to be screened and vetted.
Consular Fellows (Executive Order 13780 Sec. 9)	State expanded its Consular Fellows Program by extending non-career appointments and hiring 134 new Consular Fellows from February 2017 through February 2018, according to officials. State officials stated that the department plans to hire up to approximately 120 more Consular Fellows in the remainder of fiscal year 2018.
Refugee Program Realignment (Executive Order 13780 Sec. 6)	State suspended travel for refugees for 120 days.[a] During this time, State worked with interagency partners to review the U.S. Refugee Admissions Program application and adjudication process to identify any additional procedures or areas for improvement.

Source: GAO analysis of information provided by State. | GAO-18-470.

[a]In a June 26, 2017 ruling, the U.S. Supreme Court prohibited enforcement of entry restrictions against foreign nationals credibly claiming a bona fide relationship with a person or entity in the United States. See *Trump v. Int'l Refugee Assistance Project,* 137 S. Ct. 2080 (2017) (per curiam).

Executive Order 13780 contained several time-sensitive provisions directed to the Secretary of State. State focused on first addressing these provisions while working towards longer-term priorities outlined in the order. For instance, Executive Order 13780 Sections 2 and 6 established visa and refugee entry restrictions, which contained near-term timelines. State implemented these provisions, consistent with judicial decisions. Examples of planning and programmatic actions that State took, or officials reported taking, to implement Executive Order 13780 are described in Table 4.

For more information on specific planning or programmatic actions DHS, DOJ, and State have taken to implement the executive orders, see appendix I.

The examples we provided for DHS, DOJ, and State represent initial actions and do not constitute an exhaustive list of actions that agencies have taken, or may take in the future, to fully implement the executive orders. Agency officials anticipate that implementation of the executive orders will be a multi-year endeavor comprising present and future reporting, planning, and other actions. For example, DOJ officials noted that many of the actions that they took to implement the orders will be ongoing and responsive to additional DHS actions. Specifically, DOJ bases the number of immigration judges and AUSAs detailed to the southern border districts on court caseloads driven by ICE. If ICE hires additional officers and attorneys and arrests and files charges of removability against more foreign nationals, then DOJ may need to staff additional judges and AUSAs to meet caseload needs.

DHS, DOJ, and State Used Existing Fiscal Year 2017 Resources to Support Initial Executive Order Actions; DHS Also Received and Expended Supplemental Funds

Existing Fiscal Year 2017 Resources

Many of the initial actions agencies and components took in response to the executive orders fit within their existing fiscal year 2017 budget framework and aligned with their established missions. At the time the executive orders were issued in January and March of 2017, federal agencies were operating under existing continuing appropriations pending enactment of fiscal year 2017 appropriations; therefore the new administration's border security and immigration priorities and policies had not yet been incorporated into the budget process. As a result, it is not always possible to disaggregate which fiscal year 2017 funds were used for implementation of the executive orders versus other agency activities. For example, while the orders call for a surge in hiring at CBP and ICE, these agencies regularly hire additional personnel to offset attrition or to meet budget hiring targets as part of their normal operations.

We asked agencies to identify budgetary resources they used specifically to address the executive orders. In some cases agencies were able to quantify their expenditures; however in other cases they could not. For example, according to DOJ officials, the Executive Office for Immigration Review, which conducts immigration court proceedings, spent close to $2.4 million in existing funds to surge approximately 40 immigration judge positions to detention centers and the southwest border from March through October 2017 in response to Executive Order 13768. DHS's USCIS reported expending approximately $4.2 million detailing asylum officers to immigration detention facilities along the southern border from February 2017 through February 2018.[37] Additionally, as a result of the 120-day suspension of refugee admissions, State cancelled airline tickets for previously approved refugee applicants, which resulted in a cost of nearly $2.4 million in cancellation and unused ticket fees.[38] State officials noted that, aside from the ticket costs, other budgetary costs associated with implementing the order are difficult to disaggregate from other processing activities. For example, any budgetary costs associated with refugees who were admitted on a case-by-case basis were absorbed into overseas processing budgets. In some cases, agencies also identified cost savings or avoidances. For example, State reported a total cost avoidance of over $160 million in fiscal year 2017, partially as a result of admitting fewer refugees than originally planned under the prior administration.[39]

While the costs above were part of agencies' normal operations, we identified one case where Congress approved a DHS request to reprogram $20 million from existing programs to fund the planning and design of new physical barriers along the border, including prototype design and

[37] According to both DOJ and USCIS officials, some immigration judges and asylum officers may have been detailed to the border regardless of the executive orders as part of the agencies' regular operations.

[38] State officials told us that ticket cancellation fees totaled approximately $282,000 and the unused ticket costs were approximately $2.1 million.

[39] State officials said that these cost avoidances were a result of reduced costs for overseas processing operations, among other things. State obligated fewer funds than they budgeted for because they admitted fewer refugees.

construction.[40] Specifically, CBP reprogrammed $15 million from funds originally requested for Mobile Video Surveillance System deployments and $5 million from a border fence replacement project in Naco, Arizona.[41] Additionally, we identified another case where DHS shifted funds and notified Congress, but determined Congressional approval for reprogramming was not required. Specifically, in response to Executive Order 13768, the Secretary of Homeland Security directed ICE to reallocate any and all resources used to advocate on behalf of potentially removable foreign nationals (except as necessary to comply with a judicial order) to the new VOICE office. As part of this effort, ICE's Office of the Principal Legal Advisor determined that the creation of the VOICE office fell within ICE's authority to carry out routine or small reallocations of personnel or functions. According to officials at DHS, DOJ, and State, there were no additional requests to reprogram or transfer funds to implement the executive orders. DHS budget officials stated that any future requests from DHS components to reprogram or transfer funds would typically be considered at the midway point in the budget cycle.

All three agencies indicated that they used existing personnel to implement the executive orders and, in some cases, a substantial amount of time was spent preparing reports, planning to implement provisions, and responding to changes or new developments in the executive orders. For example, USCIS officials noted that the agency devoted a significant number of manpower hours to aligning USCIS priorities to the executive orders.[42] ICE's Office of Human Capital established a dedicated executive order hiring team to plan for the hiring surge directed by Executive Order 13768. Additionally, officials at State told us that personnel were diverted from normal operations in order to implement executive order policy

[40] As discussed above, reprogramming is shifting funds within an appropriation or fund account for purposes other than those contemplated at the time of appropriation; it is the shifting of funds from one object class to another within an appropriation or from one program activity to another. Transfer is the shifting of all or part of the budget authority in one appropriation or fund account to another. Agencies may transfer budget authority only as specifically authorized by law.

[41] Mobile Video Surveillance Systems include a telescoping mast or lift system that elevates a camera containing day and night capabilities with target illuminators and range finders.

[42] USCIS officials further noted that some USCIS initiatives aligned to the executive orders were already in progress or already of interest to USCIS and were bolstered by the order.

actions and that there were overtime costs associated with some provisions. In most cases, agencies did not specifically track or quantify the amount of time spent on these efforts; however, ICE's Office of Human Capital tracked the amount of time spent on planning for the potential surge in ICE hiring in its human resource data system. According to ICE information, ICE personnel charged approximately 14,000 regular hours (the equivalent of 1,750 8-hour days) and 2,400 overtime hours to this effort from January 2017 through January 2018.[43]

Fiscal Year 2017 Request for Supplemental Appropriations

In March 2017, the President submitted a budget amendment along with a request for $3 billion in supplemental appropriations for DHS to implement the executive orders and address border protection activities. In May 2017, an additional appropriation of approximately $1.1 billion was provided in response to this request, some of which DHS used to fund actions to implement the orders.[44] For example, CBP received $65.4 million for hiring and, according to CBP officials, used these funds to plan and prepare for the surge in Border Patrol agents directed by Executive Order 13767. As of January 2018, CBP had obligated $18.8 million and expended $14.1 million of the $65.4 million it received. Additionally, ICE received $147.9 million for custody operations. At the end of fiscal year 2017, ICE had obligated and expended nearly all—over 99.9 percent—of the funds it received.

[43] According to ICE Office of Human Capital officials, the agency is unable to provide the dollar amount or personnel costs associated with these hours.

[44] Pub. L. No. 115-31, div. F, tit. VI, 131 Stat.135, 433-35. In particular, the Consolidated Appropriations Act, 2017 included approximately $1.1 billion in additional DHS appropriations for security, enforcement, and investigations activities. Specifically, the law appropriates additional amounts of approximately $772 million for CBP and $237 million for ICE, as well as $58 million for U.S. Secret Service operations and support and $73 million for Presidential security.

Fiscal Years 2018 and 2019 Budget Requests and Fiscal Year 2018 Appropriations

Agency officials anticipate additional costs to further implement the executive orders and expect that certain provisions will require a multi-year effort. According to DHS officials, the agency expects to incorporate executive order implementation into its annual strategic and budgetary planning processes. DHS officials also noted that additional future planning and funds will be needed to fully implement actions in the orders. Agencies plan to continue to use their base budgets as well as request additional funds as needed to carry out their mission. Examples of DHS and DOJ fiscal year 2018 budget requests and appropriations to implement executive order provisions are listed below.

- CBP requested $1.6 billion and in the Consolidated Appropriations Act, 2018, received approximately $1.3 billion to build new and replace existing sections of physical barriers along the southern border.[45] CBP also projected out-year funding for construction along certain segments of the border through 2024.
- ICE requested $185.9 million for approximately 1,000 new immigration officers and 606 support staff. ICE's fiscal year 2018 appropriation included $15.6 million to support the hiring of 65 additional investigative agents, as well as 70 attorneys and support staff.[46]
- DOJ requested approximately $7.2 million to hire additional attorneys in support of the orders. According to DOJ officials, DOJ received sufficient funds in the fiscal year 2018 budget to meet the hiring goal for attorneys.

---

[45] Pub. L. No. 115-141, div. F, tit. II, § 230, 132 Stat. 348; 164 Cong. Rec. H2045, H2550, H2557 (daily ed. March 22, 2018). The Consolidated Appropriations Act, 2018 also provided $38 million for border barrier planning and design, but limited the use of funds provided for construction of new and replacement primary barriers to previously deployed fencing designs.

[46] 164 Cong. Rec. at H2550.

DHS and DOJ also requested funds for fiscal year 2019 to implement executive order provisions, examples of which are listed below.

- ICE requested $571 million to hire 2,000 immigration officers (including 1,700 deportation officers and 300 criminal investigators) and 1,312 support staff (including attorneys).
- DOJ requested $1.1 million for 17 paralegal support positions to support the additional attorneys requested in the fiscal year 2018 request.[47] DOJ also requested approximately $40 million to hire new immigration judges and their supporting staff, citing an over 25 percent increase in new cases brought forward by DHS over the course of fiscal year 2017.

DHS and DOJ components that were not directly tasked with responsibilities in the executive orders have also begun to plan for potential effects as agencies implement the orders. For example, as CBP and ICE work to meet the hiring surge in the orders, USMS anticipates a likely increase in the number of individuals who are charged with criminal immigration offenses and detained pending trial, resulting in a corresponding increase in its workload. USMS developed a multi-year impact statement which projected possible effects on USMS prisoner operations, judicial security, and investigative operations. According to DOJ officials, these efforts may inform USMS's budget requests and future year planning. For example, for fiscal year 2018 USMS requested approximately $9 million to hire 40 USMS deputies to support the executive orders.[48] For fiscal year 2019, USMS projected that the administration's policies to increase immigration enforcement and immigration-related prosecutions could result in an increase of nearly 19,000 prisoners between fiscal year 2017 and fiscal year 2019 and a

---

47 DOJ officials stated that Congress provided sufficient funding in the 2018 budget to meet DOJ's fiscal year 2019 request for paralegal positions.

48 According to DOJ officials, USMS received sufficient funds in the fiscal year 2018 budget to meet this hiring goal. In addition, these officials noted that for fiscal year 2018 USMS received a $50 million increase in Federal Prisoner Detention funding for anticipated immigration-related increases.

corresponding budget increase of approximately $105 million for immigration expenses. In addition, officials at the Federal Law Enforcement Training Centers stated that they coordinated with Border Patrol and ICE to assess future training needs and project future resource requirements based on the hiring assumptions in the executive orders. For example, the Federal Law Enforcement Training Centers requested an increase of $29 million in fiscal year 2018 and $25.7 million in fiscal year 2019 for tuition and training requirements to implement the executive orders, among other funding requested.[49]

Appendix I includes additional information on funds DHS, DOJ, and State have obligated, expended, or shifted, to implement provisions of the executive orders.

AGENCY COMMENTS

We provided a draft of this chapter to DHS, DOJ, and State for review and comment. DHS provided written comments, which are reproduced in appendix III; DOJ and State did not provide written comments. In its written comments, DHS discussed resources and legislative authorities the department believes it needs to carry out executive order requirements. All three agencies provided technical comments, which we incorporated as appropriate.

As agreed with your offices, unless you publicly announce the contents of this chapter earlier, we plan no further distribution until 30 days from the chapter date. At that time, we will send copies to the appropriate congressional committees, the Secretary of Homeland Security, the Attorney General, and the Secretary of State.

Rebecca Gambler
Director, Homeland Security and Justice

---

[49] According to DHS officials, the Consolidated Appropriations Act, 2018, did not include the $29 million the Federal Law Enforcement Training Centers requested for fiscal year 2018.

List of Requesters

The Honorable Dianne Feinstein
Ranking Member
Committee on the Judiciary, United States Senate

The Honorable Richard J. Durbin
Ranking Member
Subcommittee on Border Security and Immigration
Committee on the Judiciary, United States Senate

The Honorable Gary Peters
Ranking Member
Subcommittee on Federal Spending Oversight and Emergency Management
Committee on Homeland Security and Governmental Affairs
United States Senate

The Honorable Tammy Baldwin

The Honorable Richard Blumenthal

The Honorable Cory A. Booker

The Honorable Maria Cantwell

The Honorable Tammy Duckworth

The Honorable Kirsten Gillibrand

The Honorable Edward Markey

The Honorable Jeffrey A. Merkley

The Honorable Christopher S. Murphy

The Honorable Brian Schatz

The Honorable Chris Van Hollen

The Honorable Elizabeth Warren

The Honorable Ron Wyden
United States Senate

APPENDIX I: KEY ACTIONS AND BUDGETARY COSTS RELATED TO IMPLEMENTING EXECUTIVE ORDER 13767, 13768, AND 13780 PROVISIONS

Purpose

This appendix contains summaries of initial actions that the Department of Homeland Security (DHS), Department of Justice (DOJ), and Department of State (State) took to implement selected programmatic provisions of the President's executive orders on border security and immigration. These orders include Executive Order 13767, *Border Security and Immigration Enforcement Improvements*; Executive Order 13768, *Enhancing Public Safety in the Interior of the United States*; and Executive Order 13780, *Protecting the Nation from Foreign Terrorist Entry into the United States*.[50] These summaries also contain overviews of budget information related to implementing the executive orders, including obligations, expenditures, and budget requests where available, among

[50] Border Security and Immigration Enforcement Improvements, Exec. Order No. 13767, 82 Fed. Reg. 8793 (Jan. 30, 2017) (issued Jan. 25); Enhancing Public Safety in the Interior of the United States, Exec. Order No. 13768, 82 Fed. Reg. 8799 (Jan. 30, 2017) (issued Jan. 25); and Protecting the Nation From Foreign Terrorist Entry Into the United States, Exec. Order No. 13780, 82 Fed. Reg. 13,209 (Mar. 9, 2017) (issued Mar. 6).

other things. Table 5 lists the summaries and the executive order provisions on which they focus.

Table 5. List of Summaries and Related Executive Order Provisions

Summary title	Executive Order(s)	Provision(s)
Southern Border Barriers	13767	Section 4
Detention	13767	Section 5 and Section 6
Parole and Asylum	13767	Section 11
Hiring	13767 and 13768	Section 8 and Section 7
Federal-State Agreements	13767 and 13768	Section 10 and Section 8
Prosecution	13767 and 13768	Section 13 and Section 11
Enforcement Priorities	13768	Section 5 and Section 10
Sanctuary Jurisdictions (Sharing Immigration Status Information)	13768	Section 9
Visa Entry Restrictions and Enhanced Screening and Vetting	13780	Section 2 and Section 5
Refugee Admissions Program Realignment	13780	Section 6
Visa Interview Waiver Program	13780	Section 9

Source: GAO analysis of information from Executive Orders 13767, 13768, and 13780. I GAO-18-470.

Methodology for Selecting Executive Order Provisions

We reviewed the executive orders and placed each provision directed at DHS, DOJ, and State into one of three categories: (1) *analyses and reports*, (2) *policies*, and (3) *programs*. We defined the *analyses and reports* category as executive order provisions that direct agencies to review and analyze data, policies, processes, and operational mission areas and produce reports. We defined the *policies* category as executive order provisions that establish new or modify existing policies, guidance, or processes related to border security or immigration. We defined the *programs* category as tangible, measurable, and quantifiable executive order provisions that implement policies. We confirmed our categorization with each agency, particularly for the *programs* category, since it was sometimes ambiguous whether provisions would lead to actions that were tangible, measurable, and quantifiable. Specifically, we reviewed agency documentation, such as a DHS inventory of tasks related to the executive orders, and interviewed agency officials. In some cases, we moved policy provisions to the *programs* category if agency efforts to implement the policy were underway.

We prepared summaries for each executive order provision(s) we categorized as a *program*. For each *program*, we identified actions planned, completed, or underway at DHS, DOJ, and State as of March 2018 through reviewing documentation, interviewing agency officials, and submitting data collection instruments. For each *program* we also collected available budgetary costs—specifically, any funds requested, appropriated, obligated, and expended for executive order implementation from January 2017 through March 2018. We reviewed publicly available budget requests, congressional budget justifications, public laws, and budgetary data from agencies' internal data systems.[51] While we were able to identify certain funds directly attributed to the executive order provisions from these documents, it was not always possible to extract funds specifically meant for implementing the executive order provisions from more general budget increase requests, appropriations, or expenditures. To specifically identify funds used for the executive order provisions, we reviewed agency documentation, interviewed agency budget and program officials, and submitted written questions as necessary. In instances where we were unable to differentiate executive order provision funds from regular operating funds, we identified the larger account used for executive order funds and noted this distinction. We analyzed agency documentation on the policies, procedures, and processes for maintaining budgetary data and interviewed agency officials about their data collection practices to assess the reliability of these data. We determined that the data were sufficiently reliable for our purposes.

---

[51] There is no central intra- or interagency repository for budget information related to the executive orders. Therefore, we collected and aggregated budgetary data from systems used by individual agency components and offices.

Southern Border Barriers

Executive Order: 13767

Provision: Section 4

Provision Summary: Section 4 directs the Department of Homeland Security (DHS) to plan, design, and construct a wall or other physical barriers along the southern border, identify and allocate all sources of federal funds for such efforts, and project and develop long-term funding requirements.

Key Agency(ies) Responsible: DHS: U.S. Customs and Border Protection (CBP), U.S. Border Patrol (Border Patrol)

Program Context: Statutes enacted from 1996 through 2007 authorize DHS, subject to certain criteria, to take necessary actions to construct physical barriers and roads to deter illegal crossings in border areas experiencing high levels of illegal entry. As we previously reported in 2017, from fiscal years 2005 through 2015, CBP increased the total miles of primary border fencing on the southwest border from 119 miles to 654 miles.[52]

Department of Homeland Security Barrier Prototypes

Source: U.S. Customs and Border Protection. | GAO-18-470.

[52] The 654 miles of primary border fencing includes 354 miles of primary pedestrian fencing and 300 miles of primary vehicle fencing. GAO, *Southwest Border Security: Additional Actions Needed to Better Assess Fencing's Contributions to Operations and Provide Guidance for Identifying Capability Gaps*, GAO-17-331 (Washington, D.C.: Feb. 16, 2017).

Action Overview

CBP has taken initial steps to plan, design, and construct new and replacement physical barriers on the southern border.

- For instance, CBP began the acquisition process for a Border Wall System Program, including developing plans to construct barrier segments and awarding eight task orders with a total value of over $3 million to design and construct barrier prototypes (four made from concrete and four made from non-concrete materials).
- CBP selected San Diego, California as the first segment and plans to replace an existing 14 miles of primary and secondary barriers.[53] DHS plans to use fiscal year 2017 funding for the replacement of the primary barrier which it plans to rebuild to existing—as opposed to prototype—design standards.
- In January 2018, DHS leadership also approved cost, schedule, and performance goals for a second segment in the Rio Grande Valley in Texas, which will extend an existing barrier with 60 miles of new fencing.
- The Consolidated Appropriations Act, 2018, stated that fiscal year 2018 funds for primary pedestrian fencing are only available for "operationally effective designs deployed as of [May 5, 2017]," such as steel bollard fencing currently deployed in areas of the border.[54] As of April 2018, CBP and DHS were evaluating what, if any, impact this direction will have on the department's plans, according to DHS officials.

---

[53] Primary fencing is the first layer of fencing encountered when moving north from the southern border and may include both pedestrian and vehicle fencing; the secondary fence, located behind the primary fence, consists solely of pedestrian fencing.

[54] See Pub. L. No. 115-141, div. F, tit. II, § 230; 164 Cong. Rec. H2045, H2550, H2557 (daily ed. March 22, 2018). With respect to secondary fencing, the Consolidated Appropriations Act, 2018, specifically required that funding for such fencing in the San Diego sector only be used on designs providing cross-barrier visual situational awareness.

- Additionally, DHS waived specific legal restrictions, such as environmental restrictions, in order to begin construction of barriers in the El Centro and San Diego Border Patrol sectors in California; and the Santa Teresa, New Mexico segment of the El Paso Border Patrol Sector.[55] DHS also completed a categorical exclusion for replacement of a segment of existing barriers in El Paso, Texas.[56]

Budget Overview

To fund the barrier prototypes, Congress approved a DHS request to reprogram $20 million in fiscal year 2017. Specifically:

- CBP reprogrammed $15 million from funds originally requested for Mobile Video Surveillance System deployments.[57] The funds were originally part of the fiscal year 2015/2017 Border Security Fencing, Infrastructure, and Technology (BSFIT) Development and Deployment funding and were available due to a contract bid protest and delays associated with the Mobile Video Surveillance System Program.

---

[55] See Determinations Pursuant to Sections 102 of the Illegal Immigration Reform and Immigrant Responsibility Act of 1996, as Amended, 82 Fed. Reg. 42,829 (Sept. 12, 2017) (El Centro Sector Waiver Determination), 82 Fed. Reg. 35,984 (Aug. 2, 2017) (San Diego Sector Waiver Determination), 83 Fed. Reg. 3012 (Jan. 22, 2018) (El Paso Sector Waiver Determination). Border Patrol divides responsibility for border security operations geographically among the nine sectors along the U.S. and Mexican border, each with its own headquarters. Each sector is further divided into varying numbers of stations.

[56] Under 40 C.F.R. § 1508.4, the term "categorical exclusion" refers to a category of actions which do not significantly affect the human environment as found under relevant federal agency procedures, and for which there need not be an environmental assessment or impact statement. At DHS, certain categorical exclusions require preparation of a record of environmental consideration.

[57] Mobile Video Surveillance Systems include a telescoping mast or lift system that elevates a camera containing day and night capabilities with target illuminators and range finders.

Table 6. Requested and Appropriated Funding for Border Barrier Construction, Fiscal Years (FY) 2017 through 2019

Project and location	Border miles	Amount
FY 2017 Supplemental Appropriations (requested)		
Planning, design, and construction of the first installment of the border wall	Unspecified	$999 million
Access roads, gates, and other tactical infrastructure projects	Unspecified	$179 million
Total		$1.2 billion
FY 2017 Supplemental Appropriations (funded)		
Replacement of primary pedestrian fencing in high priority areas	20 miles	$146 million
Replacement of primary vehicle fencing with primary pedestrian fencing in high priority areas	20 miles	$146 million
Gates[a]	35 units	$49.2 million
Total		$341.2 million
FY 2018 Congressional Budget Justification (requested)		
Levee wall in Rio Grande Valley sector (Texas)	28 miles	$498 million
Border wall system[b] in Rio Grande Valley sector	32 miles	$784 million
Border wall system[b] in San Diego sector (California)	14 miles	$251 million
Total		$1.5 billion
FY 2018 Appropriation (funded)		
Primary pedestrian levee fencing in Rio Grande Valley sector	25 miles	$445 million
Primary pedestrian fencing in Rio Grande Valley sector	Unspecified	$196 million
Secondary fencing replacement in San Diego sector	14 miles	$251 million
Primary pedestrian fencing replacement along the southwest border	Unspecified	$445 million
Total		$1.3 billion
FY 2019 Congressional Budget Justification (requested)c		
Border wall system[b] in Rio Grande Valley sector	65 miles	$1.6 billion
Total		$1.6 billion

Source: GAO analysis of Department of Homeland Security (DHS) budget documentation. | GAO-18-470.

Note: Additional funds related to physical border security are not included in this table. For example, the Consolidated Appropriation Act, 2017 included $78.8 million in funding for the acquisition and deployment of border security technology and $77.4 million for new border road construction. Additionally, the Consolidated Appropriations Act, 2018, included $38 million for border barrier planning and design, $196 million for the acquisition and deployment of border security technology and $49.7 million for new border road construction.

[a]The explanatory statement (163 Cong. Rec. H3327, H3823 (daily ed. May 3, 2017)) accompanying the Consolidated Appropriation Act, 2017 (Pub. L. No. 115-31, 131 Stat. 135), indicates that $49.2 million is for 35 gates for existing barriers, without prescribing the locations for installation.

[b]CBP uses the term "wall system" to describe these planned combinations of tactical infrastructure, including primary and secondary barriers separated by an enforcement zone, access roads, lighting and surveillance technology, and interfaces for current or future technologies to support detection capabilities.

[c]According to DHS officials, the fiscal year 2019 request may be modified based on what DHS was appropriated in the Consolidated Appropriations Act, 2018.

- CBP also reprogrammed $5 million from funds originally intended for a fence replacement project in Naco, Arizona. The funds were part of fiscal year 2016 BSFIT Operations and Maintenance funding and were available as a result of unanticipated contract savings. The Naco Fence Replacement project will be completed within its original scope, according to CBP documentation.

DHS also received an appropriation in fiscal year 2017 to replace existing fencing and to install new gates; and an appropriation in fiscal year 2018 for border barrier planning and design, and to replace existing fencing and build new barriers.

As previously discussed, the Consolidated Appropriations Act, 2018, limited the use of funds provided for construction of new and replacement primary pedestrian fencing to previously deployed fencing designs. DHS has requested, but has not received, fiscal year 2019 funds for building new barriers. For more information regarding funding for future barrier construction projects along the southern border, see Table 6.

According to CBP documentation, the total cost to construct the Border Wall System Program over approximately 10 years is $18 billion. DHS headquarters conducted an independent cost estimate for the San Diego and Rio Grande Valley segments of the program, which CBP adopted as the program's life cycle cost estimate. Acquisition and operations and maintenance costs for the Rio Grande Valley segment were separately described in other DHS documents and are shown in Table 7 below.

Table 7. Fiscal Years (FY) 2018 through 2022 Rio Grande Valley, Texas Border Wall System Cost Estimate

	FY2018	FY2019	FY2020	FY2021	FY2022	Total
Acquisition	$1.35 billion	0	0	0	0	$1.35 billion
Operations & Maintenance	0	$3.27 million	$9.02 million	$12.19 million	$10.93 million	$35.41 million

Source: U.S. Customs and Border Protection. | GAO-18-470.

Detention

Executive Order: 13767

Provision: Sections 5 and 6

Provision Summary: Sections 5 and 6 pertain to detention facilities and detention of foreign nationals for violations of immigration law, pending the outcome of their proceedings or to facilitate removal. The order directs the Department of Homeland Security (DHS) to take immediate actions to construct, operate, or control facilities to detain foreign nationals at or near the southern border, and assign asylum officers to immigration detention facilities, among other things. Additionally, the order directs the Department of Justice (DOJ) to immediately assign immigration judges to immigration detention facilities.

Key Agency(ies) Responsible: DHS: U.S. Customs and Border Protection (CBP), U.S. Immigration and Customs Enforcement (ICE), U.S. Citizenship and Immigration Services (USCIS)

DOJ: Executive Office for Immigration Review (EOIR)

Program Context: ICE, through its Enforcement and Removal Operations directorate, manages the nation's immigration detention system, which houses foreign nationals detained while their immigration cases are pending or after being ordered removed from the country. DOJ's EOIR is responsible for conducting immigration court proceedings, appellate reviews, and administrative hearings, pursuant to U.S. immigration law and regulation.

Immigration Detention Facility

Source: U.S. Immigration and Customs Enforcement. | GAO-18-470.

Action Overview

- ICE and U.S. Border Patrol officials stated they consider custody determinations on a case by case basis. Additionally, officials from CBP's Office of Field Operations stated they inspect all applicants for admission in accordance with the Immigration and Nationality Act, as prescribed by the executive order and a February 2017 memorandum the Secretary of Homeland Security issued.[58]
- ICE initially intended to increase bed capacity at detention facilities in order to accommodate potential surges in apprehensions that could result from implementation of the executive order. According to ICE officials, ICE identified 1,100 additional beds available at detention facilities already in use. However, officials also stated that, as of February 2018, ICE has not needed to use these additional beds due to a decrease in the number of apprehensions.
- Additionally, ICE officials indicated no acquisition actions were needed because contracts and agreements are in place at existing detention facilities and additional beds are available for excess capacity. CBP and ICE are continuously monitoring bed space requirements based on migration volume. According to ICE officials, as of February 2018, ICE had no additional actions planned to increase bed capacity.

---

[58] See 8 U.S.C. § 1225 (regarding inspection of applicants for admission). The Immigration and Nationality Act, as amended, provides DHS with broad discretion (subject to certain legal standards) to detain or release aliens on bond, conditional parole, or terms of supervision, depending on the circumstances and statutory basis for detention. The law requires DHS to detain particular categories of aliens, such as those deemed inadmissible for certain criminal convictions or terrorist activity. See 8 U.S.C. §§ 1225, 1226, 1226a, 1231. See also Department of Homeland Security, *Implementing the President's Border Security and Immigration Enforcement Improvement Policies,* (February 2017).

- DHS's Office of Strategy, Policy and Plans convened a cross-component meeting to discuss detention standards, which govern the conditions of detainee confinement, according to DHS officials. ICE officials reported that ICE is currently re-writing its national detention standards (the standards applicable at most county jails housing immigration detainees). According to officials, the new standards are intended to make it easier for local jurisdictions to comply with standards without completely re-writing their existing policies to conform to ICE's requirements.
- USCIS officials told us they began working with ICE to identify where additional asylum officers were needed based on workload needs and space availability as soon as the executive order was issued in January 2017. From February 2017 through February 2018, USCIS deployed between 30 and 64 asylum officers during any given week along the southern border and continues to do so in response to caseload needs. USCIS continues to monitor and periodically adjust asylum officer staffing requirements, according to USCIS officials.

DOJ

DOJ officials stated that DOJ components coordinated with ICE to identify removal caseloads along the southern border that were large enough to warrant additional immigration judges. According to DOJ officials, from March 2017 through October 2017, EOIR detailed approximately 40 immigration judge positions, both in person and by video teleconference, to 19 DHS detention facilities, including many along the southern border, in response to the executive order. DOJ officials further explained that as caseloads fluctuated, some of the details ended, some in-person details were converted to video teleconference, and some details were converted to permanent immigration judge positions. EOIR often details immigration judges for operational reasons; however officials noted that the scale of this detail mobilization was larger because of the executive order.

Budget Overview

DHS

- **Fiscal Year 2017:** Because Executive Orders 13767 and 13768 were issued during fiscal year 2017, DHS submitted a budget amendment and requested supplemental appropriations to address the needs of the department in support of executive order implementation. The request proposed funding to increase daily immigration detention capacity to 45,700 detention beds by the end of fiscal year 2017. The request stated that the detention capacity was necessary to implement the administration's immigration enforcement policies for removing foreign nationals illegally entering or residing in the United States.
  - **ICE**: On May 5, 2017, ICE received a supplemental appropriation of $236.9 million for enforcement and removal operations, including $147.9 million for custody operations, $57.4 million for alternatives to detention, and $31.6 million for transportation and removal operations.[59] According to ICE documentation, almost all of the funds from that additional appropriation were obligated and expended at the conclusion of fiscal year 2017, as shown in Table 8.

Table 8. U.S. Immigration and Customs Enforcement (ICE) Fiscal Year 2017 Supplemental Appropriation Obligations and Expenditures

ICE activity	Obligated and expended
Custody Operations	$147,869,962
Alternatives to Detention	$57,392,000
Transportation Removal Program	$31,629,395
Total	$236,891,357

Source: ICE Budget Office. | GAO-18-470.

[59] ICE received an appropriation of approximately $2.6 billion, nearly $379 million over the request, for its Custody Operations, as well as the additional $236.9 million. Pub. L. No. 115-31, div. F, titles. II, VI,131 Stat. at 406-07, 435; 163 Cong. Rec. at H3811, H3823.

- **USCIS:** USCIS documentation estimated that it expended at least $4.2 million detailing asylum officers to immigration detention facilities along the southern border from February 2017 through February 2018.[60]

- **Fiscal Year 2018:** The President's budget requested an additional $1.5 billion above the 2017 annualized continuing appropriations level, for expanded detention, transportation, and removal of foreign nationals who enter, or remain in, the United States, in violation of U.S. immigration law.[61] As part of the $1.5 billion requested, the ICE congressional budget justification requested $1.2 billion in additional funds to support an average daily population (ADP) of detainees of 51,379—a 49 percent increase over fiscal year 2016 ADP (34,376).[62] The request stated that Executive Order 13768 and subsequent department guidance were expected to drive increases in the ADP due to the increase in ICE law enforcement officers and an expected increase in the average length of stay at detention facilities. ICE also requested funds for transportation and alternatives to detention. In fiscal year 2018, ICE was appropriated $4.1 billion to support enforcement and removal operations. According to DHS officials, the Consolidated Appropriations Act, 2018, provides funds for an ADP of 40,520 total beds, 10,859 lower than requested.
- **Fiscal Year 2019:** The President's budget requested $2.5 billion for detention and removal capacity. As part of the $2.5 billion

---

[60] USCIS officials noted that they combined information from two different systems to provide this cost estimate. They also cited limitations with their travel system that may have resulted in certain trips or costs not being captured in the estimate provided. In particular, the USCIS travel system does not require the traveler to identify the specific facility the traveler is operating out of, nor does its method of reporting provide an accurate accounting of each stop in a multi-destination trip, according to USCIS officials. Additionally, some of the asylum officer details were ongoing as of the date the data were pulled; therefore USCIS used the amount authorized for travel in lieu of the final amount actually expended, as those data were not available.

[61] The fiscal year 2018 and fiscal year 2019 President's budgets present the requests differently for detention and removal. The fiscal year 2018 President's Budget does not present the total requested funds; instead, it solely identifies the additional funds requested.

[62] To project its detention costs, ICE primarily relies on two variables—the average dollar amount to house one adult detainee for one day (bed rate) and the ADP of detainees.

requested, ICE's congressional budget justification states \$2.3 billion will support an ADP of 47,000.[63] According to the ICE congressional budget justification, the number of beds will sustain the fiscal year 2017 ADP level (38,106) and provide additional detention capacity stemming from the continued implementation of Executive Order 13768. ICE also requested funds for transportation and alternatives to detention.

- **Prior GAO Work:** Our prior work on immigration detention examined ICE's formulation of its budget request and cost estimate for detention resources. In April 2018, we found errors and inconsistencies in ICE's calculations for its congressional budget justifications and bed rate model. Specifically, we found that ICE made errors in its budget justifications, underestimated the actual bed rate, and its methods for estimating detention costs did not meet the characteristics of a reliable cost estimate. We also found ICE did not document its methodology for its projected ADP. We recommended that ICE assess and update its adult bed rate and ADP methodology and take steps to ensure that its budget estimating process fully addresses cost estimating best practices.[64] DHS concurred with our recommendations and plans to take actions in response to them.

DOJ

- **Fiscal Year 2017:** DOJ documentation showed it expended approximately \$2.4 million detailing immigration judge positions to immigration detention facilities from March 2017 through October 2017, either through video teleconferencing, or in-person, to adjudicate removal proceedings. EOIR officials explained the

---

[63] According to DHS officials, the fiscal year 2019 request may be modified to include additional funding for enforcement and removal operations. For example, according to DHS budget documentation, DHS plans to increase its request to \$2.8 billion for 52,000 detention beds.

[64] GAO, *Immigration Detention: Opportunities Exist to Improve Cost Estimates*, GAO-18-343 (Washington, D.C.: April 18, 2018).

funds used were unobligated balances carried over from a prior fiscal year.

- **Fiscal Year 2018:** For fiscal year 2018, DOJ requested an increase of $75 million to hire 75 additional immigration judge teams to enhance public safety and law enforcement.[65] According to DOJ officials, the agency received sufficient funds in the fiscal year 2018 budget to meet this hiring goal.
- **Fiscal Year 2019:** The fiscal year 2019 President's budget also requests an increase of $40 million for 75 new immigration judge teams at EOIR and nearly $40 million for 338 new prosecuting attorneys at ICE to ensure immigration cases are heard expeditiously. According to the President's budget, these investments are critical to the prompt resolution of newly-brought immigration charges and to reduce the 650,000 backlog of cases currently pending in the immigration courts. EOIR's fiscal year 2019 congressional budget justification includes a program increase totaling almost $65 million to provide funding for immigration judges and support staff, as well as information technology efforts. This increase supports initiatives that implement Presidential and Attorney General priority areas, among other things.

Parole and Asylum

Executive Order: 13767

Provision: Section 11

Provision Summary: Section 11 directs the Department of Homeland Security (DHS) to ensure that parole is exercised on a case-by-case basis in accordance with existing statutory criteria, and that asylum referrals and credible and reasonable fear determinations are conducted in a manner consistent with relevant statute and regulation.

Key Agency(ies) Responsible: DHS: U.S. Citizenship and Immigration Services (USCIS)

---

[65] The President's fiscal year 2018 budget states that the proposed funding for immigration judge hiring would bring the total number of funded immigration judge teams to 449.

Program Context: USCIS has discretion to authorize parole for urgent humanitarian reasons or significant public benefit, which it uses to allow an individual, who may be inadmissible or otherwise ineligible for admission to come to the United States for a temporary period. USCIS asylum officers adjudicate asylum applications filed with USCIS, and conduct credible and reasonable fear screenings to determine if certain removable foreign nationals may be eligible to seek particular forms of relief or protection in immigration court.

Action Overview

- According to DHS officials, DHS reviewed all existing category parole programs and made recommendations to modify or discontinue the programs based on the directives in Executive Order 13767 and additional guidance from the Secretary of Homeland Security.[66] USCIS officially terminated the Central American Minors Parole Program in August 2017.[67] Additionally, DHS is seeking to rescind the International Entrepreneur Parole program.[68] According to USCIS officials, as of January 2018 DHS leadership was reviewing recommendations for the remaining programs for decision.

---

[66] USCIS operates several humanitarian, or category, parole programs, through which the agency has special policies for considering parole requests from certain groups. For example, USCIS has special policies for considering parole requests from Haitian nationals with family members that are U.S. citizens or lawful permanent residents, in order to promote family unity and reduce separation time from their relatives in Haiti.

[67] See Termination of the Central American Minors Parole Program, 82 Fed. Reg. 38,926 (Aug. 16, 2017). The Central American Minors Parole Program was established in 2014 to provide special consideration of parole for certain minors in El Salvador, Guatemala, and Honduras, while still in their home country who were determined to be ineligible for refugee status.

[68] See International Entrepreneur Rule: Delay of Effective Date, 82 Fed. Reg. 31,887 (July 11, 2017) (final rule temporarily delaying effective date of International Entrepreneur Rule, 82 Fed. Reg. 5238, while DHS works to rescind the rule pursuant to Executive Order 13767). This delay rule was vacated by the U.S. District Court for the District of Columbia in *Nat'l Venture Capital Ass'n v. Duke*, No. 17- 1912, 2017 U.S. Dist. LEXIS 197738 (D.D.C. 2017). Therefore, DHS will accept applications under the International Entrepreneur Rule while moving forward with a notice of proposed rulemaking to rescind it. See Removal of International Entrepreneur Parole Program, 83 Fed. Reg. 24,415 (May 29, 2018). Under the International Entrepreneur Parole program, DHS may use its discretionary parole authority to grant a temporary period of authorized stay, on a case-by-case basis, to foreign start-up entrepreneurs who demonstrate a significant public benefit to the United States.

- The initial step for certain removable individuals to demonstrate they are eligible to be considered for particular forms of relief or protection from removal in immigration court, is a credible or reasonable fear interview with a USCIS asylum officer.[69] USCIS reviewed its credible and reasonable fear determination guidance and made select modifications pursuant to the executive order. For example, USCIS added language related to evaluating an applicant's credibility based on prior statements made to other DHS officials to establish a credible fear of persecution or torture. USCIS also issued modified guidance and provided additional training to its officers outlining the changes, according to USCIS officials.
- The Secretary directed USCIS to increase the operational capacity of the Fraud Detection and National Security (FDNS) Directorate and other operations to detect and prevent fraud in asylum and benefit adjudication processes. USCIS officials reported that from February 2017 to February 2018, between zero and five FDNS officers were deployed to southern border sites on any given week in response to the executive order.
- A February 2017 DHS memorandum entitled *Implementing the President's Border Security and Immigration Enforcement Improvement Policies*, directed the heads of USCIS, U.S. Customs and Border Protection, and U.S. Immigration and Customs Enforcement to develop uniform written guidance and training regarding proper processing of unaccompanied alien children.[70] In response, USCIS officials told us DHS and USCIS are assessing the unaccompanied alien children process, guidance, and training and finalizing a modified policy proposal, as of January 2018.

---

[69] See 8 U.S.C. §§ 1225(b) (inspection of applicants for admission, including process for determining, and definition of, "credible fear of persecution"), 1228(b) (administrative removal for a foreign national convicted of an aggravated felony at any time after admission), 1231(a)(5) (reinstatement of removal order for illegal reentry); 8 C.F.R. §§ 208.30 (credible fear determinations), 1208.30, 208.31 (reasonable fear determinations), 1208.31, 238.1, 1238.1, 241.8, 1241.8.

[70] Department of Homeland Security, *Implementing the President's Border Security and Immigration Enforcement Improvement Policies*, (February 2017).

Budget Overview

- In fiscal year 2018, USCIS requested and received a total of $43.4 million in fee spending authority for 143 positions and other expenses associated with changes in operational requirements attributable to the executive orders on border security and immigration enforcement. According to USCIS officials, the staffing resources are for the USCIS FDNS Directorate.[71] USCIS also requested and received $42 million in fee spending authority for refugee and asylum travel expenses, including travel for applicant interviews. This includes travel costs to the southwest border for asylum officers to interview detainees in support of the executive order, among other things.[72]
- In fiscal year 2019, USCIS requested a total increase of $287.5 million for all programs, projects, and activities to support changes in operational requirements driven by changes to benefit request receipt volumes and complexity of work, including implementing the executive orders.
- Additional Funds Saved and Expended:
  - According to USCIS officials, USCIS saved approximately $274,000 from not renewing contracts to administer the Central American Minors Parole Program.
  - According to USCIS documentation, USCIS expended approximately $70,300 to deploy FDNS officers along the southern border from March 2017 to February 2018.

---

[71] USCIS officials noted that a portion of these resources will also be designated for refugee and asylum caseloads, as well other related USCIS workloads.

[72] These funds also cover costs associated with overseas refugee processing. For more information related to the refugee process see Refugee Admissions Program Realignment summary.

Hiring

Executive Order: 13767 and 13768

Provision: Section 8 and Section 7

Provision Summary: Section 8 of Executive Order 13767 directs U.S. Customs and Border Protection (CBP) to hire 5,000 additional U.S. Border Patrol (Border Patrol) agents. Section 7 of Executive Order 13768 directs U.S. Immigration and Customs Enforcement (ICE) to hire 10,000 additional immigration officers.

Key Agency(ies) Responsible: Department of Homeland Security (DHS): CBP and ICE

Program Context: CBP and ICE hiring demands are driven by various factors, such as national security objectives, executive-level policies, legislative mandates, and component-specific operational requirements. Border Patrol agents are to respond to, and interdict, cross-border threats and ICE officers are responsible for apprehending individuals within the United States who may be removable for various reasons, including entering the country illegally or being convicted of certain crimes.

Source: U.S. Immigration and Customs Enforcement. | GAO-18-470.

Action Overview

DHS has taken a number of actions to implement the executive order hiring provisions. Specifically, DHS requested and the Office of Personnel Management approved a number of changes to assist DHS and its components with the executive order hiring directives. These changes include granting CBP and ICE direct hire authority and a special salary rate for polygraphers, among others.[73] DHS's Office of the Chief Human Capital Officer and DHS components' human capital offices also began additional hiring planning, such as refining component-level hiring plans, coordinating on potential joint hiring events, and targeting specific recruitment efforts, such as military veterans. CBP and ICE have also taken the following additional actions:

- **CBP**: In November 2017, CBP awarded a contract not to exceed $297 million to Accenture Federal Service LLC to help with law enforcement hiring for all CBP components. The contract is structured so the contractor receives a set dollar amount for each law enforcement officer hired—80 percent for each final offer letter and 20 percent for each law enforcement officer who enters on duty.[74] The contractor is to assist CBP in hiring 7,500 qualified agents and officers, including 5,000 Border Patrol agents, 2,000 CBP officers, and 500 Air and Marine Interdiction agents over 5 years.[75] CBP expects Accenture to be fully operational and effectively provide surge hiring capacity by June 2018, according to CBP officials.

[73] Direct-Hire Authority enables an agency to hire, after public notice is given, any qualified applicant without regard to 5 U.S.C. §§ 3309-3318, 5 C.F.R. pt. 211, or 5 C.F.R. pt. 337, subpt. A. A direct-hire authority expedites hiring by eliminating competitive rating and ranking, veterans' preference, and other procedures.

[74] The amount awarded per hire varies based on contract year and type of hire. For example, in the first 2 years, Accenture is to receive a total of approximately $40,000 for each Border Patrol agent hired.

[75] As a result of the directive to hire 5,000 additional Border Patrol agents, Border Patrol is aiming to have 26,370 agents, 5,000 above the fiscal year 2016 statutorily-established level, by the end of fiscal year 2021. In recent years however, CBP has not been able to attain statutorily-established minimum staffing levels for its Border Patrol agent positions target. Border Patrol finished fiscal year 2017 with 19,437 Border Patrol agents, or nearly 7,000 agents below the new target.

- **ICE**: According to ICE Office of Human Capital (OHC) officials, OHC is ensuring policies and procedures are in place so that ICE is ready to begin hiring additional immigration officers and support staff if funds are appropriated. In January 2018, ICE OHC also issued a contract solicitation for recruitment, market research, data analytics, marketing, hiring, and onboarding activities. ICE OHC sought to procure comprehensive hiring and recruitment services to assist ICE OHC in meeting the demands required to achieve the executive order's hiring goals and develop efficiencies to current OHC processes. ICE aimed to have a similar pricing structure as CBP's Accenture contract, according to the solicitation. Specifically, according to the solicitation, the yet to be selected contractor would receive a set dollar amount for each frontline officer hired–80 percent for each preliminary offer letter and 20 percent for each frontline officer who enters on duty.[76] The contractor would assist ICE in hiring 10,000 law enforcement agents, including 8,500 deportation officers and 1,500 criminal investigators. It would also assist in the hiring of approximately 6,500 support personnel positions. In May 2018, the contract solicitation was cancelled; however, the government anticipates re-soliciting the requirement in fiscal year 2019. According to the contract cancellation notice and an ICE OHC official, DHS cancelled the contract due to delays associated with the fiscal year 2018 budget and hiring timelines, as well as the limited number of additional ICE positions funded in the fiscal year 2018 budget. In the interim, ICE is partnering with the Office of Personnel Management to meet the executive order's hiring goals and develop efficiencies to current OHC processes, according to ICE officials.

---

[76] As of May 2018, this contract had not been awarded; therefore the amount awarded per hire has not been stipulated.

Budget Overview

- Because Executive Orders 13767 and 13768 were issued during fiscal year 2017, DHS submitted a budget amendment and requested supplemental appropriations to help address the needs of the department in support of executive order implementation. The request included funding for DHS agencies to begin building the administrative capacity necessary to recruit, hire, train and equip the additional 5,000 Border Patrol agents and 10,000 ICE officers. The Federal Law Enforcement Training Centers (FLETC), which provides training to law enforcement professionals who protect the homeland, including any new ICE and CBP personnel hired as result of the executive orders, also requested funds to support these efforts.
- On May 5, 2017, CBP received an additional appropriation of $65.4 million to improve hiring processes for Border Patrol agents, CBP officers, and Air and Marine Operations personnel, and for officer relocation enhancements.[77] Of the $65.4 million appropriated in fiscal year 2017, CBP obligated $18.8 million and expended $14.1 million as of January 2018. While ICE also received additional funding for custody operations, alternatives to detention, and transportation and removal, it did not receive supplemental funds in fiscal year 2017 specifically for hiring. DHS also requested funds for CBP, ICE, and FLETC hiring and training in fiscal year 2018 and fiscal year 2019. For additional details, see Table 9.
- According to FLETC officials, the total average cost to provide basic law enforcement training varies by agencies and position, as shown in Table 10. FLETC officials noted their partners also provide additional training unique to their missions, which is not included in the costs below.

---

[77] Pub. L. No. 115-31, div. F, tit. VI, 131 Stat. at 433.

Table 9. Department of Homeland Security (DHS) Funds Requested and Appropriated for Executive Order Hiring, Fiscal Years (FY) 2017 through 2019

U.S. Customs and Border Protection (CBP)	
FY17 Supplemental Appropriations (requested)	$65 million to build hiring capacity to recruit and onboard 5,000 U.S. Border Patrol (Border Patrol) agents
FY17 Supplemental Appropriations (funded)	$65.4 million to improve hiring processes for CBP and for relocation enhancements
FY18 requested	$100 million for 500 additional Border Patrol agents
FY18 Appropriations (funded)	$10 million above the request for CBP recruitment and retention and $10 million above the request for Border Patrol agent relocation incentives[a]
FY19 requested	$164 million for 750 additional Border Patrol agents
U.S. Immigration and Customs Enforcement (ICE)	
FY17 Supplemental Appropriations (requested)	$76 million to build hiring capacity to recruit and onboard 10,000 ICE agents and officers
FY17 Supplemental Appropriations (funded)	No funds specifically for executive order hiring
FY18 requested	$185.9 million for 1,000 additional ICE law enforcement officers and agents and 606 support staff
FY18 Appropriations (funded)	$15.7 million for 65 agents and 70 attorneys and support staff
FY19 requested	$571 million for 2,000 additional ICE law enforcement officers and agents
Federal Law Enforcement Training Centers (FLETC)	
FY17 Supplemental Appropriations (requested)	$25 million for the hiring and training of instructors to support law enforcement officer hiring and training within CBP and ICE
FY17 Supplemental Appropriations (funded)	No funds specifically for executive order hiring
FY18 requested	$29 million for training 1,000 additional ICE officers and 500 additional Border Patrol agents in response to the executive orders
FY18 Appropriations (funded)	No funds specifically for executive order hiring
FY19 requested	$25.7 million above the FY18 request for training new Border Patrol agents and ICE immigration enforcement officers

Source: Public Law 115-31, Public Law 115-141, and DHS budget documentation. | GAO-18-470.

[a]Additionally, in fiscal year 2018, approximately $204 million was redirected within CBP from salaries and expenses to enhance CBP-wide recruitment and retention activities as well as other operational requirements. See Consolidated Appropriations Act, 2018, Pub. L. No. 115-141, 132 Stat. 348, and accompanying Explanatory Statement, 164 Cong. Rec. H2045, H2547 (daily ed. March 22, 2018). According to DHS officials, approximately $8.2 million was also provided above the request for 351 new CBP officers (the executive orders did not include provisions related to hiring CBP officers).

Table 10. Average Cost Estimates to Provide Basic Law Enforcement Training at Federal Law Enforcement Training Centers (FLETC)

Component	Position	Average Cost Per Agent Incurred by Component	Average Cost Per Agent Total
U.S. Immigration and Customs Enforcement (ICE)	ICE Enforcement and Removal Deportation Officer	$26,000 incurred by ICE	$38,000
		$12,000 incurred by FLETC	
ICE	ICE Homeland Security Investigations Criminal Investigator	$35,800 incurred by ICE	$57,300
		$21,500 incurred by FLETC	
U.S. Customs and Border Protection (CBP)	U.S. Border Patrol agent	$11,000 incurred by CBP	$29,000
		$18,000 incurred by FLETC	

Source: FLETC. | GAO-18-470.

Note: According to Department of Homeland Security officials, the costs in this table do not represent the total costs to train CBP and ICE personnel.

Federal-State Agreements

Executive Order: 13767 and 13768

Provision: Section 10 and Section 8

Provision Summary: Section 10 and Section 8 of Executive Orders 13767 and 13768, respectively, direct the Department of Homeland Security (DHS) to engage with state and local entities to enter into agreements under Section 287(g) of the Immigration and Nationality Act.

Key Agency(ies) Responsible: DHS: U.S. Immigration and Customs Enforcement (ICE)

Program Context: The Illegal Immigration Reform and Immigrant Responsibility Act of 1996 added Section 287(g) to the Immigration and Nationality Act, which authorizes ICE to enter into agreements with state and local law enforcement agencies, permitting designated state and local officers to perform immigration law enforcement functions.

Action Overview

ICE officials reported expediting review of pending 287(g) requests and approved 46 additional state and local jurisdictions for the program from February 2017 through March 2018, bringing the total to 76 law enforcement agencies in 20 states. See Figure 2 for a map of additional jurisdictions approved.[78]

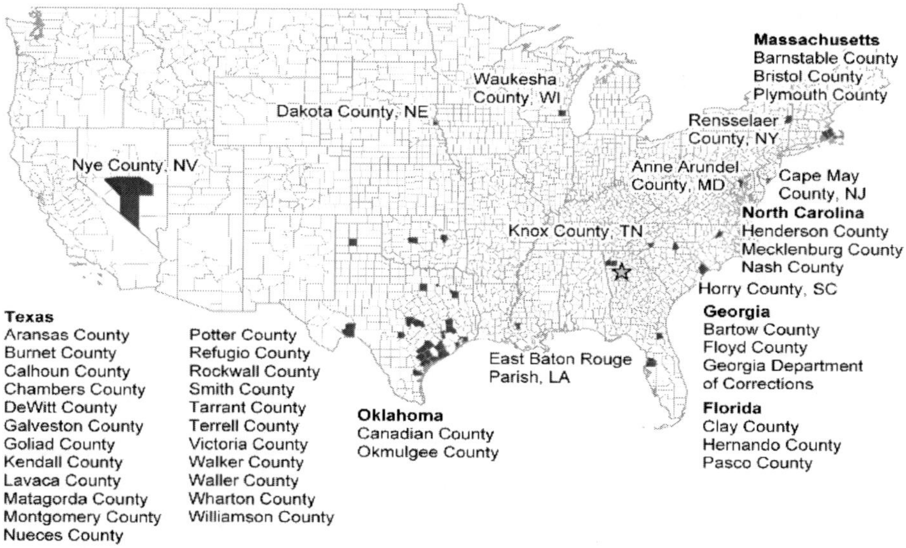

Source: U.S. Immigration and Customers Enforcement; MapInfo (map). | GAO-18-470.

Note: U.S. Immigrations and Customs Enforcement (ICE) may enter into 287(g) agreements with various entities, such as sheriff's offices, departments of correction, police departments, and local counties. The agreements ICE has entered into since February 2017 have all been with sheriff's offices, except Anne Arundel County in Maryland, Okmulgee County in Oklahoma, and the Georgia Department of Corrections.

Figure 2. Locations of Law Enforcement Agencies with New Mutually Signed 287(g) Agreements from February 2017 through March 2018.

---

[78] All current 287(g) agreements operate under a jail enforcement model, which operates solely within the confines of a jail. Under this model a potentially removable foreign national must first be arrested by local law enforcement on criminal charges and brought to the facility before any 287(g) screening activity takes place.

- According to ICE officials, ICE also conducted outreach with state and local officials and identified potential law enforcement partners with whom to enter into possible future 287(g) agreements. U.S. Customs and Border Protection (CBP) officials stated that they agreed to support ICE's program expansion efforts and provided hundreds of viable state and local law enforcement referrals to ICE to assist with this effort. For example, CBP reviewed data and conducted a gap analysis, to include a survey, to identify potential law enforcement partners for future 287(g) memorandums of agreement.
- CBP officials further noted that they introduced new language into Operation Stonegarden grant guidance that allows the use of grant funding to support CBP-identified, 287(g) law enforcement operational activities.[79] According to CBP and ICE officials, efforts to develop a 287(g) enforcement model that can be used for this purpose are pending.
- According to ICE officials, the agency is considering developing a program under which designated local law enforcement officers would be trained and authorized to serve and execute administrative warrants for individuals who are in violation of U.S. immigration laws at the time they are released from state criminal custody. ICE officials indicated that program participants would have limited authority under 287(g). For example, they would not interview individuals regarding nationality and removability, lodge detainers, or process individuals for removal. ICE has not yet finalized the program and it may evolve as ICE further develops the program, according to ICE officials.

---

[79] The Operation Stonegarden program supports enhanced cooperation and coordination among local, tribal, territorial, state, CBP, U.S. Border Patrol and other federal law enforcement agencies. It also funds investments in joint efforts to secure U.S. borders along routes of ingress from international borders to include travel corridors in states bordering Mexico and Canada, as well as states and territories with international water borders.

- ICE is also leveraging an existing Basic Ordering Agreement, a procurement tool to expedite acquisition of a substantial, but presently unknown, quantity of supplies or services, according to ICE officials.[80] A Basic Ordering Agreement is not a contract, but rather, is a written instrument of understanding, negotiated between ICE and state and local jurisdictions, to house detainees upon ICE's issuance and their acceptance of an Immigration Detainer and either a Warrant for Arrest of Alien or Warrant of Removal. For any order placed under the agreement, ICE will reimburse the provider, such as a state or local jurisdiction, for up to 48 hours of detention, under applicable regulations. The rate will be fixed at $50.00 for up to 48 hours of detention. No payment will be made for any detention beyond 48 hours.
- The Secretary of Homeland Security vested authority in CBP to accept state services to carry out certain immigration enforcement functions pursuant to Title 8, United States Code Section 1357(g). According to CBP officials, CBP also joined a 287(g) Program Advisory Board, which reviews and assesses ICE field office recommendations about pending 287(g) applications.

Budget Overview

- Participation in the 287(g) program is expected to expand further in fiscal years 2018 and 2019, according to ICE. Additionally, ICE anticipates further increase in the number of 287(g) memorandums of agreement in fiscal years 2018 and 2019.
  - In fiscal year 2018, ICE requested $24.3 million for ICE 287(g) program funding. According to the explanatory statement accompanying the Consolidated Appropriations Act, 2018, the 287(g) program was fully funded at the requested level.[81]

---

[80] 85See 48 C.F.R. § 16.703.

[81] 164 Cong. Rec. at H2552.

- In fiscal year 2019, ICE requested $75.5 million for ICE 287(g) program funding.[82]

Prosecution

> **Executive Order:** 13767 and 13768
>
> **Provision:** Sections 13 and 11
>
> **Provision Summary:** Section 13 of Executive Order 13767 directs the Department of Justice (DOJ) to establish prosecution guidelines and allocate appropriate resources to ensure that federal prosecutors prioritize offenses with a nexus to the southern border.
>
> Section 11 of Executive Order 13768 directs DOJ and the Department of Homeland Security (DHS) to develop and implement a program to ensure that adequate resources are devoted to prosecuting criminal immigration offenses, and to develop cooperative strategies to reduce the reach of transnational criminal organizations and violent crime.
>
> **Key Agency(ies) Responsible:** DOJ: Executive Office for United States Attorneys (EOUSA). DHS: Immigration and Customs Enforcement (ICE)
>
> **Program Context:** EOUSA provides executive and administrative support for United States Attorneys and Assistant United States Attorneys (AUSAs). AUSAs conduct trial work, as prosecutors, in which the United States is a party, including prosecution of criminal immigration offenses.
>
> ICE litigates charges of removability against foreign nationals and conducts criminal investigations, including investigations of immigration fraud.

Action Overview

DOJ

- The Attorney General released a memorandum with guidance for prioritizing certain immigration-related criminal offenses on April 11, 2017.[83]

---

[82] For fiscal years 2018 and 2019, the requested funds include all ICE funding for 287(g) program including funding across various programs, projects, and activities.

[83] Department of Justice, *Memorandum for All Federal Prosecutors: Renewed Commitment to Criminal Immigration Enforcement* (April 2017).

- For example, the memorandum requires that federal prosecutors consider prosecution of foreign nationals who illegally re-enter the United States after prior removal, and prioritize defendants with criminal histories. The memorandum states that further guidance and support of executing the increased priority on criminal immigration enforcement is forthcoming.
- By the end of April 2017, all 94 judicial districts designated one AUSA each to be the district border security coordinator, according to Office of the Deputy Attorney General officials. The border security coordinators are to oversee investigations and prosecutions and ensure that they are in line with the guidance in the Attorney General's April 2017 memorandum.
- Office of the Deputy Attorney General officials told us that the southern border districts developed guidelines for prioritizing misdemeanor cases involving individuals illegally entering the United States for the first time. However, according to these officials, southern border districts developed these guidelines based on an initial high volume of apprehensions, and when apprehensions decreased the guidelines were no longer necessary and never published.
- Beginning in late June 2017, EOUSA detailed three AUSAs to both the Western District of Texas and Arizona, and two AUSAs each to the Southern District of California, the District of New Mexico, and the Southern District of Texas, for a total of 12 details according to DOJ officials. The first round of details lasted for 6 months, and EOUSA extended the details of one AUSA at each southern border district for an additional 6 months. DOJ officials told us that EOUSA will continue to evaluate the need for additional details along the southern border based on the needs of the districts, as determined by the number of DHS apprehensions.

- According to DOJ officials, implementation of these provisions is ongoing and will depend largely upon DHS executive order actions—for instance, as DHS hires more enforcement personnel, criminal immigration cases may increase which could spur a need for more AUSAs.

DHS

- The Secretary of Homeland Security released a memorandum with guidance on the enforcement of immigration laws in the United States on February 20, 2017.[84] In response to this memorandum, ICE's Office of the Principal Legal Advisor sent guidance to its attorneys directing them to prioritize legal services supporting the timely removal of foreign nationals in accordance with Executive Order 13768. The guidance directed ICE to review all cases previously administratively closed based on prosecutorial discretion to determine whether the basis for closure remains appropriate under DHS's enforcement priorities.[85] The guidance also directed ICE to coordinate with the Executive Office for Immigration Review to ensure that foreign nationals charged as removable and who meet the enforcement priorities remain on active immigration court dockets and that their cases are completed as expeditiously as possible.

---

[84] Department of Homeland Security, *Enforcement of the Immigration Laws to Serve the National Interest* (February 2017).

[85] During removal proceedings, DHS's exercise of prosecutorial discretion has generally referred to requesting that an immigration judge administratively close a case because the respondent does not meet enforcement priorities. On May 17, 2018, the Attorney General determined that, except as specifically provided in regulation or a judicial settlement, immigration judges and the Board of Immigration Appeals lack general authority to administratively close removal proceedings. For cases which were administratively closed without requisite authority, if DHS or the respondent seeks reopening, the case shall be recalendared. See *Matter of CASTRO-TUM*, 27 I. & N. Dec. 271 (AG 2018).

- In response to the executive orders, ICE Homeland Security Investigations officials stated that the agency began to focus more of its resources on the investigation and criminal prosecution of immigration fraud. ICE Homeland Security Investigations added five new Document and Benefit Fraud Task Forces throughout the nation and directed field offices to increase staffing of task forces. Additionally, ICE is in the process of combining five Benefit Fraud Units into an immigration fraud center—the National Lead Development Center— that will serve as a new centralized entity that will refer cases to the task forces for enforcement action.

Budget Overview

DOJ

A summary of DOJ budget increase requests, appropriations, and expenditures related to prosecution priorities in the executive orders that we identified can be found in Table 11.

Table 11. Department of Justice Executive Office for United States Attorneys (EOUSA) Budget and Cost information Related to Executive Order Prosecution Priorities

Fiscal years 2017 and 2018 expenditures	Fiscal year 2018 budget request	Fiscal year 2018 appropriation	Fiscal year 2019 budget request
EOUSA expended approximately $358,550 out of regular operating funds, according to Department of Justice officials, for 12 AUSA details from June 2017 through December 2017.[a]	EOUSA requested $7.2 million for fiscal year 2018 to hire 70 new attorneys partially attributed to the President's executive orders on border security and immigration.	According to DOJ officials, the agency received sufficient funding to hire 70 new attorneys. In addition, officials noted that DOJ also received sufficient funding to hire paralegal positions included in the agency's fiscal year 2019 request.	EOUSA requested $1.1 million for fiscal year 2019 for 17 paralegal support positions to support the additional 70 immigration enforcement prosecutors from the fiscal year 2018 request.

Source: GAO summary of Department of Justice and federal budget information | GAO-18-470.

[a]Fiscal year 2018 data are as of February 2018, and as a result do not represent full fiscal year 2018 expenditures for detailing attorneys to the southern border.

DHS

The fiscal year 2018 President's budget request included $19.3 million for 195 attorney positions in ICE's Office of the Principal Legal Advisor.[86]

According to ICE officials, while the Consolidated Appropriations Act, 2018, included funds for 70 positions for the Homeland Security Investigations Law Division, it did not include funds for additional attorney positions for immigration litigation within the Office of the Principal Legal Advisor.[87]

The fiscal year 2019 President's budget request included $39.7 million for additional attorney resources in ICE's Office of the Principal Legal Advisor.[88]

Enforcement Priorities

Executive Order: 13768

Provision: Sections 5 and 10

Provision Summary: Sections 5 and 10 direct the Department of Homeland Security (DHS) to take action related to immigration enforcement.

Specifically, Section 5 directs DHS to prioritize the removal of certain categories of removable foreign nationals. Section 10 directs DHS to terminate the Priority Enforcement Program (PEP) and reinstitute Secure Communities, among other things.

Key Agency(ies) Responsible: DHS: U.S. Immigration and Customs Enforcement (ICE), U.S. Customs and Border Protection (CBP)

Program Context: Under PEP (from 2015 to 2017), ICE issued a request for detainer (with probable cause of removability) or information or transfer, for a priority removable individual, such as one posing a threat to national security or public safety, including a foreign national convicted of a felony, among others, under DHS's former tiered civil enforcement categories. Under Secure Communities, ICE may issue detainers for removable individuals charged, but not yet convicted, of criminal offenses, in addition to individuals subject to a final order of removal whether or not they have a criminal history.

---

86 This request for 195 attorney positions is included in ICE's overall fiscal year 2018 request for additional executive order related personnel (see Hiring summary).

87 164 Cong. Rec. at H2550 (nearly $5 million for attorneys and associated staff to support Homeland Security Investigations Law Division).

88 This request for additional attorney resources is included in ICE's overall fiscal year 2019 request for additional executive order related personnel (see Hiring summary).

Source: U.S. Immigration and Customs Enforcement. | GAO-18-470.

Action Overview

- Pursuant to Executive Order 13768, the Secretary of Homeland Security terminated PEP and reinstituted the Secure Communities program. As such, DHS is no longer required to utilize a tiered approach to civil immigration enforcement with direction to dedicate resources to those deemed of highest priority. Instead, under Section 5 of the executive order, various categories of removable individuals are general priorities for removal, and DHS personnel may initiate enforcement actions against all removable persons they encounter. Further, the DHS memorandum implementing this executive order allows ICE, CBP, and USCIS to allocate resources to prioritize enforcement activities within these categories, such as by prioritizing enforcement against convicted felons or gang members.
- As part of this effort, ICE reported it reviewed policies, regulations, and forms relevant to enforcement priorities. ICE subsequently rescinded prior enforcement priority guidance and issued new guidance directing application of the new approach to immigration enforcement prioritization. Additionally, ICE

eliminated existing forms and created a new form to place detainers on foreign nationals who have been arrested on local criminal charges and for whom ICE possesses probable cause to believe that they are removable from the United States, so that ICE can take custody of such individuals upon release.

- According to ICE officials, more than 43,300 convicted criminal aliens have been identified and removed through Secure Communities from January 25, 2017 through the end of fiscal year 2017.
    - Pursuant to Executive Order 13768 and in accordance with the Secretary of Homeland Security's memorandum entitled, *Enforcement of the Immigration Laws to Serve the National Interest*,[89] ICE's Enforcement and Removal Operations (ERO) expanded the use of the Criminal Alien Program (CAP) by increasing the use of Criminal Alien Program Surge Enforcement Team (CAPSET) operations, traditional CAP Surge operations, and the Institutional Hearing Program.[90] Specifically, ICE took the following actions:
    - ICE ERO conducted four CAPSET operations in Louisiana, Georgia, and California in fiscal year 2017, resulting in a total of 386 encounters, 275 detainers, and 261 charging documents issued, according to ICE documentation.[91]

---

[89] Department of Homeland Security, *Enforcement of the Immigration Laws to Serve the National Interest*, (February 2017).

[90] CAP provides ICE-wide direction and support in the biometric and biographic identification, arrest, and removal of priority aliens who are incarcerated within federal, state, and local prisons and jails, as well as at-large criminal aliens that have circumvented identification. The Institutional Hearing Program provides for the adjudication of immigration cases involving respondents who are incarcerated in federal, state, and local institutions for criminal offenses. Traditional CAP Surge operations focus deployment of CAP resources on conducting operations involving incarcerated aliens or criminal aliens that have circumvented identification. CAP Surge Enforcement Teams allow ERO field offices to concentrate resources in state, local, or federal detention facilities in order to identify and process large numbers of criminal aliens prior to their release from custody in an efficient manner.

[91] ICE encounters include, among other circumstances, individuals who are arrested and taken into ICE custody pursuant to the agency's civil immigration authorities. ICE may serve a charging document, known as a Notice to Appear, ordering an individuals' appearance before an immigration judge to respond to removal charges.

- ICE ERO field offices conducted CAP Surge operations, which concluded in March 2017. According to ICE documentation, the operations collectively resulted in 2,061 encounters, 668 arrests, 1,307 detainers issued, and 614 charging documents issued.
- ICE, along with the Department of Justice's Executive Office for Immigration Review and the Federal Bureau of Prisons, expanded the number of Institutional Hearing Program sites by nine, from 12 to 21. As of January 22, 2018, five of the nine Institutional Hearing Program expansion sites were operational.

- ICE officials reported that ICE also detailed over 30 percent more officers (79 officers) to support Community Shield efforts, an international law enforcement initiative to combat the growth and proliferation of transnational criminal street gangs, prison gangs, and outlaw motorcycle gangs throughout the United States.

Budget Overview

- According to ICE officials, CAP used existing resources in fiscal year 2017 to support the efforts required by Executive Order 13768.
- ICE also requested funds in fiscal years 2018 and 2019 for CAP. Specifically, ICE stated in its fiscal year 2018 and 2019 congressional budget justifications that CAP performs its duties in accordance with immigration enforcement priorities defined by Executive Order 13768.
    - In fiscal year 2018, ICE requested $412.1 million for CAP. The Consolidated Appropriations Act, 2018, funded $319.4 million for CAP, $92.6 million less than requested.[92]
    - In fiscal year 2019, ICE requested $619.1 million for CAP.

---

[92] See 164 Cong. Rec. at H2550.

- Additionally, according to the ICE fiscal year 2018 and fiscal year 2019 congressional budget justifications, the reinstitution of Secure Communities and expansion of federal-state agreements under 287(g) is expected to result in significant increases to apprehensions and removals within the United States. Subsequently ICE stated it requires additional detention and deportation officers and agents to handle this increased workload, which was incorporated as part of its request for funds to hire new law enforcement officers for the 10,000 directed in Executive Order 13768 (see Hiring summary). CAP also employs the 287(g) program in combination with Secure Communities (see Federal-State Agreements and Detention summaries).

Sanctuary Jurisdictions (Sharing Immigration Status Information)

Executive Order: 13768

Provision: Section 9

Provision Summary: Section 9 directs the Department of Justice (DOJ) and the Department of Homeland Security (DHS) to ensure that jurisdictions in willful noncompliance with 8 U.S.C. § 1373 (section 1373) are ineligible to receive federal grants. The section also directs DOJ to take appropriate enforcement action against any entity that violates section 1373, or which has in effect a policy, statute, or practice that prevents or hinders the enforcement of federal law.

Key Agency(ies) Responsible:

DOJ: Office of Justice Programs

DHS: U.S. Immigration and Customs Enforcement (ICE)

Program Context: The Attorney General determined that Section 9 will be applied solely to DOJ or DHS federal grants for jurisdictions willfully refusing to comply with section 1373. Under section 1373, a federal, state, or local government entity or official may not prohibit, or in any way restrict the exchange of information regarding citizenship or immigration status with DHS.

Action Overview

DOJ

- The Attorney General issued a May 22, 2017, memorandum clarifying the applicability of Section 9 of the executive order, which directs DOJ and DHS to ensure jurisdictions willfully prohibiting immigration status-related communication with the federal government (referred to as sanctuary jurisdictions) are not eligible for federal grants, and requiring jurisdictions applying for certain DOJ grants to certify their compliance with federal law, including section 1373. On November 20, 2017, enforcement of Executive Order 13768, section 9(a), was permanently enjoined by federal court order.[93] According to DOJ officials, no subsequent action has been taken to implement section 9(a).
- Prior to issuance of Executive Order 13768, the DOJ Inspector General conducted a compliance review of certain jurisdictions relative to 8 U.S.C. § 1373, and issued a report in May 2016 finding that 10 jurisdictions raised compliance concerns.[94] In response, DOJ placed a special condition on certain fiscal year 2016 grant awards, requiring recipients to submit an assessment of their compliance with section 1373. In November 2017, as part of the section 1373 compliance effort predating Executive Order 13768, DOJ sent letters to 29 jurisdictions expressing concern that they may not be in compliance with section 1373, and requesting

---

[93] As of April 2018, Section 9(a) remained permanently enjoined nationwide by the U.S. District Court for the Northern District of California, thereby prohibiting DOJ from taking actions to deny jurisdictions eligibility for federal grants pursuant to such section. See *Cty. Of Santa Clara v. Trump*, 275 F. Supp. 3d 1196 (N.D. Cal. Nov. 20, 2017) (the court granted the plaintiffs' motion for summary judgement regarding section 9(a) of Executive Order 13768, finding that it was unconstitutional on its face as a violation of the separation of powers doctrine and plaintiffs' tenth and 5th amendment rights).

[94] The May 2016 report also provided recommendations, such as providing clear guidance as to whether jurisdictions are expected to comply with section 1373, and requiring grant applicants to provide certifications specifying the jurisdiction's compliance with section 1373 *(Department of Justice Referral of Allegations of Potential Violations of 8 U.S.C. §1373 by Grant Recipients).*

responses regarding compliance.[95] In January 2018, DOJ sent 23 follow-up demand letters to jurisdictions seeking further documents to determine whether they are unlawfully restricting information sharing by their law enforcement officers with federal immigration authorities, and stating that failure to respond will result in records being subpoenaed.

DHS

- ICE developed weekly Declined Detainer Outcome Reports detailing jurisdictions with the highest volume of declined detainers and a list of sample crimes suspected or determined to have been committed by released individuals.[96] According to ICE officials, ICE identified data processing errors and incorrect detainer information and is working to correct these issues. ICE officials noted that they temporarily suspended the reports, and have not yet determined a specific time frame for future publications.
- DHS reviewed all DHS grant programs to determine which programs could be conditioned to require compliance with section 1373 and plans to provide this information to the Office of Management and Budget, according to DHS officials.

---

[95] See *City of Chicago v. Sessions,* 264 F. Supp. 3d 933 (N.D. Ill. 2017), *aff'd*, 2018 U.S. App. LEXIS 9862 (7th Cir. 2018) (While the U.S. District Court for the Northern District of Illinois granted a nationwide preliminary injunction against the Attorney General's imposition of two immigration-related "notice" and "access" conditions on the Byrne Justice Assistance Grants Program awards for fiscal year 2017, the court determined that the Attorney General has statutory authority to require the city to certify compliance with 8 U.S.C. § 1373 as a grant condition, and therefore denied Chicago's motion for a preliminary injunction in that regard).

[96] A detainer is a request from ICE to a government enforcement agency to provide ICE with a notice before a removable alien is released from criminal custody, and that the alien is held for a longer period of time in custody. In declining a detainer, a law enforcement agency will release a potentially removable individual upon conclusion of their term of imprisonment, instead of continuing to hold them in custody pursuant to a detainer request.

Budget Overview

- DOJ has not obligated, expended, or requested any additional funds to implement Executive Order 13768, section 9(a).
- The fiscal year 2019 President's budget proposed to amend the Illegal Immigration Reform and Immigrant Responsibility Act of 1996 to condition DHS and DOJ grants and cooperative agreements on state and local governments' cooperation with immigration enforcement.

Visa Entry Restrictions and Enhanced Screening and Vetting

Executive Order: 13780

Provision: Sections 2 and 5

Provision Summary: Section 2 directed multiple agencies, including the Department of State (State) and Department of Homeland Security (DHS), to conduct a worldwide review to identify any additional information needed from each foreign country to adjudicate immigration benefit applications and ensure that individuals applying for a visa or other immigration benefit are not a security or public safety threat. It also directed the agencies to send a report of the findings of the worldwide review to the President. This section further established visa entry restrictions applicable to foreign nationals from Iran, Libya, Somalia, Sudan, Syria, and Yemen for a 90-day period. It also stated that agencies, including State and DHS, could continue to submit additional countries for inclusion in visa entry restrictions.

Section 5 required agencies, including State, DHS, and the Department of Justice (DOJ), to develop a uniform baseline for screening and vetting to identify individuals seeking to enter the United States on a fraudulent basis or who support terrorism or otherwise pose a danger to national security or public safety.

Key Agency(ies) Responsible: State: Bureau of Consular Affairs (CA), DHS, and DOJ

Program Context: CA provides consular services in reviewing and adjudicating visa applications for those seeking to enter the United States. DHS adjudicates visa petitions, and DHS and DOJ also play roles in screening and vetting applicants. DHS and DOJ, along with State, are responsible for implementing the enhanced screening and vetting protocols established under the executive order.

Action Overview

Section 2

- An interagency working group comprised of State, DHS, the Office of the Director of National Intelligence, and National Security Council staff was formed to conduct the worldwide review to identify additional information needed from foreign countries regarding their nationals applying for U.S. immigration benefits, according to State officials. The DHS-led working group developed a set of criteria for inter-governmental information sharing for immigrant and nonimmigrant visa applications, which included three main categories: (1) identity management information, (2) national security and public-safety information, and (3) national security and public safety risk factors. The working group identified current standards and best practices for information collection and sharing under various categories of visas to create a core list of information needed from foreign governments to aid in immigration vetting in the visa adjudication process.
- State engaged with foreign governments on their information sharing practices based on the criteria identified above. In July 2017, State directed its posts to inform their respective host governments of the new information-sharing criteria and request that host governments provide the required information or develop a plan to do so. CA directed posts to engage more intensively with countries whose information-sharing and identity-management practices were preliminarily deemed "inadequate" or "at risk" and submit an assessment of mitigating factors or specific interests that should be considered in the deliberations regarding any travel restrictions. According to officials, State and its posts will continue to engage with foreign countries to address information-sharing and identify management deficiencies.

- The visa entry restrictions for nationals of listed countries lasted from June 29, 2017 through September 24, 2017. During the implementation period, if an applicant was found ineligible for a visa on other grounds unrelated to the executive order, such as prior criminal activity or immigration violations, the applicant would be refused the visa on those grounds, according to State officials. If the applicant was found to be otherwise eligible for the visa and did not qualify for an exemption or a waiver under the executive order, he or she would be refused on the basis of the executive order. CA sent several cables to posts with guidance on implementing the 90-day travel restriction, including operational guidance and updated guidance following court decisions. CA also offered trainings to consular posts on implementation of the order. A series of legal challenges ultimately led to the June 26, 2017 Supreme Court decision prohibiting enforcement of entry restrictions against foreign nationals who could credibly claim a bona fide relationship with a person or entity in the United States.[97]
- On September 24, 2017, pursuant to section 2(e) of Executive Order 13780, the President issued Presidential Proclamation 9645, which established conditional restrictions on U.S. entry for certain categories of nationals from Chad, Iran, Libya, North Korea, Syria, Venezuela, Yemen and Somalia, for an indefinite period.[98]

---

[97] See *Trump v. Int'l Refugee Assistance Project,* 137 S. Ct. 2080 (2017) (per curiam).

[98] 82 Fed. Reg. 45,161 (Sept. 27, 2017). Proclamation 9645 expanded the scope and duration of nationality-based visa entry restrictions from six to eight countries (removing Sudan, and adding Chad, North Korea, and Venezuela), and from a 90-day to an indefinite period for the revised list of countries; and contained periodic reporting requirements related to visa screening and vetting, among other things. Beginning on December 8. 2017, the Proclamation's visa entry restrictions have been fully implemented pursuant to the Supreme Court's December 4, 2017, orders staying the lower courts' injunctions (*Trump v. Int'l Refugee Assistance Project*, 138 S. Ct. 542, 2017 U.S. LEXIS 7358 (2017); *Trump v. Hawaii*, 138 S. Ct. 542, 2017 U.S. LEXIS 7357 (2017)), while the Supreme Court reviews Hawaii and Maryland federal district court rulings generally upheld by the Ninth (*Hawaii v. Trump*, 878 F.3d 662 (9th Cir. 2017) (per curiam)), and Fourth Circuits (*Int'l Refugee Assistance Project v. Trump*, 883 F.3d 233 (4th Cir. 2018)), respectively. See *Trump v. Hawaii*, 138 S. Ct. 923(2018) (The Supreme Court granted the government's certiorari petition and will therefore consider, and issue an opinion on the merits of, the Ninth Circuit's decision). On April 10, 2018, the President issued a proclamation announcing that

- According to State officials, State, DHS, DOJ, and other agencies formed a working group and developed a uniform baseline for screening and vetting standards and procedures to ensure ineligible individuals are not permitted to enter the United States, and are implementing the new requirements. The working group conducted a review of the visa screening and vetting process and established uniform standards for (1) applications, (2) interviews, and (3) system security checks, including biographic and biometric checks. According to State officials, for applications, the group identified data elements against which applicants are to be screened and vetted. For interviews, the working group established a requirement for all applicants to undergo a baseline uniform national security and public safety interview. The working group modeled its interview baseline on elements of the refugee screening interview.
- As of June 2017, State collected most of the data elements online for immigrant and nonimmigrant visas, according to State officials.
- The President issued a memorandum on February 6, 2018, directing DHS, in coordination with State, DOJ, and the Office of the Director of National Intelligence to establish a national vetting center to coordinate agency vetting efforts to identify individuals who pose a threat to national security, border security, homeland security, and public safety. The National Vetting Center will be housed in DHS, and will leverage the capabilities of the U.S. intelligence community to identify, and prevent entry of, individuals that may pose a threat to national security. On February 14, 2018, the Secretary of Homeland Security appointed a director for the National Vetting Center. The Secretary also

---

because Chad has improved its identity-management and information sharing practices sufficiently to meet U.S. baseline security standards, nationals of Chad will again be able to receive visas for travel to the United States. Maintaining Enhanced Vetting Capabilities and Processes for Detecting Attempted Entry Into the United States by Terrorists or Other Public-Safety Threats, Proclamation No. 9723, 83 Fed. Reg. 15,937 (April 13, 2018) (issued April 10).

delegated authorities of the National Vetting Center to the Commissioner of U.S. Customs and Border Protection.

Budget Overview

- State officials said that personnel worked overtime to implement Section 2 and the following Presidential Proclamation, but did not identify monetary costs or budget increases associated with implementation. DHS also dedicated several full-time staff positions to developing and implementing enhanced screening and vetting protocols, and DHS employees worked overtime to implement these provisions, according to officials.

Refugee Admissions Program Realignment

Executive Order: 13780

Provision: Section 6

Provision Summary: Section 6 directed the Department of State (State) to suspend travel of refugees seeking to enter the United States, and the Department of Homeland Security (DHS) to suspend adjudications on refugee applications, for 120 days. Section 6 further ordered that during the 120- day period, State, together with DHS, and the Office of the Director of National Intelligence review the refugee application and adjudication process to identify and implement additional procedures to ensure that refugees seeking entry into the United States under the United States Refugee Admissions Program (USRAP) do not pose a threat to U.S. security and welfare. This section also capped annual refugee admission at 50,000 in fiscal year 2017.

Key Agency(ies) Responsible: State: Bureau of Population, Refugees, and Migration (PRM)

DHS: U.S. Citizenship and Immigration Services (USCIS)

Program Context: The USRAP resettles refugees to the United States in accordance with a refugee admission ceiling set by the President each year. PRM is responsible for coordinating and managing the USRAP. USCIS is responsible for adjudicating refugee applications.

Action Overview

State

State generally suspended travel of refugees into the United States from June 29, 2017 through October 24, 2017.[99]

- State coordinated with DHS, the Office of the Director of National Intelligence, and other security vetting agencies on the 120-day review of the USRAP application and adjudication process to determine what additional procedures should be used to ensure that individuals seeking admission as refugees do not pose a threat to the security and welfare of the United States, according to State officials. Upon completion of the review, the agencies submitted a joint memorandum to the President.
- The United States admitted 53,716 refugees in fiscal year 2017, according to State officials. Throughout fiscal year 2017, State issued guidance that steered the refugee admissions program to different refugee arrival goals during different periods of time due to court decisions and budget considerations. Prior to the issuance of Executive Order 13769, which, after largely being blocked nationwide by a federal court injunction was revoked and replaced by Executive Order 13780, PRM operated at the rate of 110,000 refugees per year. After the issuance of Executive Orders 13769 and 13780, PRM officials noted that at times, State made no bookings for refugee arrivals, and also made bookings based on 50,000 arrivals, as well as 110,000 arrivals.

A series of legal challenges and resulting court injunctions culminated in the June 26, 2017, Supreme Court order limiting State's implementation

[99] In a June 26, 2017 ruling, the U.S. Supreme Court prohibited enforcement of travel restrictions against foreign nationals credibly claiming a bona fide relationship with a person or entity in the United States. See *Trump v. Int'l Refugee Assistance Project*, 137 S. Ct. 2080 (2017) (per curiam).

of this section to prospective refugees without bona fide ties to the United States.[100]

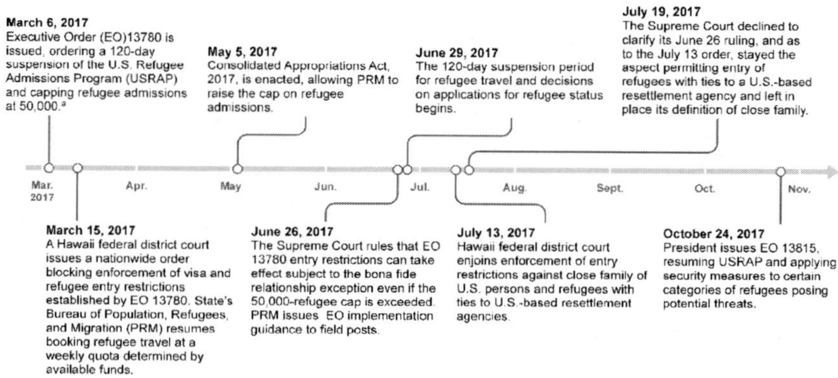

Source: GAO analysis of Information from PRM. | GAO-18-470.

[a]Executive Order 13780 revoked and replaced a prior order, Executive Order 13769, implementation of which had been largely enjoined nationwide shortly after issuance due to a federal court injunction. See *Washington V. Trump,* 2017 U.S. Dist. LEXIS 16012 (W.D. Wash. 2017), *aff'd,* 847 F.3d 1151 (9th Cir. 2017).

Figure 3. Key Milestones in Department of State Efforts to Implement the 120-Day Suspension of Refugee Admissions and 50,000 Refugee Cap in 2017.

Together with budget uncertainties, State could not enact the refugee travel suspension or 50,000-person admissions cap based on the timeline set in the executive order. Figure 3 below shows key milestones related to this section of the order.

DHS

- According to USCIS officials, USCIS is implementing new requirements and vetting procedures for refugees. For example, these officials stated that USCIS is accessing more detailed biographical information earlier in the vetting process. Additionally, these officials noted that USCIS's Fraud Detection

---

[100] "Bona fide ties" refers to the bona fide relationship to a person or entity in the United States that must have existed for a foreign national to be exempt from Executive Order 13780 travel restrictions under the Supreme Court's June 2017 decision.

and National Security unit is conducting additional reviews of applicants, including social media and other information against various databases. USCIS officials further noted that USCIS's International Operations office sent guidance to the field that established the logistical requirements of the new procedures. As of April 2018, USCIS was finalizing further guidance and training officers for the enhanced review and vetting procedures, according to USCIS officials.

- State officials said that State and DHS executed four categories of exemptions during the 120-day USRAP suspension: a Congolese woman with a life-threatening illness and her family; 29 unaccompanied refugee minors; 17 Yezidis and other religious minorities in northern Iraq who had been victims of ISIS; and 53 individuals on Nauru and Manus Islands.

Budget Overview

Table 12. Budgetary Costs and Cost-Avoidance Associated with the Refugee Suspension and Admission Cap

Costs	Cost-avoidance
The Department of State's Bureau of Population, Refugees, and Migration (PRM) reported unused airline tickets and cancellation fees totaled $2.4 million. Cancellation fees were approximately $282,000 and the ticket costs were approximately $2.1 million.[a]	PRM reported a budget savings of over $160 million in fiscal year 2017. PRM attributed these savings to refugee arrival numbers being lower than originally planned. Savings included reduced costs for overseas processing operations, among other things.

Source: GAO analysis of information provided by PRM | GAO-18-470.

[a]PRM incurred these costs as a result of the initial U.S. Refugee Admissions Program suspension in January 2017 pursuant to Executive Order 13769, which was largely blocked nationwide by federal court injunction shortly after issuance, and which Executive Order 13780 subsequently revoked and replaced. See *Washington v. Trump,* 2017 U.S. Dist. LEXIS 16012 (W.D. Wash. 2017), *aff'd,* 847 F.3d 1151 (9th Cir. 2017).

State characterized most costs in personnel resources terms. State officials told us that internally, PRM shifted priorities to implement Executive Order 13780 and to stay up-to-date on the evolving legal status of Section 6 in light of federal court orders. PRM identified some costs and savings, or cost avoidances, associated with implementing this provision, as described in Table 12.

Visa Interview Waiver Program

Executive Order: 13780

Provision: Section 9

Provision Summary: Section 9 directs the Department of State (State) to suspend the Visa Interview Waiver Program, subject to certain exceptions. To support this, the provision also directs State to expand the Consular Fellows program so that visa wait times are not unduly affected. The provision also directs State to make language training available to Consular Fellows outside of their core linguistic abilities.

Key Agency(ies) Responsible: State: Bureau of Consular Affairs (CA)

Program Context: Consular Fellows serve in U.S. embassies and consulates overseas and primarily adjudicate visa applications for foreign nationals. The Visa Interview Waiver Program formerly waived in-person interviews for certain categories of visa applicants.

Action Overview

- Following the issuance of Executive Order 13780, CA suspended the Visa Interview Waiver Program. CA instructed consular officers worldwide to require in-person interviews for all applicants between the ages of 14 and 79 except for those falling within specific statutory exceptions, including those whose interviews were formerly waived under the Visa Interview Waiver Program, according to CA officials.

- CA officials added that consular officers may still waive interviews for applicants for certain diplomatic or diplomatic-type visas, or who previously held a visa in the same category that expired less than 12 months prior to the new application.
- State exercised existing authorities to extend current Consular Fellow appointments by 12 months. In October 2017, State approved extending offers for follow-on 60-month Limited Non-Career Appointments to Consular Fellows who complete a successful initial 60-month appointment. State officials noted the first officer to accept a follow-on appointment was sworn in during April 2018. CA and State's Bureau of Human Resources updated the CA Limited Non-Career Appointments handbook to include an implementation plan for extending such appointments, and according to officials, providing language training outside of the applicant's area of core linguistic ability.
- In early 2017, State streamlined the application process for Consular Fellows and realigned resources to expedite their security clearance process, according to CA officials. From February 2017 through February 2018, State hired 134 new Consular Fellows, according to CA officials. Additionally, State officials said that they expect to hire 120 more Consular Fellows for the remainder of fiscal year 2018.
- In August 2017, the Foreign Service Institute created a 12-week Spanish Language program for Consular Fellows who received certain scores on the Spanish language exam, according to CA officials. Eleven Consular Fellows completed the program in January 2018 and 20 more are expected to complete the program in July 2018, according to CA officials. As of January 2018, five Consular fellows were being trained in a language outside their core linguistic ability, according to CA officials.

- While these actions were taken to support implementation of the executive order, CA officials also told us that hiring Consular Fellows has been a State priority for some time. CA officials said that the bureau has hired an increasing number of Consular Fellows to meet worldwide visa demand since 2012, and that providing consular services is one of State's highest priorities, as well as a national security imperative.

Budget Overview

- According to CA officials, because the Consular Fellows program is entirely funded by non-appropriated consular fees, subject to fluctuating demand for passports and visas, the expansion of the program did not have appropriations impacts. However, officials did provide per unit costs associated with aspects of expanding the Consular Fellows program. For example, Consular Fellows salaries range from approximately $48,000 to approximately $98,000 and Foreign Service Institute language courses last from 24 to 36 weeks, at a cost of $1,700 per week, per student.

APPENDIX II: EXECUTIVE ORDER REPORTS

Executive orders 13767 (Border Security and Immigration Enforcement Improvements), 13768 (Enhancing Public Safety in the Interior of the United States), and 13780 (Protecting the Nation from Foreign Terrorist Entry into the United States) include reporting requirements for the Department of Homeland Security (DHS), the Department of State (State), and the Department of Justice (DOJ).[101] Table 13 lists completed reports as of April 2018, according to DHS, State, and DOJ officials.

[101] Exec. Order No. 13767, 82 Fed. Reg. 8793 (Jan. 30, 2017) (issued Jan. 25); Exec. Order No. 13768, 82 Fed. Reg. 8799 (Jan. 30, 2017) (issued Jan. 25); and Exec. Order No. 13780, 82 Fed. Reg. 13,209 (Mar. 9, 2017) (issued Mar. 6).

Table 13. Reports Agencies Cited As Completed As of April 2018 in Response to Executive Orders 13767, 13768, and 13780

Executive Order	Executive Order section, report, and date signed or published according to agency officials	Responsible agencies
Executive Order 13767: Border Security and Immigration Enforcement Improvements	Section 4: • Comprehensive study of the security of the southern border to the President, signed Nov. 22, 2017	Department of Homeland Security (DHS)
	Section 9: • 60-day report on aid and assistance to the Mexican government, signed Mar. 27, 2017	Department of State (State), in consultation with other agencies
	Section 15: • 90-day progress report to the President, signed Sept. 28, 2017	DHS
Executive Order 13768: Enhancing Public Safety in the Interior of the United States	Section 9: • Weekly Declined Detainer Outcome Reports, published Feb. 3, 2017; Feb. 10, 2017; and Feb. 17, 2017[a]	DHS U.S. Immigration and Customs Enforcement
	Section 15: • 90-day progress report to the President, signed July 17, 2017 • 80-day progress report to the President, signed Nov. 16, 2017	DHS
	Section 16: • Quarterly reports on immigration status of all aliens incarcerated under the Federal Bureau of Prisons and U.S. Marshals Service, published on the DOJ website May 2, 2017; Aug. 1, 2017; Dec. 21, 2017; and ongoing	Department of Justice (DOJ), in consultation with DHS

Executive Order	Executive Order section, report, and date signed or published according to agency officials	Responsible agencies
Executive Order 13780:Protecting the s United States	Section 2: • 20-day worldwide country assessment of information sharing to the president, signed July 10, 2017 • 50-day country information sharing and travel restrictions to the president, assigned Sept. 15, 2017	DHS, in consultation with State and the Office of the Director of National Intelligence (ODNI)
	Section 5: • 60-day progress report to the President, signed May 22, 2017 • 100-day progress report to the President, signed July 14, 2017 • 200-day progress report to the President, signed Dec. 4, 2017	DHS, in consultation with State, DOJ, and ODNI
	Section 6: • United States Refugee Admissions Program review to the President, signed Oct. 23, 2017	State, in consultation with DHS and ODNI
	Section 11: • Transparency report on offenses and activity, terrorism and public-safety related, by foreign nationals, jointly published by DHS and DOJ on Jan. 16, 2018	DHS and DOJ

Source: GAO review of information provided by DHS, DOJ, and State. | GAO-18-470.

[a]U.S. Immigration and Customs Enforcement suspended publication of the Declined Detainer Outcome Reports to address data errors, according to agency officials.

Appendix III: Comments from the Department of Homeland Security

U.S. Department of Homeland Security
Washington, DC 20528

Homeland Security

May 23, 2018

Rebecca Gambler
Director, Homeland Security and Justice
U.S. Government Accountability Office
441 G Street, NW
Washington, DC 20548

Re: Management Response to Draft Report GAO-18-470, "BORDER SECURITY IMMIGRATION: "Initial Executive Order Actions and Resource Implications"

Dear Ms. Gambler:

Thank you for the opportunity to review and comment on the subject draft report. The U.S. Department of Homeland Security (DHS) appreciates the U.S. Government Accountability Office's (GAO) work in conducting its review and issuing this report.

The Department appreciates GAO's recognition of the actions DHS has taken, on-going, and planned to implement the President's Executive Orders (EO) relating to border security and immigration enforcement. DHS leadership and Components have endeavored to undertake a methodical, informed approach to ensuring all core DHS missions and EO requirements are resourced to the fullest extent possible. That effort began with guidance from former Secretary John Kelly on carrying out the President's EOs, resulted in a Budget Amendment to the Fiscal Year (FY) 2018 President's Budget, and continues today with the Department's requests for FY 2019 funding and legislative authorities now pending before Congress.

When it comes to critical needs, there is probably no issue more important for DHS right now than border security and immigration enforcement. The FY 2019 President's Budget makes crucial investments needed to secure our borders against threats of illegal entry. The Budget supports the recruitment, hiring, and training of 750 additional U.S. Border Patrol Agents; 2,000 additional U.S. Immigration and Customs Enforcement (ICE) law enforcement officers; and more than 1,500 support staff needed to more robustly execute the Department's border security and immigration enforcement missions. It also funds construction and renovations at the Federal Law Enforcement Training Centers to meet increased training requirements at DHS.

Investments in our layered defense at the border would include approximately 65 miles of new border wall construction in the highest-traffic zones along the Southwest Border, as well as priority tactical infrastructure, border security technology improvements, and aircraft acquisition. The Department also reiterates the importance of addressing the unfunded border wall requests from the FY 2018 Budget in addition to the investments outlined in the FY 2019 Budget. These investments ensure DHS law enforcement personnel are supported with effective surveillance technology and equipment to improve their ability to detect and interdict illegal activity.

The FY 2019 President's Budget also includes funding for 52,000 detention beds, including 2,500 beds reserved for family units, to ensure that apprehended aliens who are subject to removal from the United States – such as illegal border crossers, criminal aliens, and national security threats – are detained in safe and secure detention facilities pending their removal. For apprehended aliens who are not considered a threat to our communities, but who may pose a diminished flight risk, the President's Budget would fund ICE's Alternatives to Detention program to provide intensive supervision for up to 82,000 average daily participants through a combination of home visits, office visits, alert response, and electronic monitoring. Proposed funding for removal operations will facilitate the complex coordination required to return illegal immigrants safely and expeditiously to their home countries and pay for transportation costs.

In addition, the Budget proposes essential funding to implement the President's EO to intensify vetting of U.S.-bound travelers and individuals in our immigration system. Since the beginning of last year, DHS has undertaken historic efforts to improve every phase of the vetting process so that we can be more confident is knowing who is coming into our country – and more capable of identifying nefarious actors. This includes making applications more rigorous, deepening background checks, tightening travel and arrival screening, and enforcing foreign government information-sharing requirements. The FY 2019 Budget will facilitate the stand-up of the recently announced National Vetting Center (NVC), which will become a central U.S. Government hub for fusing intelligence, law enforcement, and homeland security data to enhance the vetting process. A detailed implementation plan is currently under development to identify NVC capacity and operational needs, which will inform future budget requests.

To achieve mission success and protect the Homeland, DHS also must have legislative authorities. Congress should pass legislation to eliminate legal loopholes that undermine border security and place our communities at risk. This includes terminating the *Flores* Settlement Agreement, amending the *Trafficking Victims Protection Reauthorizing Act*, clarifying the statutory definitions of "unaccompanied alien children" and "special immigrant juvenile," passing legislation that clearly defines an "aggravated felony," and allowing DHS to promptly remove violent criminal aliens from our nation. These solutions will provide the essential tools that the men and women of DHS need to secure our borders and defend our communities.

Enactment of the FY 2018 Consolidated Appropriations Act (P.L. 115-141) has given our frontline Components important resources to carry out EO requirements, and DHS is appreciative of the support from Congress. It cannot be overemphasized, however, that additional resources and legislative authorities are required to build on the progress made thus far.

Again, thank you for the opportunity to review and comment on this draft report. Technical comments were provided under separate cover. Please feel free to contact me if you have any questions. We look forward to working with you again in the future.

Sincerely,

JIM H. CRUMPACKER, CIA, CFE
Director
Departmental GAO-OIG Liaison Office

In: Immigration
Editor: Abel Thompson

ISBN: 978-1-53616-187-8

Chapter 2

MEXICO'S IMMIGRATION CONTROL EFFORTS*

Clare Ribando Seelke

BACKGROUND

In 2014, the United States and Mexico experienced a surge in unauthorized migration from Central America, a region that has overtaken Mexico as the primary source for immigrants apprehended at the U.S.-Mexican border. With U.S. support, Mexico has since increased its immigration control efforts. From 2015 to 2017, Mexico apprehended more than 450,000 migrants and asylum seekers from the "northern triangle" countries (El Salvador, Guatemala, and Honduras; see Figure 1). As at the U.S. southwest border, Mexico's apprehensions of migrants from the northern triangle fell in 2017 but increased by 57% in the first half of 2018 as compared to that period last year.

* This is an edited, reformatted and augmented version of Congressional Research Service, Publication No. IF10215, dated August 1, 2018.

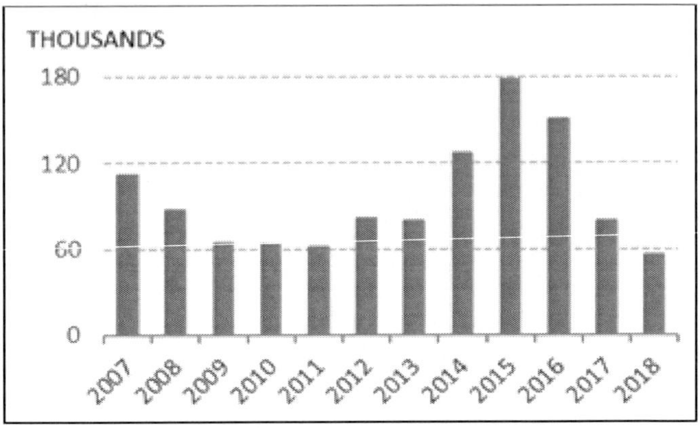

Source: Created by CRS with information from Mexico's Secretariat of Government (SEGOB).

Notes: Figures include January-June 2018.

Figure 1. Apprehensions of Migrants and Asylum Seekers in Mexico from the Northern Triangle (2007- mid-2018).

Mexico has received U.S. assistance for its immigration control efforts through the Mérida Initiative, a bilateral partnership launched in 2007 for which Congress has appropriated nearly $2.9 billion. Mexico also has received support for its humanitarian protection program through U.S. Migration and Refugee Assistance (MRA), implemented by the U.N. High Commissioner for Refugees (UNHCR) and others. Some U.S. policymakers have praised Mexico's immigration control efforts. Others have questioned Mexico's ability to protect migrants from abuse and to provide asylum to those in need of protection.

Concerns about Mexico's asylum system have increased as the Trump Administration reportedly has sought to have Mexico absorb U.S.-bound asylum seekers who transit its territory. Negotiations and migration cooperation may shift after Mexico's president-elect, Andrés Manuel López Obrador, takes office on December 1, 2018. López Obrador has pledged to work with the United States on migration issues but has suggested a focus on addressing root causes of illegal migration from southern Mexico and Central America through development programs.

MEXICO'S SOUTHERN BORDER PLAN

In July 2014, Mexican President Enrique Peña Nieto announced a new Southern Border Plan. The plan aimed to increase security at 12 ports of entry from Guatemala and Belize and along migration routes. It prioritized (1) regular and ordered migration, (2) infrastructure improvements, (3) protection of migrants, (4) regional shared responsibilities (including cooperation with Central America), and (5) interagency coordination. The Mexican government has stated that the best way to stop illegal immigration from Central America is to address the insecurity and lack of opportunities fueling recent migration flows. It cohosted, with the Trump Administration, a conference on boosting investment in Central America in June 2017.

Mexico has established 12 naval bases on the country's rivers, three security cordons stretching more than 100 miles north of the Mexico-Guatemala and Mexico-Belize borders, and a drone surveillance program. Mexico does not have a border police. Instead, its National Institute of Migration (INM) is the only agency with legal authority to detain migrants, with some assistance from the federal police. These unarmed agents have worked to increase immigration control along known migrant routes, including northbound trains and at bus stations. INM has improved the infrastructure at border crossings and created numerous mobile highway checkpoints. It also has increased the number of cases it refers to prosecutors for crimes against migrants. With U.S. support (discussed below), it is seeking to professionalize its workforce and to improve coordination and communication with the federal police, navy, army, and customs agencies.

In addition to increasing law enforcement, the plan aimed to provide basic services for migrants, including medical care, and to facilitate legal migration for tourists and laborers from Guatemala and Belize. Citizens of these countries now have access to short-term visas that allow regular reentry. Visa-processing locations are now located in Guatemala and Belize. Officials also have sought to register those already in Mexico without documentation.

Human Rights Concerns

The State Department's 2018 *Trafficking in Persons* report documents that migrants traveling through Mexico are vulnerable to human rights abuses and human trafficking. According to human rights activists, the increase in checkpoints and raids on northbound trains pushed many migrants to find more clandestine routes. Although the trains are often dangerous, these new routes leave migrants with less access to shelter and may make them more vulnerable to abuse by criminal gangs.

Many human rights groups have expressed concerns that the Southern Border Plan does little to address corruption among police and migration officials. Mexico has made some efforts to improve accountability and integrity among immigration enforcement personnel by dismissing corrupt INM agents. Mexico established a federal special prosecutor to investigate crimes involving migrants in late 2015; a few states also have prosecutors for crimes against migrants. Serious challenges remain, however. A fraction of crimes against migrants have been effectively prosecuted, and internal controls over the INM and security forces remain weak.

INM has more than 400 child protection officers to serve child migrants, but these officers are stretched thin. INM has referred some children to shelters run by Mexico's National System for Integral Family Development (DIF) or by civil society groups. Given capacity constraints, DIF has been unable to house all child migrants who have been in immigration detention centers as required by law.

Humanitarian Concerns

Studies by UNHCR and others have found that half of all children and a sizable proportion of women fleeing the northern triangle may need international protection.

Mexico has a broader definition of *refugee* than the United States. Mexico's 2011 refugee law recognizes a right to asylum based on "generalized violence; foreign aggression; internal conflicts; massive violations of human rights; and other circumstances leading to a serious disturbance of public order." Migrants' rights activists have claimed that INM agents inform very few migrants of the right to request asylum, as required by law, and that asylum, if granted, would enable them to stay in Mexico permanently.

Even with support from UNHCR, Mexico's Commission for the Aid of Refugees (COMAR) has insufficient capacity to process claims. COMAR granted refugee status to 1,426 individuals from northern triangle countries in 2017, up from 880 in 2015. The agency processed 30% of the asylum applications it received, and 48% of approved asylum claims were for Venezuelans (followed by El Salvador with 27.5%). In cases in which a migrant has an asylum application in process or is a witness to or victim of a crime in Mexico (as has happened with many Central American migrants), he or she can receive a humanitarian visa. However, since that visa is valid for only one year, the migrant could face deportation once it expires. In July 2018, the Mexican government announced a 150% budget increase and 84% staffing increase for COMAR.

U.S. Policy

The State Department has allocated more than $100 million in Mérida Initiative funding to support Mexico's southern border efforts. As of July 2018, the State Department had delivered $32 million of that assistance, mostly in the form of nonintrusive inspection equipment, mobile kiosks, canine teams, vehicles, and training in immigration enforcement.

By late 2018, U.S. funds are expected to have helped build a secure communications network for Mexican agencies in the southern border region. By 2019, U.S. funds aim to help Mexico collect biometric information that can interface with U.S. databases, at all of its migration stations.

In addition to Mérida Initiative funds, the State Department has provided MRA funding to UNHCR and others.

UNHCR estimates that it has used roughly $8.8 million in unrestricted U.S. funds in FY2016 and $8 million in FY2017 for programs in Mexico. These funds have supported efforts to improve access to asylum, give legal assistance to asylum seekers, provide alternatives to detention to asylum seekers, and increase the asylum capacity at COMAR.

DEVELOPMENTS UNDER THE TRUMP ADMINISTRATION

Under the Trump Administration, the Mérida Initiative has focused mainly on combating the business model of transnational crime groups. Bilateral cooperation on security and migration issues has continued, despite Mexico's opposition to the Administration's proposed border wall and U.S. "zero tolerance" immigration policies, which resulted in family separations. Reportedly, Mexico has resisted signing a "safe country agreement" with the Administration, which could require asylum seekers who transit Mexico to seek asylum there rather than in the United States. President-elect López Obrador may favor different policy approaches than the Trump Administration and potentially may resist establishing a safe country agreement.

The Administration's FY2019 budget request included $76.3 million for the Mérida Initiative. The House and Senate Appropriations Committees have approved their respective FY2019 Department of State, Foreign Operations, and Related Programs appropriations measures.

The report (H.Rept. 115-829) accompanying the House committee bill (H.R. 6385) recommends providing $120 million in International Narcotics Control and Law Enforcement (INCLE) aid to Mexico; it does not specify an Economic Support Funds (ESF) amount for Mexico. The report (S.Rept. 115-282) accompanying the Senate committee bill (S. 3108) recommends providing $163 million in Mérida aid, with $100 million in INCLE and $63 million in ESF. S. 3108 stipulates that $18 million of the ESF provided should be "transferred to, and merged with" funds appropriated under the Migration and Refugee Assistance account and made available to process the asylum applications of Central Americans in Mexico. It further states that "not less than $3,000,000 shall be made available for assistance to improve the capacity of the COMAR to process such applications."

In: Immigration
Editor: Abel Thompson

ISBN: 978-1-53616-187-8

Chapter 3

U.S. Immigration Laws for Aliens Arriving at the Border*

William A. Kandel

Introduction

In recent years, the migrant population arriving at the U.S.- Mexico (Southern) border without legal immigration status has shifted from being comprised predominantly of Mexican adult economic migrants to being comprised primarily of Central American adults, family units (adults with at least one child under age 18), and unaccompanied children, many of whom seek asylum in the United States. How they are processed and what options they have for legal admission and residing lawfully in the United States depend on how they attempt to enter the United States, whether they are children and/or arrive in families, what country they originate from, and if they request asylum.

* This is an edited, reformatted and augmented version of Congressional Research Service Publication No. IF11074, dated January 16, 2019.

Aliens (foreign nationals) who wish to enter the United States may request admission legally at a U.S. port of entry or may attempt to enter the United States illegally between ports of entry. The Department of Homeland Security (DHS) has broad discretion to detain aliens, including asylum seekers, during the pendency of removal proceedings that determine whether they are admissible or have other grounds to remain in the United States. Removal proceedings involve either a formal hearing before an immigration judge or a streamlined removal procedure (i.e., *expedited removal*) without hearings or significant review.

Arriving foreign nationals who seek asylum (described below) may request it at a U.S. port of entry before an admissions officer with the DHS Customs and Border Protection (CBP) Office of Field Operations, or upon apprehension between U.S. ports of entry before an agent with CBP's U.S. Border Patrol. All aliens requesting asylum are entitled to an interview with an asylum officer to assess the credibility of their asylum claims.

ILLEGAL U.S. ENTRY

Aliens entering the United States illegally face two types of penalties. First, the Immigration and Nationality Act (INA) establishes *civil* penalties for persons who are in the United States unlawfully (i.e., without legal status). These penalties apply to aliens who entered the United States illegally as well as those who entered legally but subsequently violated the terms of their admission, typically by "overstaying" their visa duration. Foreign nationals apprehended for such civil immigration violations are generally subject to removal (deportation) and placed in removal proceedings.

Second, the INA establishes *criminal* penalties for (1) persons who are convicted of entering or attempting to enter the United States illegally between ports of entry, (2) eluding examination or inspection by immigration officers, or (3) attempting to enter or obtaining entry to the United States through fraud or willful misrepresentation (generally classified as a misdemeanor). In addition, the INA provides criminal penalties for persons who are convicted of unlawfully re-entering the United States after being removed from the country previously (generally classified as a felony). Foreign nationals apprehended for criminal immigration violations are subject to prosecution by the Department of Justice (DOJ) in federal criminal courts.

Foreign nationals who attempt to enter the United States without authorization often do so between ports of entry on the U.S. border. If apprehended, they are processed and detained briefly by CBP and either transferred to the custody of another federal agency or placed directly into removal proceedings. Procedurally, removal proceedings occur after any criminal prosecution for illegal entry.

CBP typically refers apprehended aliens to DOJ for criminal prosecution if they meet criminal enforcement priorities (e.g., child trafficking, prior felony convictions, multiple illegal entries). DOJ's U.S. Marshals Service then transports these individuals to DOJ criminal detention facilities for pre-trial detention. After they have been tried—and if convicted, served a criminal sentence—they are transferred to DHS Immigration and Customs Enforcement (ICE) custody and placed in immigration detention. ICE, which represents the government in removal hearings, then commences removal proceedings.

Because children are not permitted in DOJ criminal detention with adults, prosecuting adults who cross the border illegally with their children poses unique challenges. Once DHS transfers an adult to DOJ custody, it generally treats accompanying minor children as unaccompanied alien children (UAC) and transfers them to the care and custody of the Department of Health and Human Services (HHS) Office of Refugee Resettlement (ORR) (see below). However, a California federal court ruled that if DHS separates families to enable the prosecution of adult illegal entrants, DHS is required to reunite the families after criminal proceedings conclude and any sentence is served.

UNACCOMPANIED CHILDREN

Federal law contains distinct provisions for unaccompanied alien children, defined as (1) lacking lawful immigration status in the United States, (2) under age 18, and (3) without a parent or legal guardian in the United States or one available to provide care and physical custody.

UACs are not subject to expedited removal. Instead, a UAC who immigration authorities determine to be subject to removal is generally placed in formal removal proceedings. DHS may permit a UAC to voluntarily return to his or her country in lieu of removal proceedings, but only if the UAC is a national or habitual resident of a contiguous country (i.e., Mexico and Canada), and (1) has not been, or is not at risk in his or her country of being, a victim of human trafficking; (2) does not have a credible fear of persecution in his or her country; and (3) is capable of independently withdrawing his or her application for U.S. admission. A UAC from Mexico or Canada must be screened within 48 hours of apprehension to determine whether he or she can voluntarily return.

If a UAC is not from a contiguous country or is from a contiguous country but has a credible fear of persecution, or CBP does not make a determination within the 48-hour screening period, the UAC is to be placed in the custody of ORR pending formal removal proceedings.

A child typically must be transferred to ORR within 72 hours after DHS determines he or she is a UAC. ORR must then place the UAC "in the least restrictive setting that is in the best interest of the child." UACs are typically released to sponsors, most of whom are parents or close relatives already residing in the United States. In 2018, UACs spent an average of 60 days in ORR custody.

FAMILY UNITS

Although UACs are not subject to expedited removal, accompanied alien children, such as those arriving at the border with family members, are generally treated the same as non-citizen adults, and may face either expedited or formal removal proceedings with the family unit. Generally, DHS detains children and accompanying parents in family residential centers for limited periods (typically not exceeding 20 days) before releasing them pending their removal proceedings.

ASYLUM

Many aliens arriving at the Southern border seek asylum in the United States. Asylum is a protection granted to foreign nationals physically present within the United States or at the U.S. border who meet the definition of a refugee. The INA defines refugee as a person who is outside his or her home country (a second country that is not the United States) and is unable or unwilling to return because of persecution, or a well-founded fear of persecution, on one or more of five possible criteria: (1) race, (2) religion, (3) nationality, (4) membership in a particular social group, or (5) political opinion. Asylum is not numerically limited and is granted on a case-by-case basis. Asylum can be requested by foreign nationals who have legally entered the United States and are not in removal proceedings ("affirmative" asylum, not discussed below) or those who are in removal proceedings and claim asylum as a defense to being removed ("defensive" asylum).

Arriving aliens who are inadmissible, either because they lack proper entry documents or because they attempt U.S. entry through misrepresentation or false claims to U.S. citizenship, are put into expedited removal. Aliens in expedited removal who express a fear of persecution are to be detained by ICE and given a *credible fear* interview with an asylum officer from DHS's U.S. Citizenship and Immigration Services (USCIS) to determine if the asylum claim has sufficient validity to merit a hearing before an immigration judge.

Credible fear means that there is "a significant possibility," taking into account the credibility of the statements made by the alien in support of his or her claim and such other facts as are known to the officer, that the alien could establish eligibility for asylum. Those who receive a favorable credible fear determination are placed into formal removal proceedings and given a hearing before an immigration judge, thereby placing an asylum seeker on the defensive path to asylum. Those who receive an unfavorable credible fear determination may request that an immigration judge review the case. Aliens in expedited removal who cannot demonstrate a credible fear are promptly deported.

REMOVAL

Under the formal removal process, an immigration judge from DOJ's Executive Office for Immigration Review (EOIR) determines whether an alien is removable. The immigration judge may grant certain forms of relief (e.g., asylum, cancellation of removal), and removal decisions are subject to administrative and judicial review.

Under streamlined removal procedures, which include *expedited removal* and *reinstatement of removal* (i.e., when DHS reinstates a removal order for a previously removed alien), opportunities for relief and review are generally limited. Under expedited removal, an alien who lacks proper documentation or has committed fraud or willful misrepresentation to gain admission into the United States may be removed without any further hearings or review, unless he or she indicates a fear of persecution in the home country or an intention to apply for asylum. Two other removal options, often referred to as "returns"—*voluntary departure* and *withdrawal of petition for admission*— require aliens to leave the United States promptly but exempt them from certain penalties associated with other types of removal.

Expedited removal can be applied to any alien who meets the expedited removal inadmissibility criteria described above, has not been admitted or paroled (i.e., given temporary permission to enter or remain in the United States despite being inadmissible), and cannot affirmatively show continuous physical presence for the prior two years. As a matter of policy, however, expedited removal to date has been limited to persons apprehended within 100 miles of the U.S. border and who have been present in the United States for less than 14 days. Executive Order 13767, issued on January 25, 2017, mandates that DHS expand expedited removal to the full extent of the statute. That expansion has not yet occurred.

If apprehended foreign nationals are found to be removable, ICE and CBP share the responsibility for repatriating them. CBP handles removals at the border for unauthorized aliens from Mexico and Canada, and ICE handles all removals from the U.S. interior and removals for all unauthorized aliens from noncontiguous countries.

In: Immigration
Editor: Abel Thompson

ISBN: 978-1-53616-187-8

Chapter 4

EXPEDITED REMOVAL OF ALIENS: LEGAL FRAMEWORK*

Hillel R. Smith

SUMMARY

The federal government has broad authority over the admission of non-U.S. nationals (aliens) seeking to enter the United States. The Supreme Court has repeatedly held that the government may exclude such aliens without affording them the due process protections that traditionally apply to persons physically present in the United States. Instead, aliens seeking entry are entitled only to those procedural protections that Congress has expressly authorized. Consistent with this broad authority, Congress established an expedited removal process for certain aliens who have arrived in the United States without permission.

In general, aliens whom immigration authorities seek to remove from the United States may challenge that determination in administrative proceedings with attendant statutory rights to counsel, evidentiary requirements, and appeal. Under the streamlined expedited removal process created by the Illegal Immigration Reform and Immigrant

* This is an edited, reformatted and augmented version of Congressional Research Service, Publication No. R45314, dated September 19, 2018.

Responsibility Act of 1996 and codified in Section 235(b)(1) of the Immigration and Nationality Act (INA), however, certain aliens deemed inadmissible by an immigration officer may be removed from the United States without further administrative hearings or review.

INA Section 235(b)(1) applies only to certain aliens who are inadmissible into the United States because they either lack valid entry documents or have attempted to procure their admission through fraud or misrepresentation. The statute generally permits the government to summarily remove those aliens if they are arriving in the United States. The statute also authorizes, but does not require, the government to apply this procedure to aliens who are inadmissible on the same grounds if they have been physically present in the country for less than two years.

As a matter of practice, however, immigration authorities have applied expedited removal in more limited fashion than potentially authorized by statute—in general, the process is applied strictly to (1) arriving aliens apprehended at a designated port of entry; (2) aliens who arrived in the United States by sea without being admitted or paroled into the country by immigration authorities, and who have been physically present in the United States for less than two years; or (3) aliens who are found in the United States within 100 miles of the border within 14 days of entering the country, who have not been admitted or paroled into the United States by immigration authorities. Nevertheless, expedited removal accounts for a substantial portion of the alien removals each year. And in January 2017, President Trump issued an executive order directing the Department of Homeland Security to expand expedited removal within the broader framework of INA Section 235(b)(1). The agency has yet to promulgate regulations implementing this directive.

In some circumstances, however, an alien subject to expedited removal may be entitled to certain procedural protections before he may be removed from the United States. For example, an alien who expresses a fear of persecution may obtain administrative review of his claim, and if his fear is determined credible the alien will be placed in formal removal proceedings where he can pursue asylum and related protections. Additionally, an alien may seek administrative review of a claim that he is a U.S. citizen, lawful permanent resident, admitted refugee, or asylee. Unaccompanied alien children also are statutorily exempted from expedited removal.

Given the streamlined nature of expedited removal and the broad discretion afforded to immigration officers to implement that process, challenges have been raised contesting the procedure's constitutionality. In particular, some have argued that the procedure violates aliens' due process rights because aliens placed in expedited removal do not have the opportunity to seek counsel or contest their removal before a judge or other arbiter. Reviewing courts have largely dismissed such challenges for lack of jurisdiction, or, in the alternative, rejected the claims on the grounds that aliens seeking entry into the United States generally do not have constitutional due process protections. But such cases have concerned aliens arriving at the U.S. border or designated ports of entry, and such aliens may be entitled to lesser constitutional protections than aliens located within the United States. Expanding the expedited removal process to aliens located within the interior could compel courts to tackle questions involving the relationship between the federal government's broad power over the entry and removal of aliens and the due process rights of aliens located within the United States.

INTRODUCTION

Federal immigration laws set forth procedures governing the exclusion and removal of non-U.S. nationals (aliens) who do not meet specified criteria regarding their entry or presence within the United States.[1] Typically, aliens within the United States may not be removed without due process.[2] Commensurate with these constitutional protections, the Immigration and Nationality Act (INA) generally affords an alien whose removal is sought with certain procedural guarantees, including the right to written notice of the charge of removability, to seek counsel, to appear at a hearing before an immigration judge (IJ), to present evidence, to appeal an adverse decision to the Board of Immigration Appeals (BIA), and to seek judicial review.[3]

Congress, however, has broad authority over the admission of aliens *seeking to enter* the United States.[4] The Supreme Court has repeatedly held

---

[1] *See* 8 U.S.C. §§ 1182, 1225(b)(1)(A), 1227, 1228, 1229, 1229a, 1231.

[2] *See e.g.,* Demore v. Kim, 538 U.S. 510, 523 (2003) ("'It is well established that the Fifth Amendment entitles aliens to due process of law in deportation proceedings.'") (quoting Reno v. Flores, 507 U.S. 292, 306 (1993)); Plyler v. Doe, 457 U.S. 202, 210 (1982) ("Aliens, even aliens whose presence in this country is unlawful, have long been recognized as 'persons' guaranteed due process of law by the Fifth and Fourteenth Amendments.") (citing Shaughnessy v. United States *ex rel.* Mezei, 345 U.S. 206, 212 (1953); Wong Wing v. United States, 163 U.S. 228, 238 (1896); Yick Wo v. Hopkins, 118 U.S. 356, 369 (1886)).

[3] 8 U.S.C. §§ 1229(a)(1), 1229a(b)(4); 8 C.F.R. §§ 1003.1(b), 1240.11(a)(2), 1240.15.

[4] *See e.g.,* Fiallo v. Bell, 430 U.S. 787, 792 (1977) ("This Court has repeatedly emphasized that 'over no conceivable subject is the legislative power of Congress more complete than it is over' the admission of aliens") (quoting Oceanic Navigation Co. v. Stranahan, 214 U.S. 320, 339 (1909)); Kleindienst v. Mandel, 408 U.S. 753, 765–66 (1972) ("The Court without

that the government may exclude an alien seeking to enter this country without affording him the traditional due process protections that otherwise govern formal removal proceedings; instead, an alien seeking initial entry is entitled only to those procedural protections that Congress expressly authorized.[5]

Consistent with this broad authority, Section 235(b)(1) of the INA provides for the expedited removal of arriving aliens who do not have valid entry documents or have attempted to gain their admission by fraud or misrepresentation.[6] Under this streamlined removal procedure, which Congress established through the Illegal Immigration Reform and Immigrant Responsibility Act (IIRIRA) of 1996, such aliens may be summarily removed without a hearing or further review.[7]

In limited circumstances, however, an alien subject to expedited removal may be entitled to certain procedural protections before he may be removed from the United States. For example, an alien who expresses a fear of persecution may obtain administrative review of his claim and, if the review determines that his fear is credible, the alien will be placed in "formal" removal proceedings where he can pursue asylum and related protections.[8] Additionally, an alien may seek administrative review of a

---

exception has sustained Congress' 'plenary power to make rules for the admission of aliens and to exclude those who possess those characteristics which Congress has forbidden.'") (quoting Boutilier v. Immigration and Naturalization Serv., 387 U.S. 118, 123 (1967)); *Mezei*, 345 U.S. at 210 ("Courts have long recognized the power to expel or exclude aliens as a fundamental sovereign attribute exercised by the Government's political departments largely immune from judicial control.").

[5] Zadvydas v. Davis, 533 U.S. 678, 693 (2001) ("It is well established that certain constitutional protections available to persons inside the United States are unavailable to aliens outside of our geographic borders."); United States v. Verdugo-Urquidez, 494 U.S. 259, 269 (1990) ("[W]e have rejected the claim that aliens are entitled to Fifth Amendment rights outside the sovereign territory of the United States."); Landon v. Plasencia, 459 U.S. 21, 32 (1982) ("This Court has long held that an alien seeking initial admission to the United States requests a privilege and has no constitutional rights regarding his application, for the power to admit or exclude aliens is a sovereign prerogative"); *Fiallo*, 430 U.S. at 792 ("[I]n the exercise of its broad power over immigration and naturalization, 'Congress regularly makes rules that would be unacceptable if applied to citizens.'") (quoting Mathews v. Diaz, 426 U.S. 67, 80 (1976)).

[6] 8 U.S.C. § 1225(b)(1)(A).

[7] Illegal Immigration Reform and Immigrant Responsibility Act of 1996, P.L. 104-208, § 302, 110 Stat. 3009-546, 579–80 (1996).

[8] 8 U.S.C. § 1225(b)(1)(A)(ii), (B)(ii); 8 C.F.R. §§ 208.30(f), 235.3(b)(4), 235.6(a)(1)(ii), 235.6(a)(1)(iii), 1003.42(f), 1208.30(g)(2)(iv)(B).

claim that he is a U.S. citizen, lawful permanent resident (LPR), admitted refugee, or asylee.[9] Unaccompanied alien children also are not subject to expedited removal.[10]

In addition to providing for expedited removal of certain arriving aliens, INA Section 235(b)(1) also confers the Secretary of the Department of Homeland Security (DHS) with the ability to expand the use of expedited removal to aliens present in the United States without being admitted or paroled[11] if they have been in the country less than two years and do not have valid entry documents or have attempted to gain their admission by fraud or misrepresentation.[12] In practice, the government has employed expedited removal only to (1) arriving aliens; (2) aliens who arrived in the United States by sea within the last two years, who have not been admitted or paroled by immigration authorities; and (3) aliens found in the United States within 100 miles of the border within 14 days of entering the country, who have not been admitted or paroled by immigration authorities.[13]

Nevertheless, expedited removal is a major component of immigration enforcement, and in recent years, it has been one of the most regularly employed means by which immigration authorities remove persons from the United States.[14] Furthermore, in January 2017, President Trump issued an executive order directing DHS to apply expedited removal within the broader limitations of the statute.[15] To date, however, DHS has not yet implemented this policy.

---

[9] 8 U.S.C. § 1225(b)(1)(C); 8 C.F.R. §§ 235.3(b)(5)(i), 235.3(b)(5)(iv), 235.6(a)(2)(ii).

[10] 8 U.S.C. § 1232(a)(5)(D) (providing for the placement of unaccompanied alien children in formal removal proceedings under INA § 240).

[11] Parole is a process by which an alien may be permitted to enter the United States temporarily pending his application for admission. 8 U.S.C. § 1182(d)(5); Samirah v. O'Connell, 335 F.3d 545, 547 (7th Cir. 2003) ("Parole allows an alien temporarily to remain in the United States pending a decision on his application for admission.").

[12] 8 U.S.C. § 1225(b)(1)(A)(i), (iii).

[13] *See* Notice Designating Aliens Subject to Expedited Removal Under Section 235(b)(1)(A)(iii) of the Immigration and Nationality Act, 67 Fed. Reg. 68,924 (Nov. 13, 2002); Notice Designating Aliens for Expedited Removal, 69 Fed. Reg. 48,877 (Aug. 11, 2004).

[14] Bryan Baker, *Immigration Enforcement Actions: 2016*, DHS OFFICE OF IMMIGRATION STATISTICS (Dec. 2017), https://www.dhs.gov/sites/default/files/publications/Enforcement_Actions_2016.pdf.

[15] *See* Exec. Order No. 13767, 82 Fed. Reg. 8793, 8793 (Jan. 25, 2017).

This chapter provides an overview of the statutory and regulatory framework that governs expedited removal under INA Section 235(b)(1).[16] The chapter also highlights the exceptions to expedited removal, including provisions that permit an alien to seek review of an asylum claim before he may be removed. Finally, the chapter addresses the scope of judicial review of an expedited removal order, some of the legal challenges that have been raised to the expedited removal process, and briefly considers potential legal issues that may arise if expedited removal were expanded to cover additional categories of aliens present in the United States.[17] A glossary of some terms used frequently throughout this chapter can be found in Appendix A.

BACKGROUND

The Government's Plenary Power and Constitutional Protections for Aliens Subject to Removal

The Supreme Court has long recognized the federal government's authority "to expel or exclude aliens" from the United States.[18] The Court has described this authority as a "fundamental act of sovereignty" that stems not only from Congress's legislative power, but also from "the executive power to control the foreign affairs of the nation."[19] The Court

[16] This chapter does not address the separate expedited removal procedures for arriving aliens inadmissible on security, terrorist, and related grounds; or the special removal proceedings available for certain incarcerated aliens convicted of aggravated felonies. *See* 8 U.S.C. §§ 1225(c), 1228.

[17] This chapter does not address the separate expedited removal procedures for aliens inadmissible on security, terrorist, and related grounds; or expedited removal of certain aliens convicted of aggravated felonies. *See* 8 U.S.C. §§ 1225(c), 1228.

[18] Fiallo v. Bell, 430 U.S. 787, 792 (1977); Kleindienst v. Mandel, 408 U.S. 753, 765–66 (1972); Shaughnessy v. United States *ex rel.* Mezei, 345 U.S. 206, 210 (1953); Fong Yue Ting v. United States, 149 U.S. 698, 711 (1893); Chae Chan Ping v. United States, 130 U.S. 581, 606–09 (1889).

[19] United States *ex rel.* Knauff v. Shaughnessy, 338 U.S. 537, 542 (1950); *see also Fong Yue Ting*, 149 U.S. at 711 (observing Congress's "right to exclude or to expel all aliens, or any class of aliens, absolutely or upon certain conditions, in war or in peace, being an inherent

also has repeatedly recognized that an alien's admission into the United States is a privilege, but the alien lacks a vested right to be admitted into the country.[20]

Guided by these principles, the Supreme Court has held that the government's decision to exclude an alien from entering the United States generally lies beyond the scope of judicial review.[21] Moreover, the Court has determined, "the decisions of executive or administrative officers, acting within powers expressly conferred by [C]ongress, are due process of law" for aliens seeking to enter this country.[22] Thus, the government's decision to deny entry is often deemed "final and conclusive," and immigration officials are fully "entrusted with the duty of specifying the procedures" for implementing that authority.[23]

Initially, the Supreme Court held that the government's broad authority covered not only the expulsion of foreign nationals seeking to enter the United States, but also aliens who were already within the territorial boundaries of this country.[24] The Court explained that "[t]he right of a nation to expel or deport foreigners who have not been naturalized, or taken any steps towards becoming citizens of the country, rests upon the same grounds, and is as absolute and unqualified, as the right to prohibit and prevent their entrance into the country."[25]

---

and inalienable right of every sovereign and independent nation, essential to its safety, its independence, and its welfare.").

20 Landon v. Plasencia, 459 U.S. 21, 32 (1982) ("This Court has long held that an alien seeking initial admission to the United States requests a privilege and has no constitutional rights regarding his application, for the power to admit or exclude aliens is a sovereign prerogative."); *Knauff*, 338 U.S. at 542 ("Admission of aliens to the United States is a privilege granted by the sovereign United States Government.").

21 Nishimura Ekiu v. United States, 142 U.S. 651, 660 (1892); *see also Knauff*, 338 U.S. at 543 ("[I]t is not within the province of any court, unless expressly authorized by law, to review the determination of the political branch of the Government to exclude a given alien.").

22 *Ekiu*, 142 U.S. at 660; *see also Knauff*, 338 U.S. at 544 ("Whatever the procedure authorized by Congress is, it is due process as far as an alien denied entry is concerned.").

23 *Knauff*, 338 U.S. at 543.

24 *Fong Yue Ting*, 149 U.S. at 707 (discussing the deportation of Chinese immigrants under the Chinese Exclusion Act); Wong Wing v. United States, 163 U.S. 228, 236–38 (1896) (holding that the government could summarily expel aliens already residing within the United States, but that it could not subject such aliens to criminal punishment on account of their unlawful presence without due process).

25 *Fong Yue Ting*, 149 U.S. at 707.

Gradually, the Supreme Court modified its position regarding the reach of the government's authority. For example, the Court determined that lawfully admitted aliens were entitled to Fifth Amendment due process protections in formal removal proceedings.[26] The Court explained that "'once an alien lawfully enters and resides in this country he becomes invested with the rights guaranteed by the Constitution to all people within our borders.'"[27] In these circumstances, the alien is "entitled to notice of the nature of the charge and a hearing at least before an executive or administrative tribunal."[28]

The Supreme Court eventually went further and declared that all aliens who have entered the United States—including those who entered unlawfully—may not be removed without due process.[29] The Court declared that aliens physically present in the United States, regardless of their legal status, are recognized as "persons" guaranteed due process of law by the Fifth and Fourteenth Amendments.[30] Consequently, the Court reasoned, "[e]ven one whose presence in this country is unlawful, involuntary, or transitory is entitled to that constitutional protection."[31]

Although the Supreme Court has afforded due process protections to aliens physically present in the United States, the Court has consistently held that aliens seeking to enter the country may not avail themselves of those same protections.[32] The Court has reasoned that, although "aliens

---

[26] Yamataya v. Fisher, 189 U.S. 86, 101 (1903); Kwong Hai Chew v. Colding, 344 U.S. 590, 596–98 (1953); Jay v. Boyd, 351 U.S. 345, 359 (1956); Landon v. Plasencia, 459 U.S. 21, 32–33 (1982).

[27] *Kwong Hai Chew*, 344 U.S. at 596 n. 5 (quoting Bridges v. Wixon, 326 U.S. 135, 161 (1945) (Murphy, J., concurring)); *see also Yamataya*, 189 U.S. at 101 (concluding that "an alien who has entered the country, and has become subject in all respects to its jurisdiction, and a part of its population" may not be deported without due process).

[28] *Kwong Hai Chew*, 344 U.S. at 597.

[29] Shaughnessy v. United States *ex rel.* Mezei, 345 U.S. 206, 212 (1953); Mathews v. Diaz, 426 U.S. 67, 77 (1976); Plyler v. Doe, 457 U.S. 202, 210 (1982).

[30] *Plyler*, 457 U.S. at 210 (citing *Mezei*, 345 U.S. at 212; Wong Wing v. United States, 163 U.S. 228, 238 (1896)); Yick Wo v. Hopkins, 118 U.S. 356, 369 (1886)).

[31] *Mathews*, 426 U.S. at 77; *see also* Zadvydas v. Davis, 533 U.S. 678, 693 (2001) (explaining that the Due Process Clause applies "to all 'persons' within the United States, including aliens, whether their presence here is lawful, unlawful, temporary, or permanent"); Ibrahim v. Dep't of Homeland Sec., 669 F.3d 983, 994 (9th Cir. 2012) ("Even aliens who are in the United States illegally may bring constitutional challenges.").

[32] *See* Landon v. Plasencia, 459 U.S. 21, 32 (1982) ("This Court has long held that an alien seeking initial admission to the United States requests a privilege and has no constitutional

who have once passed through our gates, even illegally, may be expelled only after proceedings conforming to traditional standards of fairness encompassed in due process of law," an alien "on the threshold of initial entry stands on a different footing" because, theoretically, he is outside of the geographic boundaries of the United States, and thus beyond the scope of constitutional protection.[33]

This distinction, known as the "entry fiction" doctrine, allows courts to treat an alien seeking admission as though he had never entered the country, even if he is, technically, physically within U.S. territory, such as at a border checkpoint or airport.[34] In those circumstances, the alien is legally considered to be "standing on the threshold of entry," and outside the territorial jurisdiction of the United States.[35] By contrast, once an alien

---

rights regarding his application, for the power to admit or exclude aliens is a sovereign prerogative."). The Supreme Court, however, has held that a returning LPR has a due process right to a hearing before he may be denied admission. *See id.* at 33 (describing Supreme Court precedent "as holding 'that the returning resident alien is entitled as a matter of due process to a hearing on the charges underlying any attempt to exclude him'") (quoting Rosenberg v. Fleuti, 374 U.S. 449, 460 (1963)); *Kwong Hai Chew*, 344 U.S. at 600–01 (holding that a returning LPR was entitled to a hearing because he retained the same constitutional rights that he enjoyed prior to leaving the United States); Matter of Huang, 19 I. & N. Dec. 749, 754 (BIA 1988) ("For purposes of the constitutional right to due process, a returning lawful permanent resident's status is assimilated to that of an alien continuously residing and physically present in the United States.") (citing *Kwong Hai Chew*, 344 U.S. at 596). Moreover, under the INA, a returning LPR is not considered an applicant for admission except in certain circumstances. 8 U.S.C. § 1101(a)(13)(C). And before IIRIRA, the Supreme Court had interpreted the term "entry" in the INA as excluding an LPR's return to the United States following "an innocent, casual, and brief excursion" outside the country. *Fleuti*, 374 U.S. at 462.

[33] *Mezei*, 345 U.S. at 212; *see also* Kaplan v. Tod, 267 U.S. 228, 230–31 (1925) (an alien denied entry and initially held at Ellis Island was, notwithstanding her subsequent transfer to the custody of another entity while awaiting removal, "still in theory of law at the boundary line and had gained no foothold in the United States") (citing Nishimura Ekiu v. United States, 142 U.S. 651, 661 (1892)).

[34] *Zadvydas*, 533 U.S. at 693 ("The distinction between an alien who has effected an entry into the United States and one who has never entered runs throughout immigration law. It is well established that certain constitutional protections available to persons inside the United States are unavailable to aliens outside of our geographic borders.").

[35] Alvarez-Garcia v. Ashcroft, 378 F.3d 1094, 1097 (9th Cir. 2004); *but see* Rodriguez v. Robbins, 804 F.3d 1060, 1082–83 (9th Cir. 2015) (holding that, "to avoid serious constitutional concerns," mandatory detention provisions for aliens subject to expedited removal should be subject to six-month time limitation because aliens seeking to enter the United States could in some cases include returning LPRs, who are not subject to the entry fiction doctrine and entitled to due process protections), *rev'd sub nom.* Jennings v. Rodriguez, 138 S. Ct. 830 (2018).

"enters" the country, "the legal circumstance changes," and he may become subject to constitutional rights and protections.[36]

The Supreme Court has applied this principle not only with respect to aliens seeking entry into the United States, but also to aliens seeking entry who are detained within the country's borders pending determinations of their admissibility. For example, in *United States* ex rel. *Knauff v. Shaughnessy*, the German wife of a U.S. citizen challenged her exclusion without a hearing under the War Brides Act.[37] The German national was detained at Ellis Island during her proceedings, and, therefore, technically within U.S. territory.[38] Nevertheless, the Supreme Court held that the government had the "inherent executive power" to deny her admission, and that "[w]hatever the procedure authorized by Congress is, it is due process as far as an alien denied entry is concerned."[39]

Similarly, in *Shaughnessy v. United States* ex rel. *Mezei*, an alien detained on Ellis Island for more than 21 months argued that the government's decision to deny admission without a hearing violated due process.[40] Citing "the power to expel or exclude aliens as a fundamental sovereign attribute exercised by the Government's political departments," the Court determined that the Executive was authorized to deny entry without a hearing, and that the decision was not subject to judicial review.[41] Further, the Court held, although the alien had "temporary harborage" inside the United States pending his exclusion proceedings, he had not effected an "entry" for purposes of immigration law, and could be "treated as if stopped at the border."[42]

Therefore, existing Supreme Court jurisprudence recognizes that the federal government has broad plenary power over the admission and exclusion of aliens seeking to enter the United States, and may deny

---

[36] *Zadvydas*, 533 U.S. at 693.
[37] United States *ex rel.* Knauff v. Shaughnessy, 338 U.S. 537, 539–40 (1950).
[38] *Id.* at 539.
[39] *Id.* at 544.
[40] Shaughnessy v. United States *ex rel.* Mezei, 345 U.S. 206, 207–09 (1953).
[41] *Id.* at 210–12.
[42] *Id.* at 212–15 (citations omitted). The Court also held that the alien could not be construed as having "entered" the country despite having previously lived in the United States. *Id.* at 213.

admission without affording due process protections such as the right to a hearing. Aliens seeking entry are thus generally entitled only to those protections that Congress explicitly authorized.[43] Conversely, an alien who has *entered* the United States is generally entitled to due process protections prior to removal.[44] Under the "entry fiction" doctrine, however, aliens who are detained within the United States pending a determination of their admissibility may be "treated, for constitutional purposes" as though they have not entered this country.[45] The extent to which the entry fiction doctrine may apply to aliens who are already within the United States remains an unresolved question. While some courts have held that aliens apprehended *near* the U.S. border may be treated as though they had not effected an entry into the country, the degree to which this principle may be applied to aliens within the interior of the United States is unclear.[46]

CREATION OF THE EXPEDITED REMOVAL PROCESS

Congress established the expedited removal process when it enacted IIRIRA in 1996.[47] Before IIRIRA, federal immigration law distinguished between arriving aliens and aliens who had entered the United States.

---

[43] *See* Guzman v. Tippy, 130 F.3d 64, 66 (2d Cir. 1997) ("An excluded alien's rights are determined by the procedures established by Congress and not by the due process protections of the Fifth Amendment.").

[44] Zadvydas v. Davis, 533 U.S. 678, 693 (2001).

[45] *Id.*

[46] *See e.g.,* Castro v. Dep't of Homeland Sec., 835 F.3d 422, 445–50 (3d Cir. 2016) (holding that aliens "apprehended within hours of surreptitiously entering the United States" could not raise a constitutional challenge to their expedited removal because they were "recent clandestine entrants" who could be treated, under the entry fiction doctrine, as aliens seeking initial admission to the country who lack constitutional protections), *cert. denied* 137 S. Ct. 1581 (2017); M.S.P.C. v. U.S. Customs and Border Prot., 60 F. Supp. 3d 1156, 1175 (D.N.M. 2014) ("Petitioner, who undisputedly crossed approximately nine miles over the border and was apprehended within 30 minutes of crossing, does not have any substantial ties to this country to place the nature of her rights near those of a permanent resident. Thus, for purposes of the constitutional right to due process, Petitioner's status is assimilated to that of an arriving alien.").

[47] Illegal Immigration Reform and Immigrant Responsibility Act of 1996, P.L. 104-208, § 302, 110 Stat. 3009-546, 579–585, 625 (1996).

Based on this distinction, there were two types of proceedings to determine whether an alien should be removed: exclusion proceedings, which were "the usual means of proceeding against an alien outside the United States seeking admission," and deportation proceedings, which applied to aliens "already physically in the United States."[48] In both types of proceedings, however, the alien had statutory rights to counsel, a hearing, and administrative and judicial review before he could be removed from the United States.[49]

Confronted with what it perceived as mounting levels of unlawful migration,[50] Congress enacted IIRIRA in 1996 and made sweeping changes to the federal immigration laws.[51] One major shift was to replace the exclusion/deportation framework, which turned on whether an alien had *physically entered* the United States, with a new framework that turned on whether an alien had been *lawfully admitted* into the country by immigration authorities.[52] Under the new framework, aliens who were lawfully admitted could be removed from the United States if they fell under the grounds of deportability listed in INA Section 237(a).[53] On the other hand, aliens who had not been admitted into the United States—whether first arriving to the United States or having entered the country without being lawfully admitted—could be denied admission and removed from the United States if they fell under the grounds of inadmissibility listed in INA Section 212(a).[54]

Secondly, IIRIRA removed the distinction between deportation and exclusion proceedings. Instead, it established a standard, "formal" removal proceeding under INA Section 240 applicable to aliens regardless of whether they are charged with being inadmissible or deportable.[55] These

---

[48] Landon v. Plasencia, 459 U.S. 21, 25 (1982).
[49] 8 U.S.C. §§ 1105a(a)(1), 1105a(b), 1225(b), 1226(b), 1251(b), 1362 (1995).
[50] S.Rept. 104-249, at 1, 3 (1996).
[51] *See generally* Illegal Immigration Reform and Immigrant Responsibility Act of 1996.
[52] *Id.* § 304, 110 Stat. at 587-88 (codified at 8 U.S.C. §§ 1229, 1229a).
[53] *Id.* § 304, 110 Stat. at 589 (codified at 8 U.S.C. § 1229a).
[54] *Id.* § 304, 110 Stat. at 593 (codified at 8 U.S.C. § 1229a).
[55] *Id.* § 304, 110 Stat. at 594 (codified at 8 U.S.C. §§ 1229, 1229a). *See also* Vartelas v. Holder, 566 U.S. 257, 262–63 (2012) (discussing changes made by IIRIRA).

formal removal proceedings generally entail the same statutory rights and protections that previously governed deportation proceedings.[56]

IIRIRA also created a new, expedited removal process generally required for certain arriving aliens.[57] This expedited removal process, codified in INA Section 235, does not apply to all arriving aliens who are believed inadmissible, but only to those who are inadmissible because they lack valid entry documents or have attempted to procure their admission through fraud or misrepresentation.[58]

Table 1. Different Forms of Administrative Removal Proceedings Pre- and Post-IIRIRA

Type of Proceedings	**Covered Aliens**	**Right to Counsel**	**Right to Administrative Hearing**	**Right to Administrative Appeal and Judicial Review**
Pre-IIRIRA Exclusion Proceedings	Arriving aliens seeking entry into the United States	Yes	Yes	Yes
Pre-IIRIRA Deportation Proceedings	Aliens who already entered the United States	Yes	Yes	Yes
Post-IIRIRA Expedited Removal Proceedings	Arriving aliens who are inadmissible because they lack valid entry documents or have sought admission through fraud (may also include aliens inadmissible on same grounds if they are present in the United States without being admitted or paroled and have been in the country less than two years)	No	No	No
Post-IIRIRA Formal Removal Proceedings	Most aliens unless they meet the criteria for expedited removal or another type of removal process	Yes	Yes	Yes

Source: 8 U.S.C. §§ 1105a(a)(1), 1105a(b), 1225(b), 1226(b), 1251(b), 1362 (1995); 8 U.S.C. §§ 1225(b)(1)(A), 1229, 1229a.

[56] IIRIRA § 304, 110 Stat. at 596-98 (codified at 8 U.S.C. §§ 1229, 1229a).
[57] *Id.* § 302, 110 Stat. at 579-84 (codified at 8 U.S.C. § 1225(b)(1)(A)(i)).
[58] *Id.*

Under this new procedure, the federal government could summarily remove these aliens without a hearing or further review unless they expressed an intent to apply for asylum or a fear of persecution.[59] In a separate provision, Congress gave the Attorney General (now the Secretary of DHS) "the sole and unreviewable discretion" to apply this procedure to "certain other aliens" inadmissible on the same grounds if (1) they were not admitted or paroled into the United States, and (2) they could not establish that they have been physically present in the United States continuously for two years at the time of their apprehension.[60]

Table 1 illustrates the differences between expedited removal proceedings, pre-IIRIRA deportation/exclusion proceedings, and post-IIRIRA formal removal proceedings.

IMPLEMENTATION AND EXPANSION OF EXPEDITED REMOVAL

Following IIRIRA, the former Immigration and Naturalization Service (INS)[61] initially applied the new expedited removal authority to circumstances mandated by the governing statute (i.e., to arriving aliens), and not to other circumstances where the Attorney General was authorized (but not required) to exercise such authority.[62] In addition, because the expedited removal provisions exempted aliens from countries in the Western Hemisphere whose governments did not have full diplomatic relations with the United States, and who arrived by aircraft at a port of

---

[59] *Id.*

[60] *Id.* § 302, 110 Stat. at 580-81 (codified at 8 U.S.C. § 1225(b)(1)(A)(iii)(I)).

[61] On March 1, 2003, the INS ceased to exist as an independent agency under the U.S. Department of Justice, and its functions were transferred to DHS. *See* Homeland Security Act of 2002, P.L. 107-296, §§ 101, 441, 451, 471, 116 Stat. 2135, 2142, 2192, 2195, 2205 (2002). Within DHS, most of the functions were transferred to three new entities: U.S. Immigration and Customs Enforcement (ICE), U.S. Citizenship and Immigration Services (USCIS), and U.S. Customs and Border Protection (CBP). *See id.* §§ 401, 411, 442, 451.

[62] Inspection and Expedited Removal of Aliens, 62 Fed. Reg. 10,312, 10,313–14 (Mar. 6, 1997); *see also* SYMPOSIUM, *Procedures for Expedited Removal and Asylum Screening Under the Illegal Immigration Reform and Immigrant Responsibility Act of 1996*, 29 CONN. L. REV. 1501, 1505, 1520 (1997).

entry,[63] Cuban nationals who arrived in the United States by aircraft were not subject to expedited removal.[64]

While the expedited removal statute governs the removal of certain aliens who are "arriving" in the United States, it does not define this group. When promulgating regulations implementing the new expedited removal authority, the INS defined the term "arriving alien" to include (1) aliens seeking admission into the United States at a port of entry, (2) aliens seeking transit through the United States at a port of entry, and (3) aliens who have been interdicted at sea and brought into the United States "by any means, whether or not to a designated port-of-entry, and regardless of the means of transport."[65]

Over the years, however, the INS and its successor agency DHS gradually expanded the implementation of expedited removal authority to cover (1) aliens who entered the United States by sea without being admitted or paroled by immigration authorities, and who have been in the country less than two years;[66] (2) aliens apprehended within 100 miles of the U.S. border within 14 days of entering the country, and who have not been admitted or paroled by immigration authorities;[67] and, (3) ultimately, Cuban nationals who met the criteria for expedited removal.[68] But despite

---

[63] 8 U.S.C. § 1225(b)(1)(F).

[64] 8 C.F.R. § 235.3(b)(1)(i) (1997). At the time IIRIRA was passed in 1996, the United States did not have diplomatic relations with Cuba. *See* Eliminating Exception to Expedited Removal Authority for Cuban Nationals Arriving by Air, 82 Fed. Reg. 4769, 4769 (Jan. 17, 2017) (noting that the United States and Cuba lacked full diplomatic relations for many years).

[65] Inspection and Expedited Removal of Aliens, 62 Fed. Reg. 444, 445 (Jan. 3, 1997); 8 C.F.R. § 1.2. In its notice of these regulations, the INS recognized that "[a]n exception is provided for Cuban nationals arriving by aircraft at a portof-entry." Inspection and Expedited Removal of Aliens, 62 Fed. Reg. at 444-45; *see also* 8 U.S.C. § 1225(b)(1)(F) (statutory exception for aliens from countries in the Western Hemisphere whose government does not have diplomatic relations with the United States and who arrived by aircraft). The INS amended the definition of "arriving alien" to exempt from expedited removal aliens who were paroled into the United States before April 1, 1997 (the effective date of IIRIRA), as well as aliens who, either before or after April 1, 1997, returned to the United States pursuant to a grant of advance parole that they applied for and obtained while physically present in the United States and prior to their departure from this country. Amendment of the Regulatory Definition of Arriving Alien, 63 Fed. Reg. 19,382, 19,382 (Apr. 20, 1998).

[66] Notice Designating Aliens Subject to Expedited Removal Under Section 235(b)(1)(A)(iii) of the Immigration and Nationality Act, 67 Fed. Reg. 68,924, 68,924 (Nov. 13, 2002).

[67] Designating Aliens for Expedited Removal, 69 Fed. Reg. 48,877, 48,877 (Aug. 11, 2004).

[68] Following the restoration of diplomatic relations with Cuba in 2015, DHS eliminated the exceptions to expedited removal that it had implemented for Cuban nationals. *See*

these expansions, the agency has never employed expedited removal to the full degree authorized by INA Section 235(b)(1), which would include both arriving aliens and, potentially, all aliens physically present in the United States without being admitted or paroled who have been in the country less than two years and who fall under the expedited removal statute's specified grounds of inadmissibility.

Table 2. Expansion of Expedited Removal

Category	Federal Register Notice	Date of Notice	Description
Arriving Aliens	62 Fed. Reg. 10,312	March 6, 1997	Aliens seeking entry at a designated port of entry, aliens seeking transit through the United States at a port of entry, and aliens who have been interdicted at sea and brought into the United States "by any means, whether or not to a designated port-of- entry, and regardless of the means of transport."
Aliens who Arrived in the United States by Sea	67 Fed. Reg. 68,924	November 13, 2002	Aliens who arrived in the United States by sea, "either by boat or other means," who (1) have not been admitted or paroled and (2) have been physically present in the United States for less than two years.
Aliens Unlawfully Present in Border Regions[a]	69 Fed. Reg. 48,877	August 11, 2004	Aliens apprehended within 100 miles of border within 14 days of entering the United States, who have not been admitted or paroled.
Cuban Nationals	82 Fed. Reg. 4769; 82 Fed. Reg. 4902	January 17, 2017	All Cuban nationals who fall within the categories of aliens currently subject to expedited removal.

[a] Discussion of DHS's implementation of this expansion from designated sectors of the U.S.-Mexico land border in 2004 to the entirety of the U.S. international borders in 2006 is found in Appendix B.

Eliminating Exception to Expedited Removal Authority for Cuban Nationals Arriving by Air, 82 Fed. Reg. at 4770; Eliminating Exception to Expedited Removal Authority for Cuban Nationals Encountered in the United States or Arriving by Sea, 82 Fed. Reg. 4902 (Jan. 17, 2017).

Table 2 shows how the INS and DHS implemented their expedited removal authority since 1997. (A more comprehensive discussion about the exercise of expedited removal authority over time can be found in Appendix B.)

INADMISSIBILITY GROUNDS THAT SERVE AS THE BASIS FOR EXPEDITED REMOVAL

As noted above, expedited removal authority currently is exercised with regard to the following three overarching categories of aliens:

1) Arriving aliens seeking entry into the United States at a designated port of entry.
2) Aliens who arrived in the United States by sea, who have not been admitted or paroled, and who have been in this country for less than two years.
3) Aliens who are encountered within 100 miles of the border, who have not been admitted or paroled, and who have been in the United States for less than 14 days.[69]

Aliens in these categories are subject to expedited removal only if they fall under the grounds of inadmissibility found in INA Section 212(a)(6)(C) and (a)(7).[70] These grounds of inadmissibility generally apply to aliens who lack valid entry documents or who attempt to procure admission through fraud or misrepresentation.[71]

More specifically, the two inadmissibility grounds apply to the following:

---

[69] 8 U.S.C. § 1225(b)(1)(A)(i), (iii)(II); 8 C.F.R. § 235.3(b)(1)(i), (ii); *see* Notice Designating Aliens Subject to Expedited Removal Under Section 235(b)(1)(A)(iii) of the Immigration and Nationality Act, 67 Fed. Reg. 68,924 (Nov. 13, 2002); Designating Aliens for Expedited Removal, 69 Fed. Reg. 48,877 (Aug. 11, 2004).

[70] 8 U.S.C. § 1225(b)(1)(A)(i).

[71] *Id.* § 1182(a)(6)(C), (a)(7).

- An alien who is not in possession of (1) a valid unexpired immigrant visa, reentry permit, border crossing identification card, or other valid entry document; and (2) a valid unexpired passport, or other suitable travel document, or document of identity and nationality if required under applicable regulations.[72] This provision applies, for example, to aliens who arrive with proper documents for entry into the United States for certain purposes, but who intend to enter the United States for reasons that require different authorizing documents.[73]
- An alien whose immigrant visa has been issued in violation of the provisions regarding the numerical limitations on the distribution of immigrant visas.[74]
- An alien whose passport will expire within six months after his authorized period of stay in the United States.[75]
- An alien who is not in possession of a valid nonimmigrant visa or border crossing identification card at the time of his application for admission.[76]

---

[72] *Id.* § 1182(a)(7)(A)(i)(I). DHS may waive this ground of inadmissibility if the alien is otherwise admissible, and was unaware that he lacked valid entry or travel documents, and could not have discovered the lack of necessary documents through reasonable diligence before his departure from outside the United States. *Id.* § 1182(a)(7)(A)(ii), (k).

[73] *See id.* § 1184(b) (providing that every alien "shall be presumed to be an immigrant until he establishes to the satisfaction of the consular officer, at the time of application for a visa, and the immigration officers, at the time of application for admission, that he is entitled to a nonimmigrant status"); Smith v. U.S. Customs & Border Prot., 741 F.3d 1016, 1021 (9th Cir. 2014) (discussing application of expedited removal statute to a Canadian national who sought entry into the United States and was deemed to be an intending immigrant because he carried large quantities of undeclared cash and flyers advertising his photography business in Arizona, and he convinced the CBP officer that he intended to work in the United States rather than come as a temporary visitor).

[74] 8 U.S.C. § 1182(a)(7)(A)(i)(II). DHS may waive this ground of inadmissibility if the alien is otherwise admissible, and was unaware that he did not have a properly issued immigrant visa, and could not have discovered it through reasonable diligence before his departure from outside the United States. *Id.* § 1182(a)(7)(A)(ii), (k).

[75] *Id.* § 1182(a)(7)(B)(i)(I). DHS may waive this requirement "(A) on the basis of unforeseen emergency in individual cases, or (B) on the basis of reciprocity with respect to nationals of foreign contiguous territory or of adjacent islands and residents thereof having a common nationality with such nationals, or (C) in the case of aliens proceeding in immediate and continuous transit through the United States pursuant to a contract with transportation companies to guarantee passage through the United States to foreign countries." *Id.* § 1182(d)(4); *see also id.* §§ 1182(a)(7)(B)(ii), 1223(c).

- An alien who seeks to procure (or has attempted to procure or has procured) a visa, other documentation, or admission into the United States or other immigration benefit through fraud or willful misrepresentation (e.g., an alien presenting a photo-substituted passport, or providing false information on a visa application).[77]
- An alien who falsely represents (or has falsely represented) himself to be a U.S. citizen.[78]

Importantly, expedited removal is available in cases where the alien is charged only with being inadmissible under these grounds. If an immigration officer determines that an alien is inadmissible on *additional grounds* (e.g., because he has engaged in specified criminal activity), then the alien will be placed in formal removal proceedings under INA Section 240.[79]

EXPEDITED REMOVAL PROCESS

INA Section 235(b)(1) instructs that an immigration officer must inspect an alien and determine whether he falls within the category of inadmissible aliens subject to expedited removal.[80] If the alien meets the

---

[76] *Id.* § 1182(a)(7)(B)(i)(II). DHS may waive this requirement "(A) on the basis of unforeseen emergency in individual cases, or (B) on the basis of reciprocity with respect to nationals of foreign contiguous territory or of adjacent islands and residents thereof having a common nationality with such nationals, or (C) in the case of aliens proceeding in immediate and continuous transit through the United States pursuant to a contract with transportation companies to guarantee passage through the United States to foreign countries." *Id.* § 1182(d)(4); *see also id.* §§ 1182(a)(7)(B)(ii), 1223(c).

[77] *Id.* § 1182(a)(6)(C)(i). This provision may be waived if the alien is the spouse, son, or daughter of a U.S. citizen or lawful permanent resident, and establishes that the denial of his admission would result in "extreme hardship" to the citizen or lawful permanent resident spouse or parent. *Id.* §§ 1182(a)(6)(C)(iii), 1182(i)(1). This waiver provision does not apply to aliens who falsely claim to be U.S. citizens. *Id.* § 1182(a)(6)(C)(iii).

[78] *Id.* § 1182(a)(6)(C)(ii). This provision does not apply if the alien's natural or adoptive parents are or were U.S. citizens, the alien permanently resided in the United States before turning 16, and the alien "reasonably believed at the time of making such representation that he or she was a citizen." *Id.* § 1182(a)(6)(C)(ii)(II).

[79] *Id.* § 1225(b)(2)(A) (inspection of other aliens); 8 C.F.R. § 235.3(c).

[80] 8 U.S.C. § 1225(a)(3), (b)(1)(A)(i).

criteria for expedited removal, the alien will be ordered removed without a hearing or further review, *unless* the alien indicates an intent to apply for asylum or a fear of persecution.[81] The alien will also be barred from reentering the United States for five years, with lengthier or even permanent bars to admission if special factors are present.[82]

While expedited removal is a more streamlined process than formal removal proceedings, it nonetheless can involve a number of determinations by multiple agencies and agency subcomponents—particularly in cases where an alien intends to apply for asylum or expresses a more generalized fear of persecution that could potentially render the alien eligible for relief from removal. U.S. Customs and Border Protection (CBP), the DHS component with primary responsibility for immigration enforcement along the border and at designated ports of entry,[83] typically takes the lead role in the expedited removal process, from the initial inspection or apprehension of the alien through the issuance of an order of expedited removal.[84] U.S. Immigration and Customs Enforcement (ICE), the DHS component primarily responsible for interior enforcement and removal, also regularly plays a significant role, such as when the alien seeks asylum or expresses a fear of persecution, and ICE takes responsibility for the alien's detention and removal.[85] Another DHS component, U.S. Citizenship and Immigration Services (USCIS), is responsible for interviewing aliens who have claimed a fear of persecution

---

[81] *Id.* § 1225(b)(1)(A)(i), (iii)(I); 8 C.F.R. § 235.3(b)(2)(i).

[82] 8 U.S.C. § 1182(a)(9)(A)(i). In the case of a second or subsequent removal, the alien is barred from seeking admission to the United States within 20 years. *Id.* If the alien is convicted of an aggravated felony, there is a permanent bar to reentry. *Id.* In addition, an alien who unlawfully enters the United States following an expedited removal is permanently barred from admission. *Id.* § 1182(a)(9)(C)(i)(II). These statutory bars, however, are subject to waivers where DHS has consented to the alien applying for admission. *Id.* § 1182(a)(9)(A)(iii), (C)(ii).

[83] *See* 6 U.S.C. § 211(c) (listing functions of CBP).

[84] *See* Jill E. Family, *The Executive Power of Process in Immigration Law*, 91 CHI.-KENT L. REV. 59, 75–76 (2016) (discussing CBP's responsibilities and expedited removal authority). Within CBP, the U.S. Border Patrol is the agency component primarily charged with the apprehension of aliens unlawfully entering the United States or who have recently entered the country unlawfully away from a designated point of entry. *See* 6 U.S.C. § 211(e)(3).

[85] *See* Family, *supra* note 84, at 63 (discussing ICE's interior enforcement responsibilities).

and assesses whether such claims are credible.[86] If such claims are not deemed credible, the agency may issue an expedited removal order.[87] Finally, IJs within the Department of Justice's Executive Office for Immigration Review may become involved in the expedited removal process when either (1) an IJ is asked to review a USCIS determination that an alien does not have a credible fear of persecution or (2) in the event that an alien is determined to have a credible fear, the alien is placed in formal removal proceedings before an IJ where the alien's claim for relief can be adjudicated.[88]

The following sections provide further explanation of the expedited removal process.

Inspection

An alien arriving in the United States *or* an alien present in the United States who has not been admitted is considered an "applicant for admission" who is subject to inspection by an immigration officer.[89] At a designated port of entry, the initial phase of the inspection process is referred to as "primary inspection."[90] During this stage, "the immigration officer literally has only a few seconds to examine documents, run basic

---

[86] *See Credible Fear Screenings*, U.S. CITIZENSHIP & IMMIGRATION SERVS., http://www.uscis.gov/unassigned/crediblefear-screenings (last modified Sept. 26, 2008).

[87] 8 C.F.R. § 208.30(g)(1)(ii).

[88] *See* 8 U.S.C. § 1225(b)(1)(B)(ii) (referral of aliens who have a credible fear of persecution to an IJ for consideration of asylum application in formal removal proceedings), (iii)(III) (providing for an IJ's review of a negative credible fear determination by USCIS).

[89] *Id.* § 1225(a)(1) (defining an "applicant for admission" as "[a]n alien present in the United States who has not been admitted or who arrives in the United States (whether or not at a designated port of arrival and including an alien who is brought to the United States after having been interdicted in international or United States waters)"), (3) ("All aliens (including alien crewmen) who are applicants for admission or otherwise seeking admission or readmission to or transit through the United States shall be inspected by immigration officers."). DHS, however, may as a matter of discretion parole an alien and defer his inspection to another location if there is insufficient documentation for the immigration officer to determine whether the alien is inadmissible. 8 C.F.R. § 235.2; *see also Deferred Inspection*, U.S. CUSTOMS & BORDER PROT., https://www.cbp.gov/contact/deferred-inspection/overview-deferred-inspection (last modified Apr. 4, 2018).

[90] Inspection and Expedited Removal of Aliens, 62 Fed. Reg. 10,312, 10,318 (Mar. 6, 1997).

lookout queries, and ask pertinent questions to determine admissibility and issue relevant entry documents."[91] If the immigration officer finds discrepancies in the alien's documents or statements, "or if there are any other problems, questions, or suspicions that cannot be resolved within the exceedingly brief period allowed for primary inspection," the alien will be referred to "secondary inspection" for "a more thorough inquiry."[92] During secondary inspection, the immigration officer often will not know if the alien is subject to expedited removal until the officer has sufficiently questioned the alien to assess whether the alien is inadmissible.[93] In order to make that determination, the immigration officer may obtain statements under oath about the purpose and intention of the applicant in coming to the United States.[94] DHS regulations provide that "[i]nterpretative assistance shall be used if necessary to communicate with the alien."[95]

At other locations (e.g., in cases where the alien is found between ports of entry), an alien who is apprehended by immigration authorities is typically taken to a U.S. Border Patrol station for inspection and processing to determine whether the alien is inadmissible and subject to expedited removal.[96]

Inadmissibility Determination and Issuance of Expedited Removal Order

DHS regulations provide that, if an immigration officer determines that an alien is inadmissible and subject to expedited removal, the officer must

---

[91] *Id.*

[92] *Id.* An alien may also be referred to secondary inspection "for routine matters, such as processing immigration documents and responding to inquiries." *Id.*

[93] *Id.*

[94] 8 U.S.C. § 1225(a)(5); *see also id.* § 1225(d)(3) ("The [Secretary] and any immigration officer shall have power to administer oaths and to take and consider evidence of or from any person touching the privilege of any alien or person he believes or suspects to be an alien to enter, reenter, transit through, or reside in the United States or concerning any matter which is material and relevant to the enforcement of this chapter and the administration of [DHS].").

[95] 8 C.F.R. § 235.3(b)(2)(i).

[96] *See* 8 U.S.C. § 1225(a)(3) (requiring all applicants for admission to be inspected by immigration officers); *Zero Tolerance Immigration Prosecutions—Family Fact Sheet*, U.S. CUSTOMS & BORDER PROT., https://www.cbp.gov/ newsroom/zero-tolerance-immigration-prosecutions-family-fact-sheet (last modified June 15, 2018) (indicating that individuals apprehended by Border Patrol are taken to stations for processing).

prepare a Record of Sworn Statement in Proceedings (Form I-867), which contains the facts of the case and any statements made by the alien.[97] The regulations require the immigration officer to record the alien's statements in response to questions concerning his identity, nationality, and inadmissibility.[98] Following questioning, the alien must be given an opportunity to read (or have read to him) the information in the Form I-867 and any statements he made during the inspection.[99] Further, the alien must sign and initial each page of the Form I-867 as well as any corrections made.[100]

DHS regulations also require the immigration officer to prepare a Notice and Order of Expedited Removal (Form I-860) containing the charges of inadmissibility against the alien, and the alien must have an opportunity to respond to the charges.[101] In addition, the regulations instruct that, in cases where an alien is suspected of being present in the United States without being admitted or paroled, the alien must be given an opportunity to show that he was admitted or paroled into the United States after inspection at a port of entry.[102]

As previously noted, an alien placed in expedited removal may be charged with being inadmissible only under the grounds involving a lack of entry documents or attempting to procure admission through fraud or

---

97 8 C.F.R. § 235.3(b)(2)(i).

98 *Id.*

99 *Id.*

100 *Id.* If the alien refuses to sign the Form I-867, the immigration officer must write "Subject refused to sign" on the signature line. *See Inspector's Field Manual* § 17.15(b)(1), U.S. CUSTOMS & BORDER PROT., http://www.aila.org/File/ Related/11120959F.pdf. Similarly, if the alien refuses to answer questions, the immigration officer should indicate that "Subject refused to answer" after each pertinent question. *Id.* The alien's refusal to sign or answer questions does not prevent expedited removal as long as there is sufficient evidence independent of the alien's statements to show that he is subject to expedited removal. *Id.*

101 8 C.F.R. § 235.3(b)(2)(i).

102 *Id.* § 235.3(b)(6). The alien has the burden of showing that he was lawfully admitted or paroled into the United States. *Id.* If he meets that burden, the immigration officer will determine whether any grounds of deportability apply under INA Section 237(a), or, if the alien was paroled and that parole has been or should be terminated, whether the alien is inadmissible under INA Section 212(a). *Id.* If the alien cannot show a lawful admission or parole, he will be ordered removed under the expedited removal provisions of INA Section 235(b)(1). *Id.*

misrepresentation.[103] If the immigration officer determines that the alien is inadmissible on other grounds, and DHS intends to pursue additional charges, the alien will be placed in formal removal proceedings under INA Section 240, and the agency may lodge the additional charges during those proceedings.[104]

An expedited order of removal becomes final after supervisory review.[105] At that point, agency regulations permit the immigration officer to serve the alien with Form I-860 and obtain the alien's signature acknowledging receipt.[106] During this process, the alien is not entitled to an administrative hearing or appeal of the expedited removal order.[107] Upon the issuance of the expedited removal order, the alien will be removed from the United States.[108]

Withdrawal of Application for Admission

As an alternative to expedited removal, DHS may permit an alien to voluntarily withdraw his application for admission if he intends, and is able, to depart the United States immediately.[109] This option allows the agency "to better manage its resources by removing inadmissible aliens quickly at little or no expense to the Government, and may be considered instead of expedited or regular removal when the circumstances of the inadmissibility may not warrant a formal removal."[110]

Under DHS policy, the immigration officer typically considers a number of factors to determine whether an alien may withdraw his application for admission, including (1) the seriousness of the immigration violation; (2) any previous findings of inadmissibility against the alien; (3)

---

[103] *Id.* § 235.3(b)(3).

[104] 8 U.S.C. § 1225(b)(2)(A); 8 C.F.R. § 235.3(b)(3), (c). Additionally, if an alien physically present in the United States who is detained pending an expedited removal screening establishes that he does not meet the criteria for expedited removal because he has been continuously present in the country for the requisite period of time prior to his apprehension (e.g., 14 days), he will be placed in formal removal proceedings under INA Section 240. 8 C.F.R. § 235.3(b)(1)(ii).

[105] 8 C.F.R. § 235.3(b)(7).

[106] *Id.* § 235.3(b)(2)(i).

[107] 8 U.S.C. § 1225(b)(1)(C); 8 C.F.R. § 235.3(b)(2)(ii).

[108] 8 C.F.R. § 235.3(b)(8).

[109] 8 U.S.C. § 1225(a)(4); 8 C.F.R. § 235.4.

[110] Inspection and Expedited Removal of Aliens, 62 Fed. Reg. 444, 445 (Jan. 3. 1997).

the intent on the part of the alien to violate the law; (4) the alien's ability to overcome the ground of inadmissibility; (5) the alien's age and health; and (6) other humanitarian or public interest considerations.[111] An alien does not have a right to withdraw his application for admission; instead, it is up to the discretion of the agency whether to permit the alien to withdraw his application and immediately leave the United States in lieu of undergoing removal proceedings.[112] Furthermore, implementing regulations provide that an alien who is allowed to withdraw his application for admission will remain detained pending his departure unless DHS determines that parole is warranted.[113]

Exceptions to Expedited Removal

Generally, an alien subject to expedited removal will be ordered removed without further hearing to contest the immigration officer's determination.[114] But there are exceptions. Notwithstanding these restrictions, further administrative review occurs if an alien in expedited removal indicates an intent to seek asylum or claims that he fears persecution if removed.[115] Administrative review also occurs if a person placed in expedited removal claims that he is a U.S. citizen, an LPR, or has been granted refugee or asylee status.[116] In these limited circumstances, DHS may not proceed with removal until the alien's claim receives consideration.

---

[111] United States v. Barajas-Alvarado, 655 F.3d 1077, 1090 (9th Cir. 2011) (citing U.S. DEP'T OF JUSTICE, IMMIGRATION & NATURALIZATION SERV., INSPECTOR'S FIELD MANUAL § 17.2(a) (2001)).

[112] 8 C.F.R. § 235.4; *see also* Inspection and Expedited Removal of Aliens, 62 Fed. Reg. at 445 ("The option to permit withdrawal is solely at the discretion of the Government, and is not a right of the alien.").

[113] 8 C.F.R. § 235.4.

[114] 8 U.S.C. § 1225(b)(1)(A)(i), (C); 8 C.F.R. § 235.3(b)(2)(ii).

[115] 8 U.S.C. § 1225(b)(1)(A)(ii); 8 C.F.R. § 235.3(b)(4).

[116] 8 U.S.C. § 1225(b)(1)(C); 8 C.F.R. § 235.3(b)(5)(i).

Credible Fear Determinations

When Congress created the expedited removal process in 1996, it also established special protections for those who claim they qualify for certain forms of relief from removal.[117] Specifically, an alien otherwise subject to expedited removal who expresses an intent to apply for asylum, a fear of persecution or torture, or a fear of returning to his country is entitled to administrative review of that claim before he can be removed.[118] In these circumstances, the statute instructs, the immigration officer must refer the alien for an interview with an asylum officer[119] to determine whether the alien has a "credible fear" of persecution or torture.[120]

A credible fear determination is a screening process that evaluates whether an alien could potentially qualify for asylum, withholding of removal, or protection under the Convention Against Torture (CAT).[121] The INA defines a "credible fear of persecution" as "a significant possibility, taking into account the credibility of the statements made by the alien in support of the alien's claim and such other facts as are known to the officer, that the alien could establish eligibility for asylum."[122] A "credible fear of torture" is defined by regulation as "a significant possibility that [the alien] is eligible for [protection] under the Convention

---

[117] Illegal Immigration Reform and Immigrant Responsibility Act of 1996, P.L. 104-208, § 302, 110 Stat. 3009 (1996) (codified at 8 U.S.C. § 1225(b)(1)(A)(i)); *see also Procedures for Expedited Removal*, *supra* note 62, at 1503.

[118] 8 U.S.C. § 1225(b)(1)(A)(i); 8 C.F.R. § 235.3(b)(4).

[119] An asylum officer is an immigration officer who "has had professional training in country conditions, asylum law, and interview techniques comparable to that provided to full-time adjudicators of [asylum] applications." 8 U.S.C. § 1225(b)(1)(E)(i). The asylum officer is "supervised by an officer" who has the same training and qualifications, and who "has had substantial experience adjudicating asylum applications." *Id.* § 1225(b)(1)(E)(ii).

[120] 8 U.S.C. § 1225(b)(1)(A)(ii); 8 C.F.R. § 235.3(b)(4). In addition, the Form I-867 prepared by the immigration officer must reflect that the alien indicated an intent to apply for asylum or had a fear of persecution. 8 C.F.R. § 235.3(b)(4).

[121] An alien is eligible for asylum if he has suffered past persecution or has a well-founded fear of future persecution on account of his race, religion, nationality, membership in a particular social group, or political opinion. 8 U.S.C. §§ 1101(a)(42), 1158(b)(1)(B)(i). An alien qualifies for withholding of removal if he can show it is more likely than not that he will be persecuted on account of one of these enumerated grounds. *Id.* § 1231(b)(3)(A); 8 C.F.R. § 208.16(b)(2). And to qualify for CAT protection, an alien must show that it is more likely than not that he will be tortured by a government official or person acting with the consent or acquiescence of that official. 8 C.F.R. §§ 208.16(c)(2), 208.18(a)(1).

[122] 8 U.S.C. § 1225(b)(1)(B)(v); *see also* 8 C.F.R. § 208.30(e)(2).

Against Torture."[123] Under this "low screening standard,"[124] the alien has to show only a "substantial and realistic possibility of success on the merits" of an application for asylum, withholding of removal, or CAT protection.[125] An alien does not have to show that it is more likely than not that he could establish eligibility for these protections to be found to have a credible fear.[126] The credible fear determination is not intended to fully assess the alien's claims, but only to determine whether those claims are sufficiently viable to warrant more thorough review.[127]

USCIS may conduct the credible fear interview at a designated port of entry or another location, such as a detention center.[128] Before the interview, the alien may consult with another person at no expense to the government; the consulted person may be present at the interview and may be permitted, at the discretion of the asylum officer, to offer a statement.[129] The alien also has the option to present evidence at the interview.[130] DHS regulations provide that the immigration officer who refers the alien for an interview must prepare Form M-444, Information about Credible Fear Interview in Expedited Removal Cases, that explains the credible fear interview process, the right to consultation before the interview, the right to request a review of the asylum officer's determination, and the consequences of failing to show a credible fear of persecution or torture.[131] The regulations direct the asylum officer to confirm that the alien received

---

[123] 8 C.F.R. § 208.30(e)(3).

[124] *See* 142 CONG. REC. S11491–02 (daily ed. Sept. 27, 1996) (statement of Sen. Hatch) (referring to "low screening standard" for credible fear determinations).

[125] *See Asylum Division Officer Training Course: Credible Fear*, U.S. CITIZENSHIP & IMMIGRATION SERVS. (Feb. 28, 2014), https://www.uscis.gov/sites/default/files/.../Asylum_and_Female_Genital_Mutilation.pdf#page=14 (citing Holmes v. Amerex Rent-a-Car, 180 F.3d 294, 297 (D.C. Cir. 1999)).

[126] *Id.* (citing Joseph E. Langlois, *Asylum Division, Office of International Affairs, Increase of Quality Assurance Review for Positive Credible Fear Determinations and Release of Updated Asylum Officer Basic Training Course Lesson Plan, Credible Fear of Persecution and Torture Determinations*, Memorandum to Asylum Office Directors, et al. (Washington, DC: 17 April 2006)).

[127] *Id.* at 14-16.

[128] 8 U.S.C. § 1225(b)(1)(B)(i); Inspection and Expedited Removal of Aliens, 62 Fed. Reg. 444, 447 (Jan. 3, 1997).

[129] 8 U.S.C. § 1225(b)(1)(B)(iv); 8 C.F.R. §§ 208.30(d)(4), 235.3(b)(4)(i)–(ii).

[130] 8 C.F.R. § 208.30(d)(4).

[131] 8 U.S.C. § 1225(b)(1)(B)(iv); 8 C.F.R. § 235.3(b)(4)(i).

Form M-444, and that he understands the credible fear interview process.[132]

The asylum officer "will conduct the interview in a nonadversarial manner, separate and apart from the general public," and the purpose of the interview "shall be to elicit all relevant and useful information bearing on whether the applicant has a credible fear of persecution or torture."[133] If the alien cannot proceed with the interview in English, the asylum officer "shall arrange for the assistance of an interpreter in conducting the interview."[134]

By regulation, during the interview, the asylum officer will create "a summary of the material facts as stated by the applicant," and, at the end of the interview, will review that summary with the alien, who must have an opportunity to correct any errors.[135] The asylum officer will then create a written record of his credible fear determination, which will include the factual summary, any additional facts he relied upon, and his decision as to whether the alien established a credible fear of persecution or torture.[136] The asylum officer's determination will not become final until it is reviewed by a supervisory asylum officer.[137]

Aliens Who Establish a Credible Fear of Persecution or Torture

An alien who has a credible fear of persecution or torture is not automatically granted relief. Rather, he is placed in formal removal proceedings governed by INA Section 240 in lieu of expedited removal.[138]

---

[132] 8 C.F.R. § 208.30(d)(2).

[133] *Id.* § 208.30(d).

[134] *Id.* § 208.30(d)(5).

[135] *Id.* § 208.30(d)(6).

[136] *Id.* § 208.30(e)(1).

[137] *Id.* § 208.30(e)(7); *see also* Inspection and Expedited Removal of Aliens, 62 Fed. Reg. 444, 447 (Jan. 3, 1997) ("The supervisory asylum officer may direct the asylum officer to interview the applicant further, or to research country conditions or other matters relevant to the decision.").

[138] 8 U.S.C. § 1225(b)(1)(B)(ii); 8 C.F.R. §§ 208.30(f), 235.6(a)(1)(ii). An alien who establishes a credible fear will be placed in formal removal proceedings for consideration of an asylum application even if he appears to be subject to one of the statutory bars to asylum (e.g., he may be safely removed to a different country, he has committed a criminal offense or other activity disqualifying him from asylum eligibility). See 8 U.S.C. § 1158(a)(2), (b)(2); 8 C.F.R. § 208.30(e)(5).

During these formal removal proceedings, the alien may be represented by counsel; challenge the basis for his removability; and pursue applications for asylum, withholding of removal, CAT protection, and other forms of relief.[139] The alien may also administratively appeal the IJ's decision and (as specified by statute) seek judicial review of a final order of removal.[140]

Aliens Who Fail to Establish a Credible Fear of Persecution or Torture

An alien's failure to establish a credible fear to the satisfaction of the asylum officer may also be subject to further review. Under INA Section 235(b)(1) and its implementing regulations, if an asylum officer determines that an alien does not have a credible fear of persecution or torture, the officer will provide the alien with written notice of that decision and inquire whether the alien would like to seek review of the decision before an IJ.[141] The alien indicates whether he wants to seek review on Form I-869, Record of Negative Credible Fear Finding and Request for Review by an IJ.[142] If the alien declines further review, the asylum officer will issue Form I-860, Notice and Order of Expedited Removal, following review by a supervisory asylum officer, and order the alien removed from the United States.[143]

The statute and regulations instruct, however, that if the alien requests review of the asylum officer's negative credible fear finding (or refuses to request or decline such review), the asylum officer will issue Form I-863, Notice of Referral to Immigration Judge, for a *de novo* review of that determination.[144] The IJ's review "shall be concluded as expeditiously as possible, to the maximum extent practicable within 24 hours, but in no case later than 7 days" after the asylum officer's decision.[145] The alien has the opportunity to be heard and questioned by the IJ during this review, which

[139] 8 U.S.C. §§ 1225(b)(1)(B)(ii), 1229a(b)(4); 8 C.F.R. §§ 208.30(f), 235.6(a)(1)(ii).
[140] 8 U.S.C. § 1252(a)(1); 8 C.F.R. § 1003.3(a)(1).
[141] 8 U.S.C. § 1225(b)(1)(B)(iii)(III); 8 C.F.R. § 208.30(g)(1).
[142] 8 C.F.R. § 208.30(g)(1).
[143] 8 U.S.C. § 1225(b)(1)(B)(iii)(I); 8 C.F.R. § 208.30(g)(1)(ii).
[144] 8 U.S.C. § 1225(b)(1)(B)(iii)(III); 8 C.F.R. §§ 208.30(g)(1)(i), 235.6(a)(2)(i), 1003.42(a), 1208.30(g)(2)(i).
[145] 8 U.S.C. § 1225(b)(1)(B)(iii)(III); 8 C.F.R. § 1003.42(e).

is limited to the issue of credible fear, and may be conducted in person or by telephonic or video conferencing.[146]

If the IJ concurs with the asylum officer's negative credible fear finding, "the case shall be returned to [DHS] for removal of the alien," and the IJ's decision "is final and may not be appealed."[147] DHS, however, may reconsider a negative credible fear finding that has been concurred upon by an IJ after providing notice to the IJ.[148] The alien may submit a request for reconsideration to the regional USCIS asylum office that conducted his initial interview, and if the request is granted, the alien will either have a second interview or receive a positive credible fear determination.[149] Based on a 1997 INS memorandum, USCIS will reconsider the alien's credible fear claim if the alien "has made a reasonable claim that compelling new information concerning the case exists and should be considered."[150]

Conversely, if the IJ finds that the alien has a credible fear of persecution or torture, the IJ will vacate the asylum officer's negative credible fear determination, and the alien will be placed in formal removal proceedings under INA § 240, where he will have an opportunity to pursue asylum, withholding of removal, or CAT protection during those proceedings.[151]

---

[146] 8 U.S.C. § 1225(b)(1)(B)(iii)(III); 8 C.F.R. § 1003.42(c); Inspection and Expedited Removal of Aliens, 62 Fed. Reg. 444, 447 (Jan. 3, 1997).

[147] 8 C.F.R. § 1208.30(g)(2)(iv)(A); *see also id.* § 1003.42(f) ("No appeal shall lie from a review of an adverse credible fear determination made by an immigration judge.").

[148] *Id.* § 1208.30(g)(2)(iv)(A); *see also* Katherine Shattuck, Comment, *Preventing Erroneous Expedited Removals: Immigration Judge Review and Requests for Reconsideration of Negative Credible Fear Determinations*, 93 WASH. L. REV. 459, 500 (2018) (noting that "this regulation supplies the official basis of a process by which asylum seekers who have received negative credible fear determinations may try to avoid expedited removal and enter [INA] section 240 removal proceedings").

[149] *See* Shattuck, *supra* note 148, at 500. If USCIS denies reconsideration, the alien remains subject to expedited removal. *Id.*

[150] *See* Memorandum from Michael A. Pearson, Exec. Assoc. Comm'r for Field Operations, Immigration & Naturalization Serv., to Reg'l Dirs., Dist. Dirs. & Asylum Office Dirs. Regarding Expedited Removal: Additional Policy Guidance (Dec. 30, 1997), https://www.aila.org/infonet/ins-expedited-removal-additional-policy.

[151] 8 C.F.R. §§ 235.6(a)(1)(iii), 1003.42(f), 1208.30(g)(2)(iv)(B).

Special Rules for Aliens Arriving from Canada

In late 2002, the United States and Canada entered into an agreement that bars certain non-Canadian nationals arriving from Canada, or who are in transit during removal from Canada, from applying for asylum and related protections in the United States.[152] Under the agreement, if such aliens express a fear of persecution or torture, they must be returned to Canada—the country of last presence—to seek protection under Canadian law rather than applying in the United States.[153] Under DHS regulations, if an alien arriving in the United States from Canada expresses a fear of persecution or torture, the asylum officer will determine whether the alien is ineligible to apply for asylum in light of the agreement, or whether he qualifies for an exception.[154] If the asylum officer (after supervisory consultation) determines that the alien does not qualify for an exception, the alien will be ineligible to apply for asylum in the United States, and will be removed to Canada, where he may pursue his claims.[155] If the alien

---

[152] Agreement Between the Government of Canada and the Government of the United States for Cooperation in the Examination of Refugee Status Claims from Nationals of Third Countries, Can.-U.S., Dec. 5, 2002, C.T.S. 2004/2, [hereinafter U.S.-Canada Agreement]. The U.S.-Canada Agreement also applies to aliens arriving in Canada from the United States who seek asylum protection. *See Canada-U.S. Safe Third Country Agreement*, CANADA.CA, http://www.cic.gc.ca/english/department/laws-policy/menu-safethird.asp (last modified June 23, 2016).

[153] U.S.-Canada Agreement, *supra* note 152, at art. V cl. a.

[154] 8 C.F.R. § 208.30(e)(6). An arriving alien from Canada (not including an alien who is being removed from Canada in transit through the United States) will be exempt from the agreement if the alien (1) "[i]s a citizen of Canada, or, not having a country of nationality, is a habitual resident of Canada"; (2) has "a spouse, son, daughter, parent, legal guardian, sibling, grandparent, grandchild, aunt, uncle, niece, or nephew who has been granted asylum, refugee, or other lawful status in the United States" (unless the alien's relative in the United States only has a nonimmigrant visitor status or visitor status under the Visa Waiver Program); (3) has "a spouse, son, daughter, parent, legal guardian, sibling, grandparent, grandchild, aunt, uncle, niece, or nephew who is at least 18 years old and has an asylum application pending" in the United States; (4) is an unaccompanied minor who "does not have a parent or legal guardian in either Canada or the United States"; (5) "[a]rrived in the United States with a validly issued visa or other valid admission document, other than for transit, issued by the United States," or, "being required to hold a visa to enter Canada, was not required to obtain a visa to enter the United States"; or (6) USCIS determines as a matter of discretion that the alien should be permitted to pursue asylum and related protections in the United States. *Id.* § 208.30(e)(6)(iii).

[155] *Id.* § 208.30(e)(6)(i). An IJ has no jurisdiction to review the asylum officer's determination. *Id.* § 1003.42(h)(1).

qualifies for an exception to the agreement, the asylum officer may determine whether the alien has a credible fear of persecution or torture.[156]

Aliens Who Claim to Be U.S. Citizens, Lawful Permanent Residents, Admitted Refugees, or Persons Who Have Been Granted Asylum

When Congress established the expedited removal process, it created an exception to the otherwise applicable expedited removal procedures for any alien who claims to be an LPR, an admitted refugee, a person who has been granted asylum (asylee), or a U.S. citizen.[157] Congress directed the implementing agency to "provide by regulation for prompt review" of an expedited removal order in these circumstances, which involve persons who claim to have some legal foothold into the United States.[158] Pursuant to the implementing regulations, an immigration officer must attempt to verify a claim of U.S. citizenship, LPR status, refugee status, or asylee status before he can issue an expedited order of removal.[159] The verification process includes "a check of all available [DHS] data systems and any other means available to the officer."[160]

Unverified Claims

DHS regulations provide that, if the immigration officer cannot verify the alien's claim that he is an LPR, refugee, asylee, or U.S. citizen, the alien will be advised of the penalties of perjury, and placed under oath or permitted to make an unsworn declaration regarding his claim of lawful status.[161] The immigration officer will obtain a written statement from the alien in his own language and handwriting "stating that he or she declares,

---

[156] *Id.* § 208.30(e)(6)(ii).

[157] Illegal Immigration Reform and Immigrant Responsibility Act of 1996, P.L. 104-208, § 302, 110 Stat. 3009-546, 579–84 (1996) (codified at 8 U.S.C. § 1225(b)(1)(C)); *see also* Landon v. Plasencia, 459 U.S. 21, 33 (1982); Rosenberg v. Fleuti, 374 U.S. 449, 460 (1963); Kwong Hai Chew v. Colding, 344 U.S. 590, 600–01 (1953) (holding that returning resident aliens are entitled to due process before being excluded).

[158] 8 U.S.C. § 1225(b)(1)(C).

[159] 8 C.F.R. § 235.3(b)(5)(i); Inspection and Expedited Removal of Aliens, 62 Fed. Reg. 444, 445 (Jan. 3, 1997).

[160] 8 C.F.R. § 235.3(b)(5)(i).

[161] *Id.*; *see* 28 U.S.C. § 1746.

certifies, verifies, or states that the claim is true and correct."[162] Following the alien's declaration, the immigration officer will issue an expedited order of removal and refer the alien to an IJ for further review.[163]

Under the regulations, if the IJ determines that the alien has not been admitted as an LPR or refugee, granted asylum status, or is not a U.S. citizen, the IJ will affirm the expedited order of removal, and DHS typically proceeds with the alien's removal.[164] There is no appeal of the IJ's decision.[165] However, if the IJ determines that the individual has been admitted as an LPR or a refugee, has been granted asylum, or is a U.S. citizen, the IJ will vacate the expedited order of removal and terminate the proceedings.[166] At this point, DHS may admit the individual or, if appropriate, commence formal removal proceedings against him under INA Section 240 "to contest his or her current retention of such status."[167] The agency, however, may not initiate removal proceedings against a U.S. citizen.[168]

Verified Claims

If, upon examination, an immigration officer verifies that an alien is a U.S. citizen, the alien may not be ordered removed and must be admitted.[169] If the immigration officer verifies that an alien is an LPR, and that he continues to hold that status, the immigration officer cannot issue an expedited order of removal against the alien.[170] Instead, the regulations require the immigration officer to determine whether the alien is considered to be applying for admission into the United States.[171]

---

162 8 C.F.R. § 235.3(b)(5)(i).
163 *Id.* §§ 235.3(b)(5)(i), 235.3(b)(5)(iv), 235.6(a)(2)(ii).
164 8 C.F.R. § 235.3(b)(5)(iv).
165 *Id.*
166 *Id.*
167 *Id.*; *see* Inspection and Expedited Removal of Aliens, 62 Fed. Reg. 444, 446 (Jan. 3, 1997); Inspection and Expedited Removal of Aliens, 62 Fed. Reg. 10,312, 10,314 (Mar. 6, 1997).
168 8 C.F.R. § 235.3(b)(5)(iv).
169 *Id.*
170 *Id.* § 235.3(b)(5)(ii).
171 *Id.*

Under the INA, an LPR will not be regarded as an applicant for admission unless he

- has abandoned or relinquished his LPR status;
- has been absent from the United States for a continuous period of more than 180 days;
- has engaged in illegal activity after departing the United States;
- has departed the United States while removal or extradition proceedings against him were pending;
- has committed a criminal offense described in INA Section 212(a)(2), such as a crime involving moral turpitude, a controlled substance offense, or a drug trafficking crime, unless the alien was previously granted a discretionary waiver or cancellation of removal; or
- is attempting to enter the United States at a time or place other than as designated by immigration officers, or has not been admitted to the United States after inspection and authorization by an immigration officer.[172]

If the immigration officer concludes that the LPR is an applicant for admission, and that he is otherwise admissible except that he lacks required documentation to enter the country, the officer may waive the documentary requirements if the alien shows good cause for failing to present documentation.[173] Alternatively, the immigration officer may defer the alien's inspection "to an onward office for presentation of the required documents."[174] On the other hand, if the immigration officer determines that an LPR seeking admission is inadmissible under INA Section 212(a) (e.g., because of certain criminal activity), the officer may initiate formal removal proceedings against the alien under INA Section 240.[175]

---

[172] 8 U.S.C. § 1101(a)(13)(C).

[173] *Id.* § 1181(b); 8 C.F.R. §§ 211.1(b)(3), 235.3(b)(5)(ii).

[174] 8 C.F.R. § 235.3(b)(5)(ii).

[175] *Id.* If a returning LPR cannot be regarded as seeking admission into the United States (based on the criteria set forth in INA Section 101(a)(13)(C)), he is not an arriving alien for immigration purposes, and DHS must allow him to return to the United States. Matter of

Under DHS regulations, if the immigration officer determines, through the verification process, that an alien has previously been admitted as a refugee or granted asylum in the United States, and that he continues to hold such status, the officer cannot issue an expedited order of removal against the alien.[176] Instead, if the alien is not in possession of a valid, unexpired refugee travel document,[177] the immigration officer may accept an application for a refugee travel document from the alien provided that he (1) did not intend to abandon his refugee or asylum status when he departed the United States; (2) did not engage in any activities outside the United States that would conflict with his refugee or asylum status (e.g., the alien engaged in persecution); and (3) has been outside the United States for less than one year.[178] If the application is approved, the immigration officer will readmit the refugee or asylee into the United States.[179] However, if the alien is not eligible to apply for a refugee travel document, the immigration officer may initiate regular removal proceedings against the alien under INA Section 240.[180]

Unaccompanied Children

Under federal statute, unaccompanied alien children are not subject to expedited removal.[181] Instead, the governing statute provides that any unaccompanied alien child (UAC)[182] who is determined by immigration

---

Pena, 26 I. & N. Dec. 613, 616 (BIA 2015). If DHS determines that the alien is subject to removal for other reasons (e.g., an alien who had obtained his LPR status through fraud or misrepresentation) and initiates formal removal proceedings, the LPR can only be charged with being deportable under INA Section 237 rather than being charged with inadmissibility under INA Section 212. *Id.* at 618–619; *see* 8 U.S.C. §§ 1182(a), 1227(a) (grounds of inadmissibility and deportability).

[176] 8 C.F.R. § 235.3(b)(5)(iii).

[177] A person who holds refugee or asylum status generally must have a refugee travel document to return to the United States after temporary travel abroad. *Id.* § 223.1(b).

[178] *Id.* §§ 223.2(b)(2)(ii), 235.3(b)(5)(iii).

[179] *Id.* §§ 223.3(d)(2)(i), 235.3(b)(5)(iii).

[180] *Id.* § 235.3(b)(5)(iii).

[181] 8 U.S.C. § 1232(a)(5)(D). This statutory provision was created by Section 235 of the William Wilberforce Trafficking Victims Protection Reauthorization Act of 2008, P.L. 110-457, § 235, 122 Stat. 5044, 5077 (2008).

[182] A UAC is defined as a child who has no lawful immigration status in the United States; has not reached the age of 18; and either has no parent or legal guardian in the United States, or has no parent or legal guardian in the United States who is available to provide care and physical custody. 6 U.S.C. § 279(g).

authorities to be subject to removal must be placed in formal removal proceedings under INA Section 240, regardless of whether the alien is found in the interior of the United States or at the border.[183] The governing statute also instructs that, during the formal removal proceedings, the UAC is eligible for voluntary departure in lieu of removal at no cost[184] and will be provided access to pro bono counsel.[185]

In limited circumstances, DHS may permit a UAC to voluntarily return to his country in lieu of removal proceedings,[186] but only if the UAC is "a national or habitual resident of a country that is contiguous with the United States" (i.e., Mexico and Canada), and the child (1) has not been a victim of human trafficking (or is not at risk of human trafficking upon return to his native country or country of last habitual residence); (2) does not have a credible fear of persecution in his native country or country of last habitual residence; and (3) is capable of independently withdrawing his application for admission to the United States.[187]

---

[183] 8 U.S.C. § 1232(a)(5)(D). The UAC will be placed in the custody of the Department of Health and Human Services' (HHS's) Office of Refugee Resettlement (ORR) pending the formal removal proceedings, and typically must be transferred to ORR within 72 hours after DHS determines that the child is a UAC. *Id.* § 1232(a)(4), (b)(3). Following transfer to ORR, the agency generally must place the UAC "in the least restrictive setting that is in the best interest of the child," and may place the child with a sponsoring individual or entity who "is capable of providing for the child's physical and mental well-being." *Id.* § 1232(c)(2)(A), (3)(A).

[184] Generally, under INA Section 240B, an IJ may permit an alien to voluntarily depart the United States at the alien's expense in lieu of being removed if the alien meets certain statutory requirements (including the posting of bond if at the conclusion of removal proceedings). *See* 8 U.S.C. § 1229c(a), (b).

[185] *Id.* § 1232(a)(5)(D), (c)(5).

[186] "Voluntary return" following a withdrawal of an application of admission is a distinct alternative to "voluntary departure" during formal removal proceeding authorized under INA Section 240B. An alien granted voluntary departure typically must pay the costs associated with departing from the United States as well as a voluntary departure bond, and is subject to a fine and certain other immigration-related penalties if he fails to depart. 8 U.S.C. § 1229c(a)(1), (a)(3), (b)(1), (b)(3), (d)(1).

[187] 8 U.S.C. § 1232(a)(2)(A), (a)(2)(B), (a)(5)(D). The federal laws concerning UACs are generally consistent with DHS's (and before that, the INS's) previously policy not to implement expedited removal with respect to unaccompanied minors, except in very limited circumstances. *See e.g.*, U.S. DEP'T OF JUSTICE, IMMIGRATION & NATURALIZATION SERV., INSPECTOR'S FIELD MANUAL § 17.15(a)(1) (2001).

DETENTION AND PAROLE OF ALIENS SUBJECT TO EXPEDITED REMOVAL

The INA generally authorizes (but does not require) immigration authorities to detain aliens pending their removal proceedings.[188] Aliens placed in expedited removal, however, are generally subject to detention pending a determination as to whether they should be removed from the United States.[189] Aliens in the expedited removal process who express a fear of persecution or an intent to apply for asylum are likewise generally subject to detention while the viability of those claims is considered.[190] But depending on a number of circumstances, including whether such aliens are apprehended at a designated port of entry or crossing the border surreptitiously, such aliens may potentially be released from detention on bond, on their own recognizance, under an order of supervision, or via the exercise of DHS's parole authority.[191] Moreover, the extended detention of alien minors and their parents is limited by a binding settlement agreement from a case in the U.S. District Court for the Central District of California now called *Flores v. Sessions*.[192]

---

[188] *See* 8 U.S.C. § 1226(a) (providing that "an alien may be arrested and detained pending a decision on whether the alien is to be removed from the United States," and that DHS may release the alien on bond of at least $1,500 or grant conditional parole). During the removal proceedings, the alien may request review of DHS's custody determination at a bond hearing before an IJ, and may appeal the IJ's custody decision to the BIA. 8 C.F.R. §§ 236.1(d)(1), 236.1(d)(3)(i), 1003.19(a).

[189] *See* 8 U.S.C. § 1225(b)(1)(B)(iii)(IV); 8 C.F.R. § 235.3(b)(2)(iii).

[190] *See* 8 U.S.C. § 1225(b)(1)(B)(ii), (iii)(IV); 8 C.F.R. § 235.3(b)(4)(ii).

[191] *See Detention and Removal of Illegal Aliens U.S. Immigration & Customs Enforcement*, DEP'T OF HOMELAND SEC. OFFICE OF INSPECTOR GEN. (Apr. 14, 2006), https://www.oig.dhs.gov/assets/Mgmt/OIG_06-33_Apr06.pdf#page=34; *Parole of Arriving Aliens Found to Have a Credible Fear of Persecution or Torture* 8.3(2)(b), U.S. IMMIGRATION & CUSTOMS ENFORCEMENT (Dec. 8, 2009), https://www.ice.gov/doclib/dro/pdf/11002.1-hdparole_of_arriving_aliens_found_credible_fear.pdf; Matter of X-K-, 23 I. & N. Dec. 731, 735–36 (BIA 2005) (holding that aliens who unlawfully enter the United States and are initially screened for expedited removal but found to have a credible fear of persecution may seek custody determination at bond hearing before an IJ during formal removal proceedings).

[192] 862 F.3d 863, 869, 874 (9th Cir. 2017). See generally CRS Report R45297, *The "Flores Settlement" and Alien Families Apprehended at the U.S. Border: Frequently Asked Questions*, by Sarah Herman Peck and Ben Harrington.

Detention of Aliens in Expedited Removal Proceedings

INA Section 235(b)(1) and its implementing regulations provide that an alien "shall be detained" pending a determination as to whether the alien should be subject to expedited removal.[193] Historically, executive branch agencies have construed this detention authority as mandatory.[194] The mandatory detention requirement applies not only during the initial expedited removal screening, but also during any determination as to whether the alien has a credible fear of persecution or torture and any administrative review of an alien's claim that he is a U.S. citizen, LPR, asylee, or refugee.[195] DHS, however, has the discretion to parole an alien on a case-by-case basis "for urgent humanitarian reasons or significant public benefit" during these expedited removal proceedings.[196] Based on this statutory authority, the agency has implemented regulations that allow parole of an alien subject to expedited removal, but only if parole "is required to meet a medical emergency or is necessary for a legitimate law enforcement objective."[197] The agency's discretionary decision to grant parole is not subject to administrative or judicial review.[198]

---

[193] 8 U.S.C. § 1225(b)(1)(B)(iii)(IV); 8 C.F.R. § 235.3(b)(2)(iii), (4)(ii), (5)(i).

[194] *See e.g.,* Matter of X-K-, 23 I. & N. Dec. at 734 (noting that the INA "provides for the mandatory detention of aliens" who are being processed for expedited removal); Inspection and Expedited Removal of Aliens, 62 Fed. Reg. 10,312, 10,315, 10,323 (Mar. 6, 1997) (observing that detention is required for aliens subject to expedited removal).

[195] 8 U.S.C. § 1225(b)(1)(B)(iii)(IV) ("Any alien subject to the procedures under this clause shall be detained pending a final determination of credible fear of persecution and, if found not to have such a fear, until removed"); 8 C.F.R. § 235.3(b)(2)(iii) ("An alien whose inadmissibility is being considered under this section or who has been ordered removed pursuant to this section shall be detained pending determination and removal"), (4)(ii) ("Pending the credible fear determination by an asylum officer and any review of that determination by an [IJ], the alien shall be detained."), (5)(i) (providing that an alien whose claim of being a U.S. citizen, LPR, asylee, or refugee cannot be verified "shall be detained pending review of the expedited removal order under this section").

[196] 8 U.S.C. § 1182(d)(5)(A); 8 C.F.R. § 235.3(b)(2)(iii), (4)(ii), (5)(i). Parole is not considered a lawful admission into the United States or a determination of admissibility, and the decision whether to grant parole is entirely subject to DHS's discretion and may be revoked at any time. 8 U.S.C. §§ 1101(a)(13)(B), 1182(d)(5)(A).

[197] 8 C.F.R. § 235.3(b)(2)(iii), (4)(ii), (5)(i).

[198] 8 U.S.C. § 1252(a)(2)(B)(ii); Rodriguez v. Robbins, 804 F.3d 1060, 1081 (9th Cir. 2015), *rev'd sub nom.* Jennings v. Rodriguez, 138 S. Ct. 830 (2018).

Detention of Aliens Who Establish a Credible Fear of Persecution or Torture

INA Section 235(b)(1) provides that aliens subject to expedited removal who establish a credible fear of persecution or torture "shall be detained" pending consideration of their applications for asylum and related protections in formal removal proceedings.[199] Under DHS regulations, the agency may parole such aliens on a case-by-case basis for "urgent humanitarian reasons" or "significant public benefit," and typically will interview the alien to determine his eligibility for parole within seven days following the credible fear finding.[200] The regulations list the following five categories of aliens who would generally meet the criteria for parole, provided that they do not present a security or flight risk:

1) aliens who have serious medical conditions;
2) women who have been medically certified as pregnant;
3) alien juveniles (defined as aliens under the age of 18) who can be released to a relative or nonrelative sponsor;
4) aliens who will be witnesses in proceedings conducted by judicial, administrative, or legislative bodies in the United States; and
5) aliens "whose continued detention is not in the public interest."[201]

While INA Section 235(b)(1) generally requires the detention of aliens who establish a credible fear of persecution or torture pending consideration of their applications for asylum and related protections

---

[199] 8 U.S.C. § 1225(b)(1)(B)(ii).

[200] 8 C.F.R. §§ 208.30(f), 212.5(b); *Parole of Arriving Aliens*, *supra* note 191, at 4.2.

[201] 8 C.F.R. §§ 212.5(b), 236.3(a). An alien's continued detention is not considered in the public interest if he establishes his identity to an immigration officer, and shows that he presents neither a flight risk nor a danger to the community. *See Parole of Arriving Aliens*, *supra* note 191, at 4.3, 8.3(2); *see also* 8 C.F.R. § 212.5(d) (providing that, in deciding whether to grant parole, agency officials may consider "relevant factors," including whether there are reasonable assurances that the alien will appear at all hearings and/or depart the United States when required to do so; the alien's community ties such as close relatives with known addresses; and any agreement to reasonable conditions such as periodic reporting requirements). If parole is denied, agency guidelines instruct that the immigration officer should advise the alien that he may request reconsideration based on changed circumstances or additional evidence relating to the alien's identity, security risk, or risk of absconding. *Parole of Arriving Aliens*, *supra* note 191, at 8.2.

(unless DHS grants parole), the mandatory detention requirement applies only to *arriving aliens*.[202] During the formal removal proceedings, such aliens are not eligible for bond hearings before an IJ under INA Section 236(a) to determine whether they should be released from custody, and may only be considered for parole by DHS.[203]

On the other hand, aliens apprehended between ports of entry (e.g., when suspected of surreptitiously crossing the border) who are initially screened for expedited removal and subsequently placed in formal removal proceedings following a positive credible fear determination are not subject to mandatory detention under INA Section 235(b)(1).[204] Instead, these aliens are subject to INA Section 236(a)'s discretionary detention authority, and, unlike arriving aliens, do not fall within the listed classes of aliens that are excluded from an IJ's custody jurisdiction during formal removal proceedings.[205] Thus, to the extent they are detained by DHS, this class of aliens may seek a redetermination of their custody status at bond hearings before an IJ.[206]

---

[202] *See* Matter of X-K-, 23 I. & N. Dec. 731, 735 (BIA 2005) (clarifying that INA Section 235(b)(1)'s mandatory detention requirement for aliens placed in formal removal proceedings "applies only to arriving aliens").

[203] *See* 8 C.F.R. § 1003.19(h)(2)(i)(B) (providing that an IJ may not review DHS's custody decisions with respect to certain categories of aliens, including "[a]rriving aliens in removal proceedings"); *Matter of X-K-*, 23 I. & N. Dec. at 735 (stating that "arriving aliens in removal proceedings are specifically excluded from the custody jurisdiction of Immigration Judges" under INA Section 236 and that such aliens "may only be considered for parole").

[204] *Matter of X-K-*, 23 I. & N. Dec. at 732, 736.

[205] *See* R.I.L-R v. Johnson, 80 F. Supp. 3d 164, 171–72 (D.D.C. 2015) (stating that INA § 236(a) governs the detention of aliens initially screened for expedited removal following their unlawful entry into the United States, and who are placed in "standard" removal proceedings after a credible fear determination); *Matter of X-K-*, 23 I. & N. Dec. at 732, 735–36 (holding that unlawful entrants who are initially screened for expedited removal but then placed in formal removal proceedings following a credible fear showing do not fall within the specific classes of aliens that are excluded from an IJ's general custody jurisdiction, and are thus eligible for custody redetermination hearings).

[206] 8 C.F.R. §§ 236.1(d)(1), 1003.19(a) (permitting an alien to seek an IJ's review of an initial custody determination by DHS); *R.I.L-R*, 80 F. Supp. 3d at 172 ("[T]he alien has the options of requesting a custody redetermination from an [IJ] within the Department of Justice and appealing an adverse redetermination decision to the [BIA]").

Detention of Other Applicants for Admission

INA Section 235(b)(2) covers applicants for admission who are *not* subject to expedited removal.[207] This provision would thus cover unadmitted aliens who are inadmissible on grounds other than those specified in INA Section 212(a)(6)(C) and (a)(7) (e.g., because of specified criminal activity); or verified LPRs who are construed to be applicants for admission (based on the narrow criteria set forth by statute) and found to be inadmissible and subject to removal.[208] The INA provides that aliens covered by INA Section 235(b)(2) "shall be detained" pending formal removal proceedings before an IJ.[209] As discussed above, arriving aliens placed in formal removal proceedings are subject to mandatory detention, and may be considered for parole by DHS only in certain circumstances (e.g., aliens with serious medical conditions, pregnant women, juveniles, witnesses, or in cases where detention "is not in the public interest").[210] But aliens apprehended within the United States following entry without inspection who are placed in formal removal proceedings are not subject to mandatory detention, and may seek review of a custody determination before an IJ.[211]

---

[207] 8 U.S.C. § 1225(b)(2); *see* Jennings v. Rodriguez, 138 S. Ct. 830, 837 (2018) (noting that 8 U.S.C. § 1225(b)(2) "is broader" and applies to applicants for admission "not covered by § 1225(b)(1)").

[208] 8 U.S.C. § 1225(b)(2)(A) (inspection of other aliens); 8 C.F.R. § 235.3(b)(3) ("If an alien appears to be inadmissible under other grounds contained in section 212(a) of the Act, and if [DHS] wishes to pursue such additional grounds of inadmissibility, the alien shall be detained and referred for a removal hearing before an immigration judge pursuant to sections 235(b)(2) and 240 of the Act for inquiry into all charges."), (5) (providing that, if a claim to LPR, refugee, or asylee status is verified, the alien is not subject to expedited removal but may be placed in formal removal proceedings if appropriate).

[209] 8 U.S.C. § 1225(b)(2)(A); 8 C.F.R. § 235.3(b)(3).

[210] 8 C.F.R. §§ 212.5(b) (listing criteria for parole of arriving aliens placed in formal removal proceedings), 235.3(c) ("[A]ny arriving alien who appears to the inspecting officer to be inadmissible, and who is placed in removal proceedings pursuant to section 240 of the Act shall be detained in accordance with section 235(b) of the Act."); *Matter of X-K-*, 23 I. & N. Dec. at 735 (clarifying that mandatory detention requirement for aliens placed in formal removal proceedings "applies only to arriving aliens").

[211] 8 C.F.R. §§ 236.1(d)(1), 1003.19(a), (h)(2)(i)(B); *Matter of X-K-*, 23 I. & N. Dec. at 735–36.

Detention of Minors and Accompanying Family Members

Table 3. Detention and Parole of Applicants for Admission Placed in Expedited Removal

Category of Aliens	Initial Expedited Removal Screening	Credible Fear Processing/ Review of Claim that Alien is a U.S. Citizen, LPR, Asylee, or Refugee	Formal Removal Proceedings (if found to have a credible fear or to be inadmissible on other grounds)
Arriving Aliens	Mandatory detention unless parole is warranted for a medical emergency or law enforcement purposes	Mandatory detention unless parole is warranted for a medical emergency or law enforcement purposes	Mandatory detention unless parole is warranted. Parole may cover aliens with serious medical conditions; women who are pregnant; juveniles; witnesses; and aliens whose detention is not in the public interest. No bond hearings before an IJ in formal removal proceedings.
Aliens apprehended within United States following entry without inspection	Mandatory detention unless parole is warranted for a medical emergency or law enforcement purposes	Mandatory detention unless parole is warranted for a medical emergency or law enforcement purposes	No mandatory detention; DHS may (but is not required to) detain alien. Alien may seek review of custody determination at bond hearing before IJ in formal removal proceedings.
Accompanied alien minors[a]	No mandatory detention; must be released promptly (alien parents in custody are typically released with their children)	No mandatory detention; must be released promptly (alien parents in custody are typically released with their children)	No mandatory detention; must be released promptly (alien parents in custody are typically released with their children)

Source: 8 U.S.C. §§ 1225(b)(1)(B)(ii), 1225(b)(1)(B)(iii)(IV), 1225(b)(2)(A), 1226(a); 8 C.F.R. §§ 212.5(b), 235.3(b)(2)(iii), 235.3(b)(3), 235.3(b)(4)(ii), 235.3(c), 236.1((d)(1), 1003.19(a), 1003.19(h)(2)(i)(B); Stipulated Settlement Agreement at 12.A, 14, Flores v. Reno, No. CV 85-4544-RJK (Px) (C.D. Cal. Jan. 17, 1997).

[a] As discussed in this chapter, *unaccompanied* alien children are not subject to expedited removal, and are placed in the custody of HHS pending formal removal proceedings under INA Section 240 (unless they meet the criteria for voluntary return). 8 U.S.C. § 1232(a)(4), (a)(5)(D), (b)(3).

As noted above, detention is generally mandatory pending expedited removal proceedings (including during any credible fear determination), and arriving aliens placed in formal removal proceedings are also subject to detention. However, a 1997 court settlement agreement (the "*Flores* Settlement") generally limits the period of time in which an alien minor may be detained by DHS.[212] Among other things, the settlement agreement requires DHS to transfer within days (subject to exception) a detained alien minor to the custody of a qualifying adult or a nonsecure facility that is licensed by the state to provide residential, group, or foster care services for dependent children.[213] Further, in 2016, the U.S. Court of Appeals for the Ninth Circuit (Ninth Circuit)[214] ruled that the *Flores* Settlement applies to both accompanied and unaccompanied minors.[215] Although the court also held that the *Flores* Settlement does not require DHS to release parents along with their children,[216] the effect of the agreement has been that DHS typically will release family units pending their removal proceedings given the difficulties of separating families who may be subject to removal. As a practical matter, DHS would face difficulties locating other relatives or licensed programs to accept the children while their parents remain in detention.[217] Additionally, a federal district court has ruled that a "government practice of family separation without a determination that the parent was unfit or presented a danger to the child"

---

[212] *See* Flores v. Sessions, 862 F.3d 863, 866, 869 (9th Cir. 2017) (discussing *Flores* Settlement).

[213] *See* Stipulated Settlement Agreement at 12.A, 14, Flores v. Reno, No. CV 85-4544-RJK (Px) (C.D. Cal. Jan. 17, 1997).

[214] This chapter references a number of decisions by federal appellate courts of various regional circuits. For purposes of brevity, references to a particular circuit in the body of this chapter (e.g., the Ninth Circuit) refer to the U.S. Court of Appeals for that particular circuit.

[215] Flores v. Lynch, 828 F.3d 898, 905–08 (9th Cir. 2016). With respect to unaccompanied minors, portions of the *Flores* Settlement effectively have been replaced by a provision of the William Wilberforce Trafficking Victims Protection Reauthorization Act of 2008, P.L. 110-457, 122 Stat. 5044, 5077 (2008), which requires DHS to transfer a UAC to ORR within 72 hours after DHS determines that the child is a UAC; and requires ORR to place the UAC "in the least restrictive setting that is in the best interest of the child." *Id.* at § 235, 5077; *see* 8 U.S.C. § 1232(b)(3), (c)(2)(A).

[216] *Flores*, 828 F.3d at 908–09 ("[P]arents were not plaintiffs in the *Flores* action, nor are they members of the certified classes. The Settlement therefore provides no affirmative release rights for parents.... ").

[217] *See id.* at 903 (listing the categories of individuals and programs to which minors may be released under the *Flores* Settlement).

likely violates due process.[218] Therefore, while DHS has broad detention authority over aliens seeking admission into the United States, the agency's ability to detain minors and their accompanying relatives is notably restricted.[219]

Table 3 shows the different detention and parole requirements for applicants for admission subject to expedited removal.

Litigation Concerning Indefinite Detention of Aliens Pending Removal Proceedings

While the INA authorizes the detention of aliens pending proceedings to determine whether they should be removed, the duration of such detention has been the subject of litigation. Previously, the Ninth Circuit upheld an injunction requiring DHS to provide aliens detained under INA Sections 235(b), 236(a), and 236(c) with individualized bond hearings after six months' detention.[220] The Ninth Circuit had expressed concern that these statutes, if construed to permit the indefinite detention of aliens pending removal proceedings, would raise "serious constitutional concerns."[221] The court acknowledged that the constitutional concerns raised by extended periods of detention generally involved aliens within the United States, and that reviewing courts had typically considered aliens

---

[218] Ms. L. v. U.S. Immigration & Customs Enforcement, 310 F. Supp. 3d 1133, 1143 (S.D. Cal. 2018), *appeal filed*, No. 18-56151 (Aug. 27, 2018).

[219] On September 7, 2018, DHS proposed new regulations that purport to incorporate the terms of the Flores Settlement with some important modifications, such as creating an alternative federal licensing scheme for DHS family detention facilities (which are not eligible for state licensing) that would enable DHS to detain minors together with their accompanying parents throughout the removal proceedings; and limiting the classes of individuals to whom a minor may be released (i.e., only to a parent or legal guardian). *See generally* Apprehension, Processing, Care, and Custody of Alien Minors and Unaccompanied Alien Children, 83 Fed. Reg. 45,486 (Sept. 7, 2018). For more discussion about the Flores Settlement and its impact on alien families, see CRS Report R45297, *The "Flores Settlement" and Alien Families Apprehended at the U.S. Border: Frequently Asked Questions*, by Sarah Herman Peck and Ben Harrington.

[220] Rodriguez v. Robbins, 804 F.3d 1060, 1090 (9th Cir. 2015), *rev'd sub nom.* Jennings v. Rodriguez, 138 S. Ct. 830 (2018).

[221] *Id.* at 1079, 1082 (citing Rodriguez v. Robbins, 715 F.3d 1127, 1142–43 (9th Cir. 2013) (upholding preliminary injunction)).

seeking initial admission into the country as having less due process protection.[222] Nonetheless, the court believed that these constitutional concerns were pertinent to INA Section 235(b), despite this provision primarily addressing aliens seeking initial entry to the United States, because it could in some circumstances apply to returning LPRs[223] who are entitled to more robust protections than aliens seeking initial entry into the United States.[224] Accordingly, the Ninth Circuit ruled that INA Sections 235(b), 236(a), and 236(c) "should be construed through the prism of constitutional avoidance" as containing implicit time limitations.[225]

In *Jennings v. Rodriguez*, the Supreme Court reversed the Ninth Circuit's decision, rejecting as "implausible" the lower court's construction of INA Sections 235(b), 236(a), and 236(c) as containing implicit time limitations.[226] The Court reasoned that both INA Sections 235(b) and 236(c) were textually clear in generally requiring the detention of covered aliens during removal proceedings, and that nothing in INA Section 236(a) *required* bond hearings after an alien was detained under that authority.[227] The Court remanded the case to the Ninth Circuit to address, in the first instance, the plaintiffs' constitutional claim that their indefinite detention under these provisions violated their due process rights.[228] Therefore, while

---

[222] *Id.* at 1082.

[223] *See* 8 U.S.C. § 1101(a)(13)(C) (setting forth six categories of lawful permanent residents who are considered applicants for admission).

[224] *Rodriguez*, 804 F.3d at 1082–83 (citing *Rodriguez*, 715 F.3d at 1141–42); *see also* Landon v. Plasencia, 459 U.S. 21, 32–33 (1982) (holding that LPRs are entitled to due process); Jay v. Boyd, 351 U.S. 345, 359 (1956); Kwong Hai Chew v. Colding, 344 U.S. 590, 596–98 (1953).

[225] *Rodriguez*, 804 F.3d at 1079, 1083, 1085 (citing *Rodriguez*, 715 F.3d at 1135, 1138, 1141).

[226] Jennings v. Rodriguez, 138 S. Ct. 830, 842 (2018).

[227] *Id.* at 842–43, 846–48.

[228] *Id.* at 851. Previously, in *Zadvydas v. Davis*, 533 U.S. 678 (2001), the Supreme Court held that the indefinite detention of lawfully admitted aliens who had been ordered removed following formal removal proceedings, but whose removal could not foreseeably be effectuated, "would raise a serious constitutional problem." *Id.* at 690. The Court ruled that the INA implicitly limited an alien's detention to a period reasonably necessary to bring about the alien's removal from the United States, and concluded that, after six months, the alien could not be detained unless the government produced evidence showing a significant likelihood that the alien would be removed in the reasonably foreseeable future (however, the Court suggested that indefinite detention would be permissible if the statute "appl[ied] narrowly to 'a small segment of particularly dangerous individuals'" such as terrorists). *Id.* at 691-92 (quoting Kansas v. Hendricks, 521 U.S. 345, 356 (1997)); *see id.* at 699-702. In *Jennings*, the Supreme Court distinguished *Zadvydas* because the statute at issue in that case

the Supreme Court has upheld DHS's *statutory* authority to detain aliens potentially indefinitely pending their removal proceedings, the Court has left unresolved the issue of whether such detention is constitutionally permissible.

LIMITATIONS TO JUDICIAL REVIEW OF AN EXPEDITED ORDER OF REMOVAL

An alien who is in expedited removal proceedings generally has no right to a hearing or administrative appeal of an immigration officer's determination that he should be removed from the United States.[229] In addition to these restrictions, the alien has no statutory right to seek judicial review of the expedited order of removal except in limited circumstances.[230]

Statutory Framework

Under Section 242 of the INA, the federal courts of appeals generally have jurisdiction to review a final order of removal,[231] and a petition for review may be filed in the circuit court in the jurisdiction where the

(INA § 241) did not clearly provide that an alien's detention after an initial 90- day period was required; accordingly, in *Zadvydas*, the Court could appropriately construe that statute as containing an implicit time limitation to avoid the constitutional issue raised if the statute was read to permit the indefinite detention of an alien who, though ordered removed, could not foreseeably be transferred to another country. *Jennings*, 138 S. Ct. at 843. On the other hand, the Court reasoned, INA Sections 235(b) and 236(c) provided for detention for a specified period of time, and the statutes were textually clear in generally requiring the detention of covered aliens during removal proceedings. *Id.* at 844, 846. Moreover, in *Demore v. Kim*, 538 U.S. 510 (2003), which involved a challenge to INA Section 236(c)'s mandatory detention provision for criminal aliens pending formal removal proceedings, the Court had ruled that "[d]etention during removal proceedings is a constitutionally permissible part of that process." *Id.* at 527–28, 531.

[229] 8 U.S.C. § 1225(b)(1)(A)(i), (C); 8 C.F.R. § 235.3(b)(2)(ii).

[230] 8 U.S.C. § 1252(a)(2)(A).

[231] For purposes of judicial review, an order of removal becomes final when the BIA affirms the order on appeal. *See* Abdisalan v. Holder, 774 F.3d 517, 521 (9th Cir. 2014); 8 U.S.C. § 1101(a)(47)(B)(i); 8 C.F.R. § 1241.1(a).

Immigration Court proceedings were completed.[232] INA Section 242(a)(2)(A), however, expressly precludes judicial review of an expedited order of removal unless the alien's claim falls within one of the exceptions referenced in INA Section 242(e).[233] The jurisdictional bar applies to claims that an immigration officer improperly placed an alien in expedited removal proceedings; challenges to an immigration officer's credible fear determination; arguments challenging the procedures and policies implemented by DHS to expedite removal; and claims contesting the expedited removal order itself.[234] Additionally, although INA Section 242(a)(2)(D) typically grants the courts jurisdiction to review constitutional claims or questions of law raised in a petition for review that would otherwise be foreclosed on jurisdictional grounds, this provision does not apply to petitions challenging expedited removal orders.[235]

---

[232] 8 U.S.C. § 1252(a)(1), (b)(2).

[233] Specifically, Section 242(a)(2)(A) of the INA provides that no court shall have jurisdiction to review—

(1) "[E]xcept as provided in [INA Section 242(e)], any individual determination or to entertain any other cause or claim arising from or relating to the implementation or operation of an order of removal pursuant to section 1225(b)(1) of this title";

(2) "[E]xcept as provided in [INA Section 242(e)], a decision by the [Secretary] to invoke the provisions of such section";

(3) "[T]he application of such section to individual aliens, including the determination made under section 1225(b)(1)(B) [no credible fear]"; or

(4) "[E]xcept as provided in [INA Section 242(e)], procedures and policies adopted by the [Secretary] to implement the provisions of section 1225(b)(1) of this title."

Id. § 1252(a)(2)(A).

[234] *See* United States v. Barajas-Alvarado, 655 F.3d 1077, 1082 (9th Cir. 2011) ("Congress expressly deprived courts of jurisdiction to hear a direct appeal from an expedited removal order."); Shunaula v. Holder, 732 F.3d 143, 146 (2d Cir. 2013) (noting that, with limited exceptions arising in habeas petitions, INA Section 242(a)(2)(A) "deprives this court of jurisdiction to hear challenges relating to the [Secretary's] decision to invoke expedited removal, his choice of whom to remove in this manner, his 'procedure and policies,' and the 'implementation or operation' of a removal order") (quoting 8 U.S.C. § 1252(a)(2)(A)).

[235] *See* 8 U.S.C. § 1252(a)(2)(D) (allowing courts to exercise jurisdiction notwithstanding "subparagraph (B) or (C) [of section 242(a)(2)], or [ ] any other provision of this chapter (*other than this section*) which limits or eliminates judicial review") (emphasis added); Fernandez-Ruiz v. Gonzales, 410 F.3d 585, 587 (9th Cir. 2005) ("In short, Congress repealed all jurisdictional bars to our direct review of final removal orders other than those remaining in 8 U.S.C. § 1252 (in provisions *other than* (a)(2)(B) or (C)) following the amendment of that section by the REAL ID Act.") (emphasis added), *rev'd en banc on other grounds*, 466 F.3d 1121 (9th Cir. 2006).

The statutory bar to review of an expedited order of removal, however, is not without *any* exception. There are limited circumstances where an alien may seek review of an expedited order of removal.

Habeas Corpus Proceedings

Under INA Section 242(e)(2), an alien subject to an expedited order of removal may challenge the underlying order in a habeas corpus proceeding.[236] The district court's jurisdiction, however, is strictly limited to the following three narrow issues:

1) whether the petitioner in the habeas action is an alien;
2) whether the petitioner was ordered removed under INA Section 235(b)(1)'s expedited removal provisions; and
3) whether the petitioner can prove by a preponderance of the evidence that he is an LPR, that he has been admitted as a refugee, or that he has been granted asylum.[237]

INA Section 242(e)(5) provides that, in reviewing whether the petitioner was ordered removed under the expedited removal provisions, the district court's inquiry "shall be limited to whether such an order in fact was issued and whether it relates to the petitioner."[238] However, "[t]here shall be no review of whether the alien is actually inadmissible or entitled to any relief from removal."[239] If the court determines that the petitioner is an alien who was not ordered removed under the expedited removal statute, or that he was lawfully admitted for permanent residence, admitted as a refugee, or granted asylum, "the court may order no remedy or relief other than to require that the petitioner be provided a hearing" in formal

---

[236] 8 U.S.C. § 1252(e)(2).

[237] *Id.* Because the statute permits consideration of whether the petitioner is an alien, such habeas challenges would also encompass claims that the petitioner is a U.S. citizen. *Id.*

[238] *Id.* § 1252(e)(5).

[239] *Id.*

removal proceedings under Section 240 of the INA.[240] Further, the alien may seek judicial review of any final order of removal issued in those proceedings.[241]

Challenges to the Expedited Removal System

Under INA Section 242(e)(3), an alien subject to an expedited order of removal may challenge the validity of the expedited removal system by filing a lawsuit in the U.S. District Court for the District of Columbia.[242] The district court's review, however, is limited to determining one of the following issues:

1) whether the expedited removal statute or its implementing regulations is constitutional; or
2) whether a regulation, written policy directive, written policy guideline, or written procedure issued by DHS to implement expedited removal is consistent with the statute or other laws.[243]

A lawsuit raising a systemic challenge to expedited removal must be brought within 60 days after implementation of the challenged statutory provision, regulation, directive, guideline, or procedure.[244] The D.C. District Court has held that the 60-day requirement "is jurisdictional rather than a traditional limitations period," and, therefore, the period runs from the initial implementation of the challenged provision or policy, rather than from the date they were applied to a particular alien.[245]

Finally, an alien challenging the validity of the expedited removal system may file a notice of appeal within 30 days of the district court's

---

[240] *Id.* § 1252(e)(4)(B).
[241] *Id.*; *see also id.* § 1252(a)(1), (b).
[242] *Id.* § 1252(e)(3)(A).
[243] *Id.*
[244] *Id.* § 1252(e)(3)(B).
[245] Am. Immigration Lawyers Ass'n v. Reno, 18 F. Supp. 2d 38, 44–47 (D.D.C. 1998).

order.[246] The statute instructs the appellate courts to conduct review in an expedited manner.[247]

Collateral Challenges Raised as a Defense during Criminal Proceedings for Unlawful Reentry into the United States

In some cases, an alien who is criminally charged with unlawful reentry after removal may collaterally challenge an expedited order of removal. Under INA Section 276, an alien who "has been denied admission, excluded, deported, or removed or has departed the United States while an order of exclusion, deportation, or removal is outstanding," and subsequently "enters, attempts to enter, or is at any time found in, the United States" shall be subject to criminal penalty.[248] The INA provides that, in prosecutions for unlawful reentry, the courts do not have jurisdiction to consider any claim challenging the validity of an expedited order of removal, including a determination that an alien failed to show a credible fear of persecution.[249]

In *United States v. Mendoza-Lopez*, however, the Supreme Court held that an alien who is prosecuted for unlawful reentry may challenge the validity of an underlying removal order during his criminal proceedings if the removal proceeding "effectively eliminates the right of the alien to obtain judicial review" of that order.[250] The Court reasoned that "where a determination made in an administrative proceeding is to play a critical role in the subsequent imposition of a criminal sanction, there must be *some* meaningful review of the administrative proceeding."[251] The Court thus declared that, at a minimum, "where the defects in an administrative

---

246 8 U.S.C. § 1252(e)(3)(C).
247 *Id.* § 1252(e)(3)(D).
248 *Id.* § 1326(a). The statute allows an exception if DHS expressly consented to the alien reapplying for admission, or if the alien shows that he was not required to obtain advance permission to reenter the United States. *Id.* § 1326(a)(2).
249 *Id.* § 1225(b)(1)(D). The statute also bars challenges to validity of an expedited removal order in the context of a prosecution for unlawful entry under INA Section 275, 8 U.S.C. § 1325.
250 United States v. Mendoza-Lopez, 481 U.S. 828, 838–39 (1987).
251 *Id.* at 838 (emphasis in original).

proceeding foreclose judicial review of that proceeding, an alternative means of obtaining judicial review must be made available before the administrative order may be used to establish conclusively an element of a criminal offense."[252]

In response to the Supreme Court's decision, Congress enacted a new clause to the unlawful reentry statute, which provides that an alien charged with unlawful reentry may challenge the validity of an underlying removal order if (1) he exhausted any administrative remedies that may have been available to seek relief against the order; (2) the prior removal proceedings in which the order was issued deprived the alien of the opportunity to seek judicial review; and (3) the entry of the order was "fundamentally unfair."[253]

Subsequently, the Ninth Circuit determined that "the principle established by *Mendoza-Lopez* is equally applicable in the expedited removal order context."[254] The Ninth Circuit ruled that the Supreme Court's rationale that aliens must have "some meaningful review" of their underlying removal orders if they serve as a basis for criminal prosecution is applicable to a criminal defendant "regardless of whether the defendant was a nonadmitted alien or an alien in the United States when the removal order was issued."[255] The Ninth Circuit thus held that a defendant charged with the crime of unlawful reentry may challenge an expedited removal order that serves as the basis for prosecution if he contends that the expedited removal order is "fundamentally unfair."[256] According to the Ninth Circuit, an expedited removal proceeding is "fundamentally unfair"

---

[252] *Id.*

[253] 8 U.S.C. § 1326(d); United States v. Gonzalez-Flores, 804 F.3d 920, 926 (9th Cir. 2015), *cert denied sub nom.*, Gonzalez-Flores v. United States, 136 S. Ct. 1234 (Feb. 29, 2016).

[254] United States v. Barajas-Alvarado, 655 F.3d 1077, 1083 (9th Cir. 2011).

[255] *Id.* at 1083–84.

[256] *Id.* at 1085. Further, for purposes of 8 U.S.C. § 1326(d), an alien challenging an expedited removal order would likely be able to show that he exhausted any available remedies to seek relief from the order because the expedited removal provisions do not provide for administrative review except in limited circumstances (e.g., when an alien placed in expedited removal is seeking asylum, claiming to be a lawful permanent resident, etc.). 8 U.S.C. § 1225(b)(1)(A)– (C). The alien would also likely be able to show that he had no meaningful opportunity for judicial review of the expedited removal order because the statute forecloses appeal of that order. *Id.* § 1252(a)(2)(A).

if it deprives the alien of due process and results in prejudice.[257] The Ninth Circuit, for example, has determined that expedited removal proceedings are fundamentally unfair if the immigration officer failed to obtain interpretative assistance, provide the alien with notice of the charge and nature of the proceedings, and afford the alien an opportunity to review his sworn statement—as DHS regulations require.[258]

In sum, the INA generally limits the ability of an alien to challenge an underlying expedited removal order in a subsequent criminal prosecution for unlawful reentry in violation of the order. That order can be challenged only in limited circumstances, primarily centering on whether the entry of the order was "fundamentally unfair."[259]

CONSTITUTIONAL AND LEGAL CHALLENGES TO EXPEDITED REMOVAL

Given its summary nature and comparatively limited procedural protections, the expedited removal process has been subject to legal challenges since its implementation in 1997. However, in part because of the strict limitations to judicial review of an expedited order of removal, courts have largely dismissed such challenges for lack of jurisdiction, or, in the few occasions where courts have entertained such challenges, rejected them on substantive grounds. Nevertheless, these cases raise important issues concerning the breadth and scope of the expedited removal statute and the constitutionality of its provisions.

---

[257] *Barajas-Alvarado*, 655 F.3d at 1085–88 (citing United States v. Arias-Ordonez, 597 F.3d 972, 976 (9th Cir. 2010)).

[258] United States v. Raya-Vaca, 771 F.3d 1195, 1204–06 (9th Cir. 2014); *Barajas-Alvarado*, 655 F.3d at 1088. *See also* 8 C.F.R. § 235.3(b)(2)(i).

[259] *Barajas-Alvarado*, 655 F.3d at 1087–88. Outside of the Ninth Circuit, at least one other Circuit has considered an alien's collateral challenge in criminal proceedings to an expedited removal order issued under INA Section 235(b)(1), but without addressing the threshold question of whether an alien charged with unlawful reentry may challenge the prior expedited removal order as "fundamentally unfair." *See* United States v. Santos-Pulido, 815 F.3d 443, 445–46 (8th Cir. 2016) (concluding that alien failed to show that her expedited removal proceeding violated her right to due process where she argued that she had a right to withdraw her application for admission).

Challenges to the Expedited Removal System: American Immigration Lawyers Association v. Reno

In 1997, shortly after IIRIRA's implementation, a group of immigrant assistance organizations and aliens who had been removed challenged the new expedited removal statute and regulations in the federal district court for the District of Columbia.[260] In *American Immigration Lawyers Association v. Reno*, the plaintiffs argued, among other things, that the expedited removal procedures offered insufficient protections for aliens seeking entry into the United States because they did not afford an opportunity to consult with family or counsel during that process, or to contest and seek further review of an expedited removal order.[261] The plaintiffs also claimed that the expedited removal procedures violated aliens' due process rights because those aliens could be erroneously removed from the country without additional protections provided in formal removal proceedings.[262]

The district court held that the limited protections afforded by the expedited removal statute reasonably "advance[d] Congress's twin goals of creating a fair yet expedited process," and fell well within the statute's command that an alien be summarily removed "without further hearing or review."[263] The court also cited Congress's broad legislative authority over the admission of aliens, and the "long-standing precedent" that aliens seeking to enter the United States— including those detained just within the border—have no constitutional due process protections concerning

---

[260] Am. Immigration Lawyers Ass'n v. Reno, 18 F. Supp. 2d 38, 44–46 (D.D.C. 1998). As discussed in the preceding section, judicial review of an expedited order of removal is permitted if a lawsuit is filed in the D.C. District Court within 60 days after implementation of the expedited removal provision, regulation, directive, guideline, or procedure, and the court's review is limited to (1) whether the expedited removal statute and its implementing regulations is constitutional, or (2) whether a regulation, written policy directive, written policy guideline, or written procedure issued by DHS to implement expedited removal is consistent with the statute or other laws. 8 U.S.C. § 1252(e)(3).

[261] *Am. Immigration Lawyers Ass'n*, 18 F. Supp. 2d at 44–59, 66–67.

[262] *Id.*

[263] *Id.* at 52, 56 (citing 8 U.S.C. § 1225(b)(1)(A)(i)).

their applications for admission, apart from what Congress provided by statute.[264]

The plaintiffs appealed the district court's order to the D.C. Circuit.[265] In a published decision, the D.C. Circuit affirmed the dismissal of the plaintiffs' complaints "substantially for the reasons stated in the [district] court's thorough opinion."[266] The court also held that the organizational plaintiffs lacked standing to challenge the expedited removal procedures because there was nothing in the statute governing judicial review of an expedited order of removal that permitted litigants to bring claims on behalf of aliens subject to expedited removal.[267]

Challenges to Expedited Removal in Individual Cases

Although the U.S. District Court for the District of Columbia rejected a legal challenge to the expedited removal system itself, some courts have addressed challenges to the application of expedited removal in individual cases. Despite the jurisdictional limitations governing review of expedited removal orders,[268] courts have entertained such challenges in a few notable cases. The majority of reviewing courts, however, have dismissed such challenges based on jurisdictional limitations.

---

[264] *Id.* at 58–60. The court also ruled that it lacked jurisdiction to review the plaintiffs' contention that, in practice, expedited removal resulted in extended detentions, the signing of documents without explanation or translation, and a lack of food, water, and restroom access. *Id.* at 57–58. The court explained that INA Section 242(e)(3)(A)(ii) expressly limited the court's review "to a 'regulation, written policy directive, written policy guideline, or written procedure,'" rather than *unwritten* policies or practices. *Id.* (quoting 8 U.S.C. § 1252(e)(3)(A)(ii)). The court, however, was "troubled by the effects of Congress's decision to immunize the unwritten actions of an agency from judicial review, particularly where, as here, so much discretion is placed in the hands of individual INS agents who face only a supervisor's review of their decisions." *Id.* at 58. The court thus cautioned the INS "to comply with its own regulations, policies, and procedures in providing aliens with the treatment, facilities, and information required by the agency's regulations, policies, and procedures." *Id.*

[265] Am. Immigration Lawyers Ass'n v. Reno, 199 F.3d 1352, 1356–57 (D.C. Cir. 2000).

[266] *Id.* at 1357.

[267] *Id.* at 1358–64.

[268] 8 U.S.C. § 1252(a)(2)(A).

For example, a federal district court in Michigan held that INA Section 242(e)(2) allowed the court to consider in habeas corpus proceedings whether the expedited removal statute was "lawfully applied" to the petitioners.[269] Because INA Section 242(e)(2) permits judicial inquiry in habeas proceedings into "whether the petitioner was ordered removed" under the expedited removal statute, the district court determined it could consider "whether such an order in fact was issued and whether it relates to the petitioner."[270] Such review, the court reasoned, necessarily entails a determination by a reviewing court of whether the expedited order was "lawfully applied" to the alien.[271] Applying this standard, the court struck down the implementation of expedited removal to a group of Lebanese nationals who had entered the United States with fraudulent advance parole documents because they were not "arriving aliens" subject to the statute.[272]

In a separate case, the Third Circuit disagreed with the Michigan federal district court's determination that judicial review in habeas proceedings of whether an expedited removal order "relates to the petitioner" includes consideration of whether the order was "lawfully applied."[273] The Third Circuit found that this construction of the statute was "not just unsupported, but also flatly contradicted by the plain language of the [expedited removal] statute itself," which explicitly bars judicial review of the application of expedited removal to individual

---

[269] Am.-Arab Anti-Discrimination Comm. v. Ashcroft, 272 F. Supp. 2d 650, 660–63 (E.D. Mich. 2003).

[270] *Id.*; *see* 8 U.S.C. § 1252(e)(5) ("In determining whether an alien has been ordered removed under [INA Section 235(b)(1)], the court's inquiry shall be limited to whether such an order in fact was issued and whether it relates to the petitioner.").

[271] *Am.-Arab Anti-Discrimination Comm.*, 272 F. Supp. 2d at 660–63.

[272] *Id.* at 668. The court concluded that the expedited removal system was intended to be applied to aliens seeking admission at a port of entry, and that "neither the expedited removal statute nor the definition of 'arriving alien' appear[ed] to have been applied to aliens who are deemed arriving aliens *simply or solely* by virtue of the application of the entry fiction doctrine." *Id.* at 665–66 (emphasis in original). Notably, the court issued its decision before DHS began to implement expedited removal with respect to aliens who were already within the United States (in 2004). Hence, the court focused its analysis on whether the petitioners were "arriving aliens." *Id.*

[273] Castro v. Dep't of Homeland Sec., 835 F.3d 422, 432 (3d Cir. 2016), *cert. denied*, 137 S. Ct. 1581 (2017); *see also* 8 U.S.C. § 1252(e)(5).

aliens.[274] Similarly, the Fifth Circuit has held that a district court in habeas proceedings could not consider whether the agency properly applied the expedited removal statute to an alien.[275] The court observed that the statutory language permitting habeas review of "whether the petitioner was ordered removed" expressly limits such inquiry to "whether such an order in fact was issued and whether it relates to the petitioner," and that "the matter ends there."[276]

Outside of the habeas context, some courts have exercised jurisdiction to review expedited removal orders that served as predicates for unlawful reentry prosecutions under INA Section 276.[277] As discussed in the preceding section, the Ninth Circuit has held that, under INA Section 276(d), a court may review whether an alien's underlying expedited removal proceedings were "fundamentally unfair" when the resulting expedited removal order serves as a basis for the unlawful reentry prosecution.[278] Applying this standard, the court found that an arriving alien's contention that his expedited removal violated his right to counsel

---

[274] *Castro*, 835 F.3d at 432–33; *see also* 8 U.S.C. § 1252(a)(2)(A)(iii) (barring review of application of expedited removal statute to an alien). The Third Circuit also rejected the petitioners' claim that INA § 242(e)(2)'s jurisdictional limitations in habeas cases violated the Suspension Clause, which provides that "[t]he Privilege of the Writ of Habeas Corpus shall not be suspended, unless when in Cases of Rebellion or Invasion the public Safety may require it." *Castro*, 835 F.3d at 434, 444–50 (quoting U.S. CONST. art. I, § 9, cl. 2). The court held that the petitioners were not entitled to constitutional protections under the Suspension Clause "because the Supreme Court has unequivocally concluded that 'an alien seeking initial admission to the United States requests a privilege and has no constitutional rights regarding his application,'" and because the petitioners were "recent clandestine entrants," they were essentially aliens seeking admission to the United States who could not raise a constitutional challenge to their removal "in an effort to force judicial review beyond what Congress has already granted them." *Id.* at 445–46, 449–50 (quoting Landon v. Plasencia, 459 U.S. 21, 32 (1982)).

[275] Brumme v. Immigration and Naturalization Serv., 275 F.3d 443, 447–48 (5th Cir. 2001).

[276] *Id.* at 448 (quoting 8 U.S.C. § 1252(e)(5)). *See also* De Rincon v. Dep't of Homeland Sec., 539 F.3d 1133, 1139–40 (9th Cir. 2008) (holding that district court lacked jurisdiction to review alien's due process challenge to the summary nature of her expedited removal proceedings because alien did not contest the order on any of the three specified grounds for habeas review set forth in INA § 242(e)(2), and, moreover, she had no constitutional right to due process at the border); M.S.P.C. v. U.S. Customs and Border Prot., 60 F. Supp. 3d 1156, 1163, 1175 (D.N.M. 2014) (rejecting alien's "expansive reading" of INA § 242(e)(2) as permitting habeas review of whether she should have been subject to expedited removal, and further rejecting alien's constitutional challenge to statute's jurisdictional limitations because, as a recent surreptitious entrant, she had no constitutional due process rights).

[277] United States v. Barajas-Alvarado, 655 F.3d 1077, 1080 (9th Cir. 2011).

[278] *Id.* at 1083–84.

lacked merit because nonadmitted aliens have no right to representation, and "are entitled only to whatever process Congress provides."[279] By contrast, in another unlawful reentry case, the Ninth Circuit held that an alien was entitled to due process during his expedited removal proceedings because he was already within the United States when he was apprehended, and that the immigration officer's failure to provide the alien notice of his inadmissibility charge and an opportunity to review his sworn statement violated due process.[280]

Apart from habeas and criminal reentry cases, the courts have addressed challenges to expedited removal orders raised in petitions for review filed directly with the federal courts of appeals. In these cases, the petitioners have argued that their expedited removal proceedings violated their right to due process because they were detained, had no right to counsel, and did not have an opportunity to contest their charges of inadmissibility.[281] As discussed in this chapter, an alien subject to a final order of removal generally may file a petition for review of that order in the judicial circuit where the administrative removal proceedings were completed.[282] The courts of appeals, however, have dismissed petitions for review challenging expedited removal orders, citing INA Section 242(a)(2)(A)'s language barring judicial review of claims arising in the context of expedited removal proceedings.[283] The courts have further determined that, although INA Section 242(a)(2)(D) restores jurisdiction to review constitutional claims or questions of law raised in a petition for review that is otherwise subject to jurisdictional limitations, this exception does not apply to the statutory provisions barring judicial review of an

---

[279] *Id.* at 1088 (citing United States *ex rel.* Knauff v. Shaughnessy, 338 U.S. 537, 544 (1950)).

[280] United States v. Raya-Vaca, 771 F.3d 1195, 1203–06 (9th Cir. 2014). *See* 8 C.F.R. § 235.3(b)(2)(i) (detailing the procedural requirements during expedited removal).

[281] *See e.g.,* Pena v. Lynch, 815 F.3d 452, 455 (9th Cir. 2015); Shunaula v. Holder, 732 F.3d 143, 145 (2d Cir. 2013); Khan v. Holder, 608 F.3d 325, 330 (7th Cir. 2010); Turgerel v. Mukasey, 513 F.3d 1202, 1205 (10th Cir. 2008).

[282] 8 U.S.C. § 1252(a)(1), (b)(1), (b)(2).

[283] *See id.* § 1252(a)(1) (providing for "[j]udicial review of a final order of removal (*other than* an order of removal without a hearing pursuant to section 1225(b)(1) of this title)") (emphasis added), (a)(2)(A) (barring review of expedited removal); *Pena*, 815 F.3d at 456; *Turgerel*, 513 F.3d at 1205–06; *Khan*, 608 F.3d at 327; *Shunaula*, 732 F.3d at 145–47.

expedited removal order.[284] Although some courts have expressed concern that the expedited removal process is "fraught with risk of arbitrary, mistaken, or discriminatory behavior," reviewing courts have nonetheless ruled that they are not "free to disregard jurisdictional limitations" imposed by statute on the review of expedited removal orders.[285]

Potential Expansions of Expedited Removal and Legal Implications

Since the enactment of the expedited removal statute, immigration authorities have implemented expedited removal with respect to three overarching categories of aliens: (1) those who arrive in the United States at a designated port of entry; (2) those who arrived in the United States by sea, and who have been in the country for less than two years; and (3) those found within 100 miles of the U.S. border, within 14 days of entering the country.[286] The overwhelming majority of aliens subject to expedited removal, in other words, have been inspected or apprehended at a designated port of entry or near the international border when attempting to enter, or shortly after entering, the United States.[287]

But as previously discussed, the expedited removal statute permits the Secretary of DHS to apply expedited removal to any alien inadmissible due to a lack of entry documents or because he sought to obtain entry through fraud or misrepresentation, regardless of the alien's location, provided that the alien has not been admitted or paroled and has been in the country for less than two years.[288] Thus, DHS has the statutory authority to expand expedited removal on a much larger geographic and temporal scale.

---

[284] *Pena*, 815 F.3d at 456; *Turgerel*, 513 F.3d at 1206; *Khan*, 608 F.3d at 328–29.

[285] *Khan*, 608 F.3d at 329; *accord* Castro v. Dep't of Homeland Sec., 835 F.3d 422, 432–33 (3d Cir. 2016), *cert. denied* 137 S. Ct. 1581 (2017).

[286] Jennifer M. Chacon, *Essay: Immigration and the Bully Pulpit*, 130 HARV. L. REV. F. 243, 261 (2017).

[287] *See* Shattuck, *supra* note 148, at 474 (expedited removal "deputizes individual immigration officers near borders and ports of entry to issue removal orders against individuals found ineligible to enter the United States.").

[288] 8 U.S.C. § 1225(b)(1)(A)(iii)(II).

To that end, on January 25, 2017, President Trump issued an executive order directing the DHS Secretary to apply expedited removal within the broader framework of INA Section 235(b)(1).[289] Less than a month later, then-DHS Secretary John Kelly announced a series of border security and immigration enforcement initiatives.[290] Among other measures, Secretary Kelly announced that "[t]o ensure the prompt removal of aliens apprehended soon after crossing the border illegally, the Department will publish in the *Federal Register* a new Notice Designating Aliens Subject to Expedited Removal Under [INA] Section 235(b)(1)(a)(iii)," which may "depart from the limitations set forth in the designation currently in force."[291] As reasons for this policy change, Secretary Kelly pointed to a "surge of illegal immigration at the southern border," a "historic backlog" of immigration court cases, and an increase in the number of apprehensions between ports of entry on the southern border.[292] In response, some immigrant rights advocates reportedly "denounced the proposed expansion ... warning that the policy would strip more immigrants of due process rights to seek asylum or other legal protections that would allow them to remain in the country."[293]

While federal statute clearly confers DHS with authority to employ expedited removal in a broader fashion, extending the process to aliens away from the border or its functional equivalent would likely prompt legal challenge. As previously discussed, the Supreme Court has long recognized that, while aliens seeking entry into the United States have no

---

[289] Exec. Order No. 13767, 82 Fed. Reg. 8793, 8796 (Jan. 25, 2017) ("The Secretary shall take appropriate action to apply, in his sole and unreviewable discretion, the provisions of section 235(b)(1)(A)(i) and (ii) of the INA to the aliens designated under section 235(b)(1)(A)(iii)(II).").

[290] *See* Memorandum from John Kelly, Sec'y of Homeland Sec., to Kevin McAleenan, Acting Comm'r, U.S. Customs & Border Prot., et al., Regarding Implementing the President's Border Security and Immigration Enforcement Improvement Policies (Feb. 20, 2017), https://www.dhs.gov/sites/default/files/publications/17_0220_S1_Implementing-the-Presidents-Border-SecurityImmigration-Enforcement-Improvement-Policies.pdf.

[291] *Id.* at 6, 11.

[292] *Id.* at 6.

[293] Abigail Hauslohner & David Nakamura, *In Memo, Trump Administration Weighs Expanding the Expedited Deportation Powers of DHS*, WASH. POST (Jul. 14, 2017), http://wapo.st/2t0phNX?tid=ss_mail&utm_term=.69c7e3b24f36.

constitutional rights regarding their applications for admission,[294] aliens who have *entered* the United States, even unlawfully, are entitled to some due process protections before they can be removed.[295] Such due process protections typically involve the right to a hearing and a meaningful opportunity to be heard.[296] As discussed in this chapter, an alien subject to expedited removal has no right to a hearing or further review of a determination that he should be removed from the United States.[297] Thus, expanding expedited removal to cover aliens present in *any* part of the United States could come into conflict with these constitutional notions. Moreover, although some courts have, in light of the entry fiction doctrine, determined that aliens apprehended near the border may not avail themselves of these constitutional protections,[298] the extent to which this

---

[294] *See e.g.,* Landon v. Plasencia, 459 U.S. 21, 32 (1982) ("This Court has long held that an alien seeking initial admission to the United States requests a privilege and has no constitutional rights regarding his application"); United States *ex rel.* Knauff v. Shaughnessy, 338 U.S. 537, 544 (1950) ("Whatever the procedure authorized by Congress is, it is due process as far as an alien denied entry is concerned").

[295] *See e.g.,* Zadvydas v. Davis, 533 U.S. 678, 693 (2001) ("But once an alien enters the country, the legal circumstance changes, for the Due Process Clause applies to all 'persons' within the United States, including aliens, whether their presence here is lawful, unlawful, temporary, or permanent"); Plyler v. Doe, 457 U.S. 202, 210 (1982) ("Aliens, even aliens whose presence in this country is unlawful, have long been recognized as "persons" guaranteed due process of law by the Fifth and Fourteenth Amendments."); Shaughnessy v. United States *ex rel.* Mezei, 345 U.S. 206, 212 (1953) ("[A]liens who have once passed through our gates, even illegally, may be expelled only after proceedings conforming to traditional standards of fairness encompassed in due process of law"). *See also* David A. Martin, *Graduated Application of Constitutional Protections for Aliens: The Real Meaning of* Zadvydas v. Davis, 2001 SUP. CT. REV. 47, 97 (2001) ("Practice has traditionally treated an entrant without inspection (EWI) more favorably, for purposes of constitutional and statutory claims, than parolees or applicants for admission at the border.").

[296] Mathews v. Eldridge, 424 U.S. 319, 333 (1976) ("The fundamental requirement of due process is the opportunity to be heard 'at a meaningful time and in a meaningful manner.'") (quoting Armstrong v. Manzo, 380 U.S. 545, 552 (1965)); *see also* Kwong Hai Chew v. Colding, 344 U.S. 590, 597 (1953) (recognizing that due process requires "notice of the nature of the charge and a hearing at least before an executive or administrative tribunal"); Salgado-Diaz v. Gonzales, 395 F.3d 1158, 1162 (9th Cir. 2005) ("Immigration proceedings, although not subject to the full range of constitutional protections, must conform to the Fifth Amendment's requirement of due process.").

[297] 8 U.S.C. § 1225(b)(1)(A)(i); 8 C.F.R. § 235.3(b)(2)(ii).

[298] *See e.g.,* Castro v. United States Dep't of Homeland Sec., 835 F.3d 422, 445–50 (3d Cir. 2016) (holding that aliens "apprehended within hours of surreptitiously entering the United States" could not raise a constitutional challenge to their expedited removal because they were "recent clandestine entrants" who could be treated as aliens seeking initial admission to the country who lack constitutional protections), *cert. denied*, 137 S. Ct. 1581 (2017); M.S.P.C. v. U.S. Customs and Border Prot., 60 F. Supp. 3d 1156, 1175 (D.N.M. 2014)

principle may be applied to aliens in the interior, or who have developed ties to the United States, is far from certain.[299]

However, the Supreme Court, at times, has appeared to view *admission* into the United States by immigration authorities as the key factor that determines whether an alien is entitled to constitutional protections. For example, in *Landon v. Plasencia*, the Supreme Court stated that "once an alien gains admission to our country and begins to develop the ties that go with permanent residence his constitutional status changes accordingly."[300] The Court has also suggested that the length of time that an alien has spent in the United States may inform the scope and degree of constitutional protections.[301] These principles might support the argument that expedited removal can be applied on a wider basis to aliens within the interior of the United States who have been in the country for relatively short periods of time.

("Petitioner, who undisputedly crossed approximately nine miles over the border and was apprehended within 30 minutes of crossing, does not have any substantial ties to this country to place the nature of her rights near those of a permanent resident. Thus, for purposes of the constitutional right to due process, Petitioner's status is assimilated to that of an arriving alien.").

299 *See* Jennifer Lee Koh, *Removal in the Shadows of Immigration Court*, 90 S. CAL. L. REV. 181, 197–98 (2017) (describing expansion of expedited removal away from ports of entry "as an example of the shifting nature of the immigration border and the border's increased disassociation from settled physical boundaries," and arguing that an expansion into the interior of the United States "would constitute a radical boost to the scope of CBP's powers.").

300 *Landon*, 459 U.S. at 32; *see also Kwong Hai Chew*, 344 U.S. at 596 n.5 ("'The Bill of Rights is a futile authority for the alien seeking admission for the first time to these shores. But once an alien *lawfully* enters and resides in this country he becomes invested with the rights guaranteed by the Constitution to all people within our borders.'") (quoting Bridges v. Wixon, 326 U.S. 135, 161 (1945) (Murphy, J., concurring) (emphasis added).

301 *See e.g.*, United States v. Verdugo-Urquidez, 494 U.S. 259, 265 (1990) (explaining that, for purposes of the Fourth Amendment, constitutional protections extend "to a class of persons who are part of a national community or who have otherwise developed sufficient connection with this country to be considered part of that community"); *Landon*, 459 U.S. at 32 (emphasizing the "ties" that an alien develops with the United States in determining the degree of constitutional protections); Johnson v. Eisentrager, 339 U.S. 763, 770 (1950) (an alien is "accorded a generous and ascending scale of rights as he increases his identity with our society"); Yamataya v. Fisher, 189 U.S. 86, 101 (1903) (holding that "an alien who has entered the country, and has become subject in all respects to its jurisdiction, and a part of its population" may not be deported without due process). *See also* Martin, *supra* note 295, at 99 (claiming that, when unlawfully present aliens accrue lengthy periods of presence in the United States, they develop social connections that "deserve some weight in deciding on the exact protections owed them").

But notwithstanding the language in *Landon,* the Supreme Court has continued to describe an alien's physical presence in the United States, whether lawful or unlawful, as the critical factor in assessing whether due process attaches.[302] Therefore, if DHS undertakes a future expansion of expedited removal, the courts may be confronted with further challenges to the agency's implementation of that procedure down the road. Until now, courts have addressed such challenges only within the confines of enforcement actions at or near the border. If DHS implements expedited removal on a broader scale throughout the United States, the courts may need to address critical questions concerning the scope of the federal government's plenary power over the admission of aliens, and the limits of that "sovereign prerogative" with respect to aliens already present in the United States.[303]

APPENDIX A. GLOSSARY

- **Admission** – The lawful entry of an alien into the United States after inspection and authorization by an immigration officer.
- **Alien** – Any person who is not a citizen or national of the United States.
- **Applicant for Admission** – By statute, an alien present in the United States who has not been admitted by immigration authorities or who arrives in the United States (whether or not at a designated port of entry and including an alien who is brought to the United States after having been interdicted in international or U.S. waters).
- **Arriving Alien** – By regulation, an alien coming or attempting to come into the United States at a designated port of entry, or an alien seeking transit through the United States at a port of entry, or

[302] *See e.g.,* Zadvydas v. Davis, 533 U.S. 678, 693 (2001); Plyler v. Doe, 457 U.S. 202, 210 (1982); Matthews v. Diaz, 426 U.S. 67, 77 (1976); Shaughnessy v. United States *ex rel.* Mezei, 345 U.S. 206, 212 (1953).

[303] *Landon*, 459 U.S. at 32.

an alien interdicted in international or U.S. waters and brought into the United States by any means, whether or not to a designated port of entry (and regardless of the means of transport).

- **Asylee** – A person in the United States who has applied for and received asylum.
- **Asylum** – A form of relief available for aliens who arrive in or are physically present in the United States who establish that they suffered past persecution or have a well-founded fear of future persecution on account of their race, religion, nationality, membership in a particular social group, or political opinion.
- **Board of Immigration Appeals (BIA)** – The highest administrative body responsible for interpreting and applying federal immigration laws; a component of the Department of Justice's Executive Office of Immigration Review, the BIA has jurisdiction to hear appeals from decisions issued by immigration judges and certain DHS officials.
- **Credible Fear** – A significant possibility, taking into account the credibility of the statements made by the alien in support of the alien's claim and such other facts as are known to the asylum officer, that the alien could establish eligibility for asylum, withholding of removal, or protection under the Convention Against Torture.
- **Deportability** – The status of being subject to removal following a lawful admission into the United States.
- **Expedited Removal** – A streamlined removal process that applies to certain arriving aliens and other aliens physically present in the United States who are inadmissible on the grounds that they lack valid entry documents or have attempted to procure their admission through fraud or misrepresentation.
- **Formal Removal Proceedings** – A formal removal process under INA Section 240 in which an alien subject to removal is issued a notice to appear at a hearing before an immigration judge, where the alien may contest his removability, obtain counsel, present evidence, and apply for any available forms of relief from removal.

- **Immigration Judge (IJ)** – An attorney employed by the Department of Justice's Executive Office for Immigration Review who conducts and adjudicates removal proceedings.
- **Inadmissibility** – The status of being ineligible for admission into the United States for certain disqualifying grounds (e.g., lack of valid entry documents, fraud).
- **Lawful Permanent Resident(LPR)** – An alien who has been lawfully accorded the privilege of residing permanently in the United States in accordance with the immigration laws.
- **Parole** – Permission to enter the United States pending a determination as to whether an alien should be admitted; typically granted as a matter of discretion for urgent humanitarian reasons or significant public benefit, but not regarded as a lawful admission of the alien for immigration purposes.
- **Port of Entry** – A location designated as a place for the authorized entry of persons and merchandise into the United States, whether arriving by land, air, or sea. It may include designated locations along the international borders or within the interior of the United States (e.g., international airports).
- **Refugee** – A person outside of the United States who has been granted permission to enter the United States because he suffered past persecution or has a wellfounded fear of future persecution on account of his race, religion, nationality, membership in a particular social group, or political opinion, and is not firmly resettled in another country.
- **U.S. Border Patrol** – An agency component within CBP that is primarily charged with the apprehension of aliens unlawfully entering the United States or who have recently entered the country unlawfully away from a designated point of entry along the border.
- **U.S. Citizenship and Immigration Services (USCIS)** – An agency within DHS that adjudicates petitions for immigration benefits and naturalization; conducts credible fear interviews of

aliens at the border who seek asylum or express a fear of persecution or torture.

- **U.S. Customs and Border Protection (CBP)** – An agency within the Department of Homeland Security (DHS) that is primarily responsible for immigration enforcement along the border and at designated ports of entry.
- **U.S. Immigration and Customs Enforcement (ICE)** – An agency within DHS that is primarily responsible for immigration enforcement in the interior of the United States, including the detention and removal of aliens.

APPENDIX B. IMPLEMENTATION AND EXPANSION OF EXPEDITED REMOVAL: 1997-2017

The following discussion is a more comprehensive overview of the Executive's implementation and expansion of expedited removal following the passage of IIRIRA in 1996.

Arriving Aliens

Initially, the former INS limited the application of its expedited removal authority to aliens arriving in the United States.[304] In order to clarify the scope of the term "arriving alien," the INS issued regulations that defined the term to include aliens seeking admission into the United States at a port of entry, aliens seeking transit through the United States at a port of entry, and aliens who have been interdicted at sea and brought into the United States "by any means, whether or not to a designated port-of-entry, and regardless of the means of transport."[305]

---

[304] Inspection and Expedited Removal of Aliens, 62 Fed. Reg. 10,312, 10,313–14 (Mar. 6, 1997); *see also Procedures for Expedited Removal*, *supra* note 62, at 1505, 1520.

[305] Inspection and Expedited Removal of Aliens, 62 Fed. Reg. 444, 445 (Jan. 3, 1997); 8 C.F.R. § 1.2. In its notice of these regulations, the INS recognized that "[a]n exception is provided

In response to opposition to the inclusion of aliens interdicted at sea in the definition of "arriving alien," the INS pointed to BIA precedent holding that "the mere crossing into the territorial waters of the United States has never satisfied the test of having entered the United States," and reasoned that "[a]liens who have not yet established physical presence on land in the United States cannot be considered as anything other than arriving aliens."[306] Furthermore, the INS declared, "[t]he inclusion of aliens interdicted at sea in the definition of arriving alien will support the Department's mandate to protect the nation's borders against illegal immigration."[307]

The INS further determined that "[a]n arriving alien remains an arriving alien even if paroled pursuant to INA Section 212(d)(5), and even after any such parole is terminated or revoked."[308] The INS explained that the inclusion of paroled aliens was based on the language of INA Section 212(d)(5), which indicated that the parole of an alien did not constitute an admission into the United States, and that the alien would be considered an applicant for admission once the purpose of the parole had been served.[309]

Looking ahead, the INS "reserve[d] the right to apply expedited removal procedures to additional classes of aliens *within the limits set by the statute*, if, in the Commissioner's discretion, such action is

---

for Cuban nationals arriving by aircraft at a portof-entry." Inspection and Expedited Removal of Aliens, 62 Fed. Reg. at 444-45; *see also* 8 U.S.C. § 1225(b)(1)(F) (statutory exception for aliens from countries in the Western Hemisphere whose government does not have diplomatic relations with the United States and who arrived by aircraft). The INS concluded that the expedited removal statute, coupled with other references to "arriving aliens" located elsewhere in the INA, "seemed to differentiate more clearly between aliens at ports-of-entry and those encountered elsewhere in the United States," and interpreted the term "arriving alien" primarily in reference to aliens encountered at ports of entry. Inspection and Expedited Removal of Aliens, 62 Fed. Reg. at 10,312–13.

[306] Inspection and Expedited Removal of Aliens, 62 Fed. Reg. at 10,313 (citing Matter of G, 20 I. & N. Dec. 764 (BIA 1993)).

[307] *Id.*; *see also* Sale v. Haitian Ctrs. Council, Inc., 509 U.S. 155, 187–88 (1993) (holding that statutory and treaty protections that governed the treatment of refugees within the United States had no extraterritorial application to Haitian migrants interdicted on the high seas).

[308] Inspection and Expedited Removal of Aliens, 62 Fed. Reg. at 444–45.

[309] Inspection and Expedited Removal of Aliens, 62 Fed. Reg. at 10,313. However, if an alien was paroled into the United States before April 1, 1997, *or* was paroled on or after April 1, 1997, pursuant to a grant of advance parole which the alien applied for and received in the United States prior to his departure from and return to the United States, the alien will not be considered an "arriving alien" for purposes of expedited removal. 8 C.F.R. § 1.2.

operationally warranted."[310] This expanded category of aliens, the INS explained, "may be localized, in response to specific needs within a particular region, or nationwide, as appropriate."[311] The agency declared that "a proposed expansion of the expedited removal procedures may occur at any time and may be driven either by specific situations such as a sudden influx of illegal aliens motivated by political or economic unrest or other events or by a general need to increase the effectiveness of enforcement operations at one or more locations."[312]

The INS, however, recognized that expanding the reach of expedited removal would "involve more complex determinations of fact and will be more difficult to manage," and indicated that, for the time being, it would apply the new procedures "on a more limited and controlled basis."[313] Therefore, upon IIRIRA's passage, the new expedited removal statute covered only arriving aliens in the United States, which, in turn, encompassed (1) aliens arriving at a port of entry, (2) aliens in transit at a port of entry, and (3) aliens interdicted at sea who have been brought into the United States.[314] Nevertheless, at the outset, the INS's expedited removal authority "dramatically affect[ed] the pool of persons subject to expedited procedures."[315]

---

[310] Inspection and Expedited Removal of Aliens, 62 Fed. Reg. at 10,314 (emphasis added).

[311] Inspection and Expedited Removal of Aliens, 62 Fed. Reg. at 444–45.

[312] Inspection and Expedited Removal of Aliens, 62 Fed. Reg. at 10,314; *see also* 8 C.F.R. § 235.3(b)(1)(ii) ("The Commissioner shall have the sole discretion to apply the provisions of section 235(b)(1) of the Act, at any time, to any class of aliens described in this section").

[313] Inspection and Expedited Removal of Aliens, 62 Fed. Reg. at 10,313–14.

[314] Subsequently, in 1998, the INS amended its definition of "arriving alien" to exempt from expedited removal aliens who were paroled into the United States before April 1, 1997 (the effective date of IIRIRA), as well as aliens who, either before or after April 1, 1997, returned to the United States pursuant to a grant of advance parole that they applied for and obtained while physically present in the United States and prior to their departure from this country. Amendment of the Regulatory Definition of Arriving Alien, 63 Fed. Reg. 19,382, 19,382 (Apr. 20, 1998). The agency explained that, as a matter of policy, this group of paroled aliens was "not best regarded as arriving aliens for purposes of the applicability of expedited removal" because it covered aliens who were initially paroled well before expedited removal came into effect, and aliens previously present in the United States for lengthy periods of time who departed from and later returned to the United States on advance parole. *Id.*

[315] *Procedures for Expedited Removal*, *supra* note 62, at 1520.

Criminal Aliens Held in Texas Correctional Facilities (Proposed but Not Implemented)

In 1999, the INS considered, but ultimately did not implement, a "pilot program" that would have extended expedited removal to aliens who (1) had been convicted of unlawful entry; (2) had not been admitted or paroled into the United States, and had been physically present in the United States for less than two years; and (3) were serving criminal sentences in designated correctional facilities in Texas.[316]

To support its proposed expansion, the INS cited INA Section 235(b)(1)(A)(iii) and its implementing regulations, which gave it the authority to apply expedited removal to aliens who entered the United States without being admitted or paroled, and who have not been in the United States for at least two years.[317] Citing a lack of detention space and an increase in the number of criminal alien apprehensions, the INS determined that a more effective procedure to remove aliens serving short criminal sentences was warranted.[318] Despite this proposed expansion, neither the INS nor DHS implemented this policy.

Aliens Who Arrived in the United States by Sea

In 2002, the INS authorized expedited removal for a "newly designated class" of aliens: those who arrived in the United States by sea, "either by boat or other means," and who (1) have not been admitted or paroled, and (2) have not been physically present in the United States for a continuous period of at least two years at the time of their apprehension.[319]

---

[316] Advance Notice of Expansion of Expedited Removal to Certain Criminal Aliens Held in Federal, State, and Local Jails, 64 Fed. Reg. 51,338, 51,338–39 (Sept. 22, 1999).

[317] *Id.* at 51,339; *see* 8 U.S.C. § 1225(b)(1)(A)(iii); 8 C.F.R. § 235.3(b)(1)(ii).

[318] Advance Notice of Expansion of Expedited Removal, 64 Fed. Reg. at 51,339.

[319] Notice Designating Aliens Subject to Expedited Removal Under Section 235(b)(1)(A)(iii) of the Immigration and Nationality Act, 67 Fed. Reg. 68,924, 68,924 (Nov. 13, 2002).

As it had done before, the INS cited INA Section 235(b)(1)(A)(iii) as the statutory authority for expanding expedited removal to aliens "who arrive illegally by sea."[320] The INS noted that this expansion did not include aliens who arrived in the United States at a designated port of entry, or who were interdicted at sea and brought into the United States, because they were already subject to the expedited removal process for arriving aliens.[321] In addition, the INS did not apply its expansion to Cuban nationals who arrived in the United States by sea because of the "longstanding U.S. policy to treat Cubans differently from other aliens."[322]

Therefore, apart from Cuban nationals, all aliens who unlawfully arrived by sea in the United States, in a location other than a port of entry, would now be subject to expedited removal, and, with limited exceptions, detained pending any determination as to whether they had a credible fear of persecution.[323] The INS claimed that this expansion would "assist in deterring surges in illegal migration by sea, including potential mass migration, and preventing loss of life."[324] The agency explained that "[a] surge in illegal migration by sea threatens national security by diverting valuable U.S. Coast Guard and other resources from counterterrorism and homeland security responsibilities."[325] In addition, channeling the original legislative intent behind IIRIRA's amendments, the agency determined that its decision was "necessary to remove quickly from the United States aliens who arrive illegally by sea and who do not establish a credible fear."[326] The INS thus announced that it would implement expedited removal for aliens who arrived in this country by sea on or after November 13, 2002.[327]

---

[320] *Id.* at 68,924.
[321] *Id.*
[322] *Id.* at 68,925.
[323] *Id.* at 68,924–25.
[324] *Id.*at 68,924.
[325] *Id.*
[326] *Id.*
[327] *Id.* at 68,925.

Aliens Unlawfully Present in the United States within 100 Miles of the Border

A few years later, in 2004, DHS (which had now replaced the INS) authorized CBP to implement expedited removal for aliens who were unlawfully present in the United States without being admitted or paroled, if (1) they were apprehended within 100 miles of the border, and (2) they had not been physically present in the United States for a continuous period of at least 14 days.[328] As the statutory basis for this expansion, the agency again cited INA Section 235(b)(1)(A)(iii), which gave it the discretion to apply expedited removal to aliens who were physically present in the United States without being admitted or paroled, and who could not establish their continuous physical presence in this country for up to two years.[329]

In support of its decision to extend expedited removal to border areas, DHS pointed to "an urgent need to enhance [its] ability to improve the safety and security of the nation's land borders, as well as the need to deter foreign nationals from undertaking dangerous border crossings, and thereby prevent the needless deaths and crimes associated with human trafficking and alien smuggling operations."[330] DHS thus determined that expanding the reach of expedited removal to aliens encountered shortly after they unlawfully entered the United States through the border would improve national security, "increase the deterrence of illegal entries by ensuring that apprehension quickly leads to removal," and "impair the ability of smuggling organizations to operate."[331]

Ultimately, though, DHS limited its new designation of expedited removal to aliens who were neither nationals of Mexico nor Canada, and Mexican and Canadian nationals who had histories of criminal or immigration violations.[332] With regard to non-Mexican and non-Canadian nationals ("third-country nationals"), DHS explained that there were

---

[328] Designating Aliens for Expedited Removal, 69 Fed. Reg. 48,877, 48,877 (Aug. 11, 2004).
[329] *Id.* at 48,878.
[330] *Id.* at 48,879.
[331] *Id.* at 48,879–80.
[332] *Id.* at 48,878.

logistical difficulties of initiating formal removal proceedings against nearly 1 million aliens apprehended each year, particularly along the southern border with Mexico, and that, while the majority of those aliens were Mexican nationals who could be "voluntarily returned" to Mexico without any formal removal process, aliens from other countries could not simply be returned to Mexico.[333] Instead, they had to be detained pending arrangements for their return by aircraft, or pending formal removal proceedings.[334] Given the agency's lack of resources to detain all third-country nationals, DHS explained, many of these aliens were released with instructions to appear for their removal proceedings, only to subsequently disappear in the United States.[335] For these reasons, DHS had a greater incentive to apply expedited removal to third-country nationals in border areas, than it did for Mexican and Canadian nationals.[336] On the other hand, given the agency's interest in improving national security and public safety, Mexican and Canadian nationals with prior criminal or immigration violations would be subject to expedited removal.[337]

DHS also limited the scope of its new expedited removal designation to border areas. The agency recognized that INA Section 235(b)(1)(A)(iii) did not geographically restrict expedited removal for aliens present in the United States without being admitted or paroled, and that the statute permitted expedited removal for aliens who could not establish their continuous physical presence in this country for up to two years.[338] Nevertheless, the agency concentrated its enforcement resources "upon unlawful entries that have a close spatial and temporal nexus to the border."[339] Therefore, instead of implementing expedited removal nationwide, DHS limited it to "aliens who are apprehended immediately proximate to the land border and have negligible ties or equities in the U.S."[340] The agency determined that an area within 100 miles of the border

---

[333] *Id.*
[334] *Id.*
[335] *Id.*
[336] *Id.*
[337] *Id.* at 48,878–79.
[338] *Id.*
[339] *Id.* at 48,879.
[340] *Id.*

was "immediately proximate" to the border "because many aliens will arrive in vehicles that speedily depart the border area, and because other recent arrivals will find their way to near-border locales seeking transportation to other locations within the interior of the U.S."[341] DHS also cited to agency regulations that had already established that the 100-mile range was a "reasonable distance" from the external boundary of the United States.[342]

Accordingly, DHS limited its new application of expedited removal to aliens apprehended within 14 days after they entered the United States, and within 100 miles of any international land border.[343] Aliens falling into this category would be detained pending their removal and any determination as to whether they feared persecution.[344] Consistent with other expedited removal designations, however, DHS excluded Cuban nationals because their removal to Cuba "[could not] presently be assured and for other U.S. policy reasons."[345]

DHS indicated that it would implement expedited removal for aliens apprehended in border areas beginning on August 11, 2004.[346] Based on this latest expansion, DHS could now apply its expedited removal authority not only to aliens who arrived in the United States at ports of entry or by sea, but also to aliens who were encountered within this country's border regions *between* ports of entry.[347]

Expansion to Entire Southwest Border

Initially, DHS limited the implementation of its new expedited removal authority to parts of the southwestern United States, specifically the border sectors of Tucson, Arizona; Yuma, Arizona; McAllen, Texas;

---

[341] *Id.*

[342] *Id.*; *see* 8 C.F.R. § 287.1(a)(2).

[343] Designating Aliens for Expedited Removal, 69 Fed. Reg. at 48,878.

[344] *Id.* at 48,879.

[345] *Id.* at 48,879–80.

[346] *Id.* at 48,880.

[347] DHS noted, however, that although it was geographically restricting expedited removal to border areas, it retained the discretion to implement "the full nationwide enforcement authority of the statute through publication of a subsequent Federal Register notice." *Id.* at 48,879.

Laredo, Texas; San Diego, California; and El Centro, California.[348] On September 14, 2005, DHS announced the expansion to three additional border sectors in Del Rio, TX; Marfa, TX; and El Paso, TX—thereby implementing the policy across the entire Southwest border.[349] Former Secretary of Homeland Security Michael Chertoff, who headed the agency at the time, declared that the expansion "gives Border Patrol agents the ability to gain greater control of our borders and to protect our country against the terrorist threat."[350] Further, according to DHS, the expedited removal process "will disrupt the vicious human smuggling cycle that occurs along the southwest border."[351] Following the announcement, DHS implemented expedited removal along the entire land border with Mexico.

Expansion to Entire U.S. Border

A few months later, on January 30, 2006, DHS announced the implementation of expedited removal along the entire U.S.-Canadian border and all U.S. coastal areas.[352] Noting decreased unlawful border crossings since expedited removal began in the southwestern United States, Secretary Chertoff asserted that expanding the process along all borders "will provide DHS agents and officers with an additional tool to protect our nation's boundaries and quickly remove those who entered our country illegally."[353] According to the agency, expedited removal had proven to be "an effective border management process that swiftly returns illegal aliens to their countries of origin while maintaining protections for those who fear persecution."[354] DHS also pointed to the disruption of "human smuggling cycles" as a factor warranting the expansion of expedited removal.[355] Therefore, with this expansion in place, DHS could now

---

[348] Press Release, U.S. Dep't of Homeland Sec., DHS Expands Expedited Removal Authority Along Southwest Border (Sept. 14, 2005), http://www.hsdl.org/?view&did=477118.

[349] *Id.*; *see also* Designating Aliens for Expedited Removal, 69 Fed. Reg. at 48,878 (identifying border sectors where expedited removal would be implemented).

[350] Press Release, *supra* note 348.

[351] *Id.*

[352] Press Release, U.S. Dep't of Homeland Sec., DHS Streamlines Removal Process Along Entire U.S. Border (Jan. 30, 2006), https://www.hsdl.org/?abstract&did=476965.

[353] *Id.*

[354] *Id.*

[355] *Id.*

implement expedited removal in the northern border sectors of Blaine, WA; Spokane, WA; Havre, MT; Grand Forks, ND; Detroit, MI; Buffalo, NY; Swanton, VT; and Houlton, ME.[356]

Cuban Nationals Arriving in the United States

On July 20, 2015, the United States formally restored diplomatic relations with Cuba.[357] In addition, on January 12, 2017, former President Barack Obama announced an end to the longstanding "wet-foot, dry-foot" policy, which allowed Cubans who arrived on American soil the right to remain in the United States and apply for lawful permanent resident status, while those who were detained at sea were returned to Cuba.[358]

In response to the restoration of diplomatic relations, DHS eliminated the exception to expedited removal for Cuban nationals who arrive in the United States at a designated port of entry by aircraft.[359] The agency observed, moreover, that the policy justifications for exempting Cuban nationals were no longer valid given Cuba's agreement to facilitate the return of Cuban nationals ordered removed from the United States.[360] In addition, DHS determined that "a significant increase in attempts by Cuban nationals to illegally enter the United States" meant that an exception for Cuban nationals would significantly undermine efforts to remove aliens who had no authorization to be in this country.[361] Therefore, Cuban

---

[356] Designating Aliens for Expedited Removal, 69 Fed. Reg. 48,877, 48,880 (Aug. 11, 2004).

[357] Karen De Young, *Cuba and U.S. Quietly Restore Full Diplomatic Ties After 5 Decades*, WASH. POST, July 20, 2015, http://wapo.st/1TLMGtS?tid=ss_tw&utm_term=.c7a5c88b1750.

[358] *See* United States v. Dominguez, 661 F.3d 1051, 1067 (11th Cir. 2011) (discussing "special treatment to Cuban nationals who come to the United States").

[359] Eliminating Exception to Expedited Removal Authority for Cuban Nationals Arriving by Air, 82 Fed. Reg. 4769, 4769–70 (Jan. 17, 2017); *see* 8 U.S.C. § 1225(b)(1)(F) (providing that expedited removal does not apply "to an alien who is a native or citizen of a country in the Western Hemisphere with whose government the United States does not have full diplomatic relations and who arrives by aircraft at a port of entry").

[360] Eliminating Exception to Expedited Removal Authority for Cuban Nationals Arriving by Air, 82 Fed. Reg. at 4770.

[361] *Id.*

nationals who arrived in the United States at a designated port of entry by aircraft were now subject to expedited removal.

DHS additionally eliminated the exception for Cuban nationals who arrive in the United States by sea, who have not been admitted or paroled, and who have not been physically present in this country for less than two years.[362] DHS also removed the exception for Cuban nationals who are encountered within 100 miles of the border, who have not been admitted or paroled, and who have not been in the United States for less than 14 days.[363] The agency again cited the restoration of diplomatic relations between the United States and Cuba and other "significant changes" in the relationship between the two countries as factors that warranted a change in policy that "reflect[ed] these new realities."[364] Therefore, regardless of the manner in which they came to the United States, Cuban nationals were now subject to expedited removal if they met the statutory criteria for that process.

---

[362] Eliminating Exception to Expedited Removal Authority for Cuban Nationals Encountered in the United States or Arriving by Sea, 82 Fed. Reg. 4902 (Jan. 17, 2017).

[363] *Id.*

[364] *Id.* at 4904.

In: Immigration
Editor: Abel Thompson
ISBN: 978-1-53616-187-8

Chapter 5

THE TRUMP ADMINISTRATION'S "ZERO TOLERANCE" IMMIGRATION ENFORCEMENT POLICY*

William A. Kandel

SUMMARY

For the last several years, Central American migrant families have arrived at the U.S.-Mexico border in relatively large numbers, many seeking asylum. While some request asylum at U.S. ports of entry, others do so after entering the United States "without inspection" (i.e., illegally) between U.S. ports of entry. On May 7, 2018, the Department of Justice (DOJ) implemented a "zero tolerance" policy toward illegal border crossing both to discourage illegal migration into the United States and to reduce the burden of processing asylum claims that Administration officials contend are often fraudulent.

Under the zero tolerance policy, DOJ prosecuted all adult aliens apprehended crossing the border illegally, with no exception for asylum seekers or those with minor children. DOJ's policy represented a change

* This is an edited, reformatted and augmented version of Congressional Research Service Publication No. R45266, updated February 26, 2019.

in the level of enforcement of an existing statute rather than a change in statute or regulation. Prior Administrations prosecuted illegal border crossings relatively infrequently.

Criminally prosecuting adults for illegal border crossing requires detaining them in federal criminal facilities where children are not permitted. While DOJ and the Department of Homeland Security (DHS) have broad statutory authority to detain adult aliens, children must be detained according to guidelines established in the Flores Settlement Agreement (FSA), the Homeland Security Act of 2002, and the Trafficking Victims Protection Reauthorization Act of 2008. A 2015 judicial ruling held that children remain in family immigration detention for no more than 20 days. If parents cannot be released with them, children are treated as unaccompanied alien children and transferred to the Department of Health and Human Services' (HHS's) Office of Refugee Resettlement (ORR) for care and custody.

The widely publicized family separations were a consequence of the Trump Administration's zero tolerance policy, not the result of an explicit family separation policy. Since the zero tolerance policy was implemented, up to 3,000 children may have been separated from their parents. In addition, thousands more were separated prior to the public announcement of the policy change.

Following mostly critical public reaction, President Trump issued an executive order on June 20, 2018, mandating that DHS maintain custody of alien families during the pendency of any criminal trial or immigration proceedings. DHS Customs and Border Protection (CBP) subsequently stopped referring most illegal border crossers to DOJ for criminal prosecution. A federal judge then mandated that all separated children be promptly reunited with their families. Another rejected DOJ's request to modify the FSA to extend the 20-day child detention guideline. DHS has since reverted to some prior immigration enforcement policies, and family separations continue to occur based upon DHS enforcement protocols in place prior to the 2018 zero tolerance policy.

Administration officials and immigration enforcement advocates argue that measures like the zero tolerance policy are necessary to discourage migrants from coming to the United States and submitting fraudulent asylum requests. They maintain that alien family separation resulting from the prosecution of illegal border crossers mirrors that which occurs regularly under the U.S. criminal justice system policy where adults with custody of minor children are charged with a crime and may be held in jail, effectively separating them from their children.

Immigrant advocates contend that migrant families are fleeing legitimate threats from countries with exceptionally high rates of gang violence, and that family separations resulting from the zero tolerance policy are cruel and violate fundamental human rights—such as the ability to request asylum. They maintain that the zero tolerance policy was hastily implemented and lacked planning for family reunification following criminal prosecutions. Some observers question the Trump Administration's capacity to marshal sufficient resources to prosecute all illegal border crossers without additional resources. Others criticize the family separation policy in light of less expensive alternatives to detention.

In prior years, most individuals apprehended were single adult males. Family unit apprehensions, which increased from just over 11,000 in FY2012 to 99,901 in the first four months of FY2019, and apprehensions of unaccompanied alien children are occurring within the context of otherwise relatively low historical levels of total alien apprehensions. In addition, the national origin of recently apprehended family units and unaccompanied children has shifted to mostly Central American from long-term trends of mostly Mexican.

INTRODUCTION

In recent years, Central American migrant families have been arriving at the U.S.-Mexico border in relatively large numbers, many seeking asylum.[1] While some request asylum at U.S. ports of entry, others do so after attempting to enter the United States illegally between U.S. ports of entry.[2] On May 7, 2018, Attorney General Jeff Sessions announced that the Department of Justice (DOJ) implemented a "zero tolerance" policy toward illegal border crossing, both to discourage illegal migration into the

---

[1] Asylum is a protection granted to a foreign national physically present within the United States or at the U.S. border who meets the definition of a refugee. A refugee is a person who is outside his or her home country (a second country that is not the United States) and is unable or unwilling to return because of persecution, or a well-founded fear of persecution, on account of five possible criteria: (1) race, (2) religion, (3) nationality, (4) membership in a particular social group, or (5) political opinion. INA 1101(a)(42)(A). In recent years, particularly following the surge of unaccompanied children at the Southwest border in 2014, courts have grappled with whether the statutory definition of asylum can encompass threats like gang violence. In some cases, asylum has been granted on such grounds.

[2] A port of entry is a harbor, border town, or airport through which people and goods may enter a country. The United States currently has 328 ports of entry. For background information related to ports of entry and border security, see CRS Report R43356, *Border Security: Immigration Inspections at Ports of Entry*; and CRS Report R42138, *Border Security: Immigration Enforcement Between Ports of Entry*.

United States and to reduce the burden of processing asylum claims that Administration officials contend are often fraudulent.[3]

Under the zero tolerance policy, DOJ prosecuted 100% of adult aliens[4] apprehended crossing the border illegally, making no exceptions for whether they were asylum seekers or accompanied by minor children. Illegal border crossing is a *misdemeanor*[5] for a first time offender and a *felony*[6] for anyone who has previously been "denied admission, excluded, deported, or removed, or has departed the United States while an order of exclusion, deportation or removal is outstanding and thereafter enters, attempts to enter or is found in the U.S."[7] Both such criminal offenses can be prosecuted by DOJ in federal criminal courts.

DOJ's "100% prosecution"[8] policy represented a change in the level of enforcement of an existing statute rather than a change in statute or regulation.[9] The recent Bush and Obama Administrations prosecuted illegal border crossings relatively infrequently, in part to avoid having DOJ resources committed to prosecuting sizeable numbers of misdemeanors. At different times during those Administrations, illegal entrants would be criminally prosecuted in an attempt to reduce illegal migration, but exceptions were generally made for families and asylum seekers.

---

[3] U.S. Department of Justice, Office of Public Affairs, "Attorney General Sessions Delivers Remarks Discussing the Immigration Enforcement Actions of the Trump Administration," May 7, 2018.

[4] *Alien* refers to anyone who is not a citizen or a national of the United States; INA §101(a)(3), 8 U.S.C. §1101(a)(3). In this chapter, alien is synonymous with *foreign national*. *Unauthorized alien* refers to a foreign national who is unlawfully present in the United States and who either entered the United States illegally ("without inspection") or entered lawfully and temporarily ("with inspection") but subsequently violated the terms of his/her admission, typically by "overstaying" a visa duration.

[5] A misdemeanor, under federal law, is a criminal offense that is generally regarded as less serious than a felony and punishable by a fine and/or imprisonment for a period of one year or less. See 18 U.S.C. § 3559; see also Black's Law Dictionary, 10th ed., 2014.

[6] A felony is a criminal offense punishable by a term of imprisonment for more than one year or by death. See 18 U.S.C. § 3559; see also Black's Law Dictionary, 10th ed., 2014.

[7] 8 U.S.C. §1326.

[8] DHS's Immigration and Customs Enforcement (ICE) referred to the "zero tolerance" policy as the "100% prosecution" policy. CRS consultation with ICE Legislative Affairs, June 8, 2018.

[9] See Tim O'Shea, Theresa Cardinal Brown, "Why Are families Being Separated at the Border? An Explainer," Bipartisan Policy Center, June 13, 2018; and Weekend Edition Saturday, "Jeh Johnson On Immigration And Trump," *National Public Radio*, June 9, 2018.

Illegal border crossers who are prosecuted by DOJ are detained in federal criminal facilities. Because children are not permitted in criminal detention facilities with adults, detaining adults who crossed illegally requires that any minor children under age 18 accompanying them be treated as unaccompanied alien children (UAC)[10] and transferred to the care and custody of the Department of Health and Human Services' (HHS's) Office of Refugee Resettlement (ORR).

The widely publicized family separations were therefore a *consequence* of the Administration's policy of 100% prosecution of illegal border crossing, and not the result of a direct policy or law mandating family separation. Since the policy was implemented, "under 3,000" children may have been separated from their parents, including at least 100 under age 5.[11]

The family separations have garnered extensive public attention. The Trump Administration and immigration enforcement advocates maintain that the zero tolerance policy was necessary to disincentivize migrants from coming to the United States and clogging immigration courts with fraudulent requests for asylum.[12] Immigrant advocates contend that migrant families are fleeing legitimate threats of violence and that family separations resulting from the zero tolerance policy were cruel and violated fundamental human rights.[13]

---

[10] Unaccompanied alien children (UAC) are defined in statute as children who lack lawful immigration status in the United States, who are under the age of 18, and who either are without a parent or legal guardian in the United States or without a parent or legal guardian in the United States who is available to provide care and physical custody; 6 U.S.C. §279(g)(2). In this chapter, children refers to minors under age 18 unless otherwise indicated. For more information, see CRS Report R43599, *Unaccompanied Alien Children: An Overview*.

[11] U.S. Department of Health and Human Services, "HHS Issues Statement on Ms. L, et al., Status Report Regarding Plan for Compliance for Remaining Class Members," press release, July 13, 2018. This figure was also reported in several news reports including Dan Diamond, "HHS says hundreds more migrant kids may have been separated than earlier count," *Politico*, July 5, 2018; and Caitlin Dickerson, "Trump Administration in Chaotic Scramble to Reunify Migrant Families," *New York Times*, July 5, 2018.

[12] U.S. Department of Justice, Office of Public Affairs, "Attorney General Sessions Delivers Remarks Discussing the Immigration Enforcement Actions of the Trump Administration," May 7, 2018.

[13] See for example, American Immigration Council, "Asylum in the United States, Fact Sheet," May 14, 2018; and International Justice Resource Center, Asylum and the Rights of Refugees, accessed by CRS on July 12, 2018, at https://ijrcenter.org/refugee-law/.

This chapter briefly reviews the statutory authority for prosecuting persons who enter the United States illegally between U.S. ports of entry, and the policies and procedures for processing apprehended illegal border entrants and any accompanying children. It explains enforcement policies under past Administrations and then discusses the Trump Administration's zero tolerance policy on illegal border crossers and the attendant family separations. The chapter concludes by presenting varied policy perspectives on the zero tolerance policy and briefly reviews recent related congressional activity. An appendix examines recent trends in the apprehension of family units at the U.S. Southwest border.

This chapter describes policies and circumstances that continue to change. Information presented in it is current as of the publication date but may become outdated quickly.

ENFORCEMENT AND ASYLUM POLICY FOR ILLEGAL BORDER CROSSERS

Aliens who wish to enter the United States may request admission legally[14] at a U.S. port of entry or may attempt to enter illegally by crossing the border surreptitiously between U.S. ports of entry. Aliens who wish to request asylum may do so at a U.S. port of entry before an officer with the Department of Homeland Security (DHS) Customs and Border Protection (CBP) Office of Field Operations or upon apprehension between U.S. ports of entry before an agent with CBP's U.S. Border Patrol. DHS has broad statutory authority both to detain aliens not legally admitted, including asylum seekers, and to remove aliens who are found to be either inadmissible at ports of entry or removable once in the United States. Aliens requesting asylum at the border are entitled to an interview assessing the credibility of their asylum claims.[15]

---

[14] For more information on legal admissions, see CRS Legal Sidebar LSB10150, An Overview of U.S. Immigration Laws Regulating the Admission and Exclusion of Aliens at the Border; and CRS Report R45020, A Primer on U.S. Immigration Policy.

[15] INA §235(b)(1), 8 U.S.C. §1225(b)(1).

Illegal U.S. Entry

Aliens who enter the United States illegally between ports of entry face two types of penalties. They face civil penalties for illegal presence in the United States, and they face criminal penalties for having entered the country illegally. Both types of penalties are explained below.

The Immigration and Nationality Act (INA) establishes *civil* penalties for persons who are in the United States unlawfully (i.e., without legal status). These penalties apply to foreign nationals who entered the United States illegally as well as those who entered legally but subsequently violated the terms of their admission, typically by "overstaying" their visa duration. Foreign nationals who are apprehended for such civil immigration violations are generally subject to removal (deportation) and are placed in formal or streamlined removal proceedings (described below in "Removal")

The INA also establishes *criminal* penalties for (1) persons who enter or attempt to enter the United States illegally between ports of entry, (2) persons who elude examination or inspection by immigration officers, or (3) persons who attempt to enter or obtain entry to the United States through fraud or willful misrepresentation.[16] In addition, the INA provides criminal penalties for persons who unlawfully re-enter the United States after they were previously removed from the country.[17] Foreign nationals apprehended for criminal immigration violations are subject to prosecution by DOJ in federal criminal courts. This chapter only addresses criminal penalties for illegal entry and re-entry between ports of entry.

Foreign nationals who attempt to enter the United States without authorization often do so between U.S. ports of entry on the U.S. border. If apprehended, they are processed by CBP. They are typically housed briefly in CBP detention facilities before being transferred to the custody of another federal agency or returned to their home country through

---

[16] INA §275, 8 U.S.C. §1325 treats "improper" entry by aliens (first-time illegal entry) as a federal misdemeanor, punishable by fines and/or up to six months in prison.

[17] INA §276, 8 U.S. C. §1326 treats illegal re-entry as a felony, punishable by fines and/or up to two years in prison. Higher penalties apply for migrants with criminal records.

streamlined removal procedures (discussed below). All apprehended aliens, including children, are placed into removal proceedings that occur procedurally after any criminal prosecution for illegal entry. Removal proceedings generally involve formal hearings in an immigration court before an immigration judge, or expedited removal without such hearings (see "Removal" below).

In general, CBP refers apprehended aliens for criminal prosecution if they meet criminal enforcement priorities (e.g., child trafficking, prior felony convictions, multiple illegal entries). Such individuals are placed in the custody of the U.S. Marshals Service (DOJ's enforcement arm) and transported to DOJ criminal detention facilities for pre-trial detention. After individuals have been tried—and if convicted, have served any applicable criminal sentence—they are transferred to DHS Immigration and Customs Enforcement (ICE) custody and placed in immigration detention.[18] ICE, which represents the government in removal hearings, commences removal proceedings.

If CBP does not refer apprehended aliens to DOJ for criminal prosecution, CBP may either return them to their home countries using streamlined removal processes or transfer them to ICE custody for immigration detention while they are in formal removal proceedings.[19]

Asylum

Many aliens at the U.S.-Mexico border seek asylum in the United States. Asylum is not numerically limited and is granted on a case-by-case basis. Asylum can be requested by foreign nationals who have already entered the United States and are not in removal proceedings ("affirmative" asylum) or those who are in removal proceedings and claim

---

[18] Sentences for first-time illegal entry under INA §275 are typically a matter of days or weeks, with pre-trial detention usually counted as part of the sentence; Tim O'Shea, Theresa Cardinal Brown, "Why Are families Being Separated at the Border? An Explainer," Bipartisan Policy Center, June 13, 2018.

[19] For more information on formal and streamlined removal processes, see CRS Report R43892, *Alien Removals and Returns: Overview and Trends*.

asylum as a defense to being removed ("defensive" asylum). The process in each case is different.[20]

Arriving aliens who are inadmissible, either because they lack proper entry documents or because they attempt U.S. entry through misrepresentation or false claims to U.S. citizenship, are put into a streamlined removal process known as expedited removal (described below in "Removal").[21] Aliens in expedited removal who express a fear of persecution are detained by ICE and given a "credible fear" interview with an asylum officer from DHS's U.S. Citizenship and Immigration Services (USCIS).[22] The purpose of the interview is to determine if the asylum claim has sufficient validity to merit an asylum hearing before an immigration judge. Those who receive a favorable credible fear determination are taken out of expedited removal, placed into formal removal proceedings, and given a hearing before an immigration judge, thereby placing the asylum seeker on the defensive path to asylum. Those who receive an unfavorable determination may request that an immigration judge review the case. Aliens in expedited removal who cannot demonstrate a credible fear are promptly deported.

---

[20] For more information on the two ways of obtaining asylum, see U.S. Citizenship and Immigration Services, "Obtaining Asylum in the United States," updated October 19, 2015, accessed by CRS on February 20, 2019, at https://www.uscis.gov/humanitarian/refugees-asylum/asylum/obtaining-asylum-united-states.

[21] INA §212(a)(7) and §212(a)(6)(C) are inadmissibility sections that apply to expedited removal. Expedited removal was introduced as part of the Illegal Immigration and Immigrant Responsibility Act of 1996. According to the statute (INA §235(b)(1)(A)(iii)), expedited removal can be applied to an alien who meets the expedited removal inadmissibility criteria described above, has not been admitted or paroled, and cannot affirmatively show continuous physical presence for the prior two years. As a matter of policy, however, expedited removal to date has been limited to persons apprehended within 100 miles of the U.S. border and who have been present in the United States for less than 14 days. Executive Order 13767 issued on January 25, 2017, instructs the DHS Secretary to implement the expansion of expedited removal to the full extent of the statute. That implementation has not yet occurred.

[22] Credible fear means that there is "a significant possibility," taking into account the credibility of the statements made by the alien in support of the alien's claim and such other facts as are known to the officer, that the alien could establish eligibility for asylum. INA §235(b)(1)(B)(v); 8 U.S.C. §1225(b)(1)(B)(v).

Detention

The INA provides DHS with broad authority to detain adult aliens who are in removal proceedings.[23] However, child detention operates under different policies than that of adults. All children are detained according to broad guidelines established through a court settlement agreement (applicable to all alien children) and two statutes (applicable only to unaccompanied alien children).

The 1997 Flores Settlement Agreement (FSA) established a nationwide policy for the detention, treatment, and release of all alien children, both accompanied and unaccompanied. The Homeland Security Act of 2002 charged ORR with providing temporary care and ensuring custodial placement of UAC with suitable and vetted sponsors.[24] Finally, the William Wilberforce Trafficking Victims Protection Reauthorization Act of 2008 (TVPRA) directed DHS to ensure that all UAC be screened by DHS for possible human trafficking.[25] The TVPRA mandated that UAC from countries other than Mexico or Canada—along with all UAC apprehended in the U.S. interior—be transferred to the care and custody of ORR, and then be "promptly placed in the least restrictive setting that is in the best interest of the child."[26] In the course of being referred to ORR, UAC are also put into formal removal proceedings, ensuring they can request asylum or other types of immigration relief before an immigration judge.

---

23 For background information, see archived CRS Report RL32369, *Immigration-Related Detention*.

24 P.L. 107-296, §462, codified, as amended, at 6 U.S.C. §279(g)(2).

25 P.L. 110-457, §235.

26 For unaccompanied alien children from Mexico or Canada, CBP personnel must screen each child within 48 hours of apprehension to determine if he or she (1) is at risk of becoming a trafficking victim, (2) has a possible asylum claim, and (3) is unable to make an independent decision to voluntarily return to his/her country of nationality or last habitual residence. If any response is affirmative, CBP must refer the child to ORR within 72 hours of this determination. If CBP personnel determine the minor to be inadmissible under the INA (i.e., if responses are not affirmative), they can permit the minor to voluntarily return to his/her country of nationality or last habitual residence. For more information, see CRS Report R43599, *Unaccompanied Alien Children: An Overview*.

As a result of a 2015 judicial interpretation of the Flores Settlement Agreement, children accompanying apprehended adults cannot be held in family immigration detention with their parents for more than 20 days, on average. If the parents cannot be released with them, such children are typically treated as UAC and referred to ORR.

Removal

Under the formal removal process, an immigration judge from DOJ's Executive Office for Immigration Review (EOIR) determines whether an alien is removable. The immigration judge may grant certain forms of relief (e.g., asylum, cancellation of removal), and removal decisions are subject to administrative and judicial review.

Under streamlined removal procedures, which include *expedited removal* and *reinstatement of removal* (i.e., when DHS reinstates a removal order for a previously removed alien), opportunities for relief and review are generally limited. Under expedited removal (INA §235(b)), an alien who lacks proper documentation or has committed fraud or willful misrepresentation to gain admission into the United States may be removed without any further hearings or review, unless he or she indicates a fear of persecution in their home country or an intention to apply for asylum.[27]

If apprehended foreign nationals are found to be removable, ICE and CBP share the responsibility for repatriating them.[28] CBP handles removals at the border for unauthorized aliens from the contiguous countries of Mexico and Canada, and ICE handles all removals from the U.S. interior and removals for all unauthorized aliens from noncontiguous countries.[29]

---

[27] Two other removal options, often referred to as "returns"—*voluntary departure* and *withdrawal of petition for admission*—require aliens to leave the United States promptly but exempt them from certain penalties associated with other types of removal. For background information, see CRS Report R43892, *Alien Removals and Returns: Overview and Trends*.

[28] Ibid.

[29] For more detail on laws governing border enforcement, see CRS Legal Sidebar LSB10150, *An Overview of U.S. Immigration Laws Regulating the Admission and Exclusion of Aliens at the Border*.

Prosecution of Aliens Charged with Illegal Border Crossing in Prior Administrations

Prior to the Trump Administration, aliens apprehended between ports of entry who were not considered enforcement priorities (e.g., a public safety threat, repeat illegal border crosser, convicted felon, suspected child trafficker) were typically not criminally prosecuted for illegal entry but would be placed directly into civil removal proceedings for unauthorized U.S. presence.[30]

In addition, aliens apprehended at and between ports of entry who sought asylum and were found to have credible fear generally were not held in immigration detention if DHS did not assess them as public safety risks. Rather, they were administratively placed into removal proceedings, instructed by DHS to appear at their immigration hearings, and then released into the U.S. interior. This policy became more prevalent after 2015 when a federal judge ruled that children could not be kept in immigration detention for more than 20 days.[31]

DHS officials justified the "catch and release" approach in the past because of the lack of detention bed space and the considerable cost of detaining large numbers of unauthorized aliens and family units for the lengthy periods, often stretching to years, between apprehension by CBP and removal hearings before an EOIR judge.[32] Immigration enforcement advocates criticized the catch and release policy because of the failure of many apprehended individuals to appear subsequently for their immigration hearings.[33]

---

[30] CRS consultation with ICE Legislative Affairs, June 8, 2018.

[31] The federal judge ruled that under the Flores Settlement Agreement, minors detained as part of a family unit cannot be detained in unlicensed facilities for longer than "a presumptively reasonable period of 20 days," at which point, such minors must be released or transferred to a licensed facility. Since most jurisdictions do not offer licensure for family residential centers, and because none of ICE's family detention centers is licensed, DHS rarely detains families for more than 20 days. See Flores v. Lynch, 212 F. Supp. 3d 907 (C.D. Cal. 2015).

[32] Lori Robertson, "Did the Obama Administration Separate Families," *FactCheck.org*, June 20, 2018.

[33] For more information, see Mark Metcalf, "Absent attendance and absent enforcement in America's immigration courts," Center for Immigration Studies, March 19, 2017.

According to some observers, prior Administrations made more use of alternatives to detention that permitted DHS to monitor families who were released into the U.S. interior.[34] Such practices are needed to monitor the roughly 2 million aliens in removal proceedings given that ICE's current budget funds less than 50,000 beds, which are prioritized for aliens who pose public safety or absconder risks.[35]

Data are not available on the rate and/or absolute number of family separations resulting from illegal border crossing prosecutions under prior Administrations, limiting the degree to which comparisons can be made with the Trump Administration's zero tolerance policy.[36]

DHS states that the agency referred an average of 21% of all illegal border crossing "amenable adults" for prosecution from FY2010 through FY2016.[37] DHS maintains that it has an established policy of separating children from adults when it

- cannot determine the family relationship or otherwise verify identity,

---

[34] See for example, Ana Campoy, "The $36-a-day alternative to jailing immigrant families favored by Obama," Quartz, June 23, 2018; Alex Nowrasteh, "Alternatives to Detention Are Cheaper than Universal Detention," Cato Institute, June 20, 2018; and Alexia Fernández Campbell, "Trump doesn't need to put families in detention centers to enforce his immigration policy. There are better options," *Vox*, June 22, 2018. For more information on alternatives to detention, see United Nations High Commission for Refugees, "Guiding Questions for the assessment of Alternatives to Detention," *UNHCR Beyond Detention Toolkit*, May 2018; and American Immigration Lawyers Association, "The Real Alternatives to Detention," Document 17071103, July 11, 2017. For a critical perspective on alternatives to detention, see Dan Cadman, "Are 'Alternative to Detention' Programs the Answer to Family Detention?, Center for Immigration Studies, June 28, 2018.

[35] U.S. Department of Homeland Security, Office of the Inspector General, "U.S. Immigration and Customs Enforcement's Alternatives to Detention (Revised)," OIG-15-22, February 4, 2015. For FY2019, ICE is requesting funding for 47,000 detention beds (44,500 for adults, 2,500 for families); see U.S. Immigration and Customs Enforcement, FY2109 Congressional Budget Justification, Operations and Support, pp. 13-14.

[36] As of this writing, CRS has open requests with DHS for data on family separations under the Obama Administration. Other observers have similar pending requests. See, for example, Lori Robertson, "Did the Obama Administration Separate Families," *FactCheck.org*, June 20, 2018.

[37] U.S. Department of Homeland Security, "Myth vs. Fact: DHS Zero-Tolerance Policy," press release, June 18, 2018. However, as some observers note, this percentage does not reveal how many children were separated from the adults who were referred for prosecution. See Lori Robertson, "Did the Obama Administration Separate Families?", *FactCheck.org*, June 20, 2018.

- determines that the child is being smuggled or trafficked or is otherwise at risk with the parent or legal guardian, or
- determines that the parent or legal guardian may have engaged in criminal conduct and refers them for criminal prosecution.[38]

Prosecution of Aliens Charged with Illegal Border Crossing in the Trump Administration

On April 6, 2018, Attorney General Jeff Sessions announced a "zero tolerance" policy under which *all* illegal border crossers apprehended *between U.S. ports of entry* would be criminally prosecuted for illegal entry or illegal re-entry.[39] This policy made no exceptions for asylum seekers and/or family units.[40] To facilitate this policy, the Attorney General announced that he would send 35 additional prosecutors to U.S. Attorney's Offices along the Southwest border and 18 additional immigration judges to adjudicate cases in immigration courts near the Southwest border.[41]

Consequently, if a family unit was apprehended crossing illegally between ports of entry, the zero tolerance policy mandated that CBP refer all illegal adult entrants to DOJ for criminal prosecution. Accompanying children, who are not permitted to be housed in adult criminal detention settings with their parents, were to be processed as unaccompanied alien children in accordance with the TVPRA. They were transferred to the

---

[38] Ibid.

[39] Office of the Attorney General, *Memorandum for Federal Prosecutors Along the Southwest Border*, "Zero-Tolerance for Offenses Under 8 U.S.C. §1325(a)," April 6, 2018. The policy was implemented on May 7, 2018; U.S. Department of Justice, Office of Public Affairs, "Attorney General Sessions Delivers Remarks Discussing the Immigration Enforcement Actions of the Trump Administration," May 7, 2018.

[40] Immigration and human rights advocates caution that prosecuting persons who cross into the United States in order to present themselves before a CBP officer and request asylum raises concerns about whether the United States is abiding by a number of human rights and refugee-related international protocols. See, for example, Jonathan Blitzer, "The Trump Administration Is Completely Unravelling the U.S. Asylum System," *The New Yorker*, June 11, 2018.

[41] U.S. Department of Justice, Office of Public Affairs, "Justice Department Announces Additional Prosecutors and Immigration Judges For Southwest Border Crisis," May 2, 2018.

custody of ORR, which houses them in agency-supervised, state-licensed shelters. If feasible given the circumstances, ORR attempted to place them with relatives or legal guardian sponsors or place them in temporary foster care.[42]

ORR has over 100 shelters in 17 states,[43] and during the implementation of the zero tolerance policy were reportedly at close to full capacity.[44] Consequently, at one point, the agency was evaluating options for housing children on Department of Defense (DOD) installations to handle the surge of separated children resulting from increased prosecution of parents crossing between ports of entry.[45]

As noted earlier, after adults have been tried in federal courts for illegal entry—and if convicted, have served their criminal sentences—they are transferred to ICE custody and placed in immigration detention. Typically, parents are then reunited in ICE family detention facilities with their children who have either remained in ORR custody or have been placed with a sponsor. Requests for asylum can also be pursued at this point.

---

[42] Most unaccompanied alien children who arrive at the Southwest border alone are placed with sponsors or in ORRarranged foster care; for more information, see CRS Report R43599, *Unaccompanied Alien Children: An Overview*. It is not clear whether such placements are as likely for UAC who arrive with parents. During the peak of the UAC apprehension surge in 2014, UAC spent an average of 35 days in ORR shelters. Most recently, ORR reported that the average length of stay in its shelters was 57 days. U.S. Department of Health and Human Services, Administration for Children and Families, Office of Refugee Resettlement, *Fact Sheet*, "Unaccompanied Alien Children Program," June 15, 2018.

[43] U.S. Department of Health and Human Services, Office of Refugee Resettlement, "Unaccompanied Alien Children Frequently Asked Questions," website, July 9, 2018, accessed by CRS on February 20, 2019.

[44] One article at the end of May 2018 reported ORR shelter capacity at 95%; see Nick Miroff, "Trump's 'zero tolerance' at the border is causing child shelters to fill up fast," *Washington Post*, May 29, 2018. CRS was unable to obtain a figure for current ORR shelter capacity as of this writing.

[45] Letter from Alex M. Azar II, Secretary, U.S. Department of Health and Human Services, to The Honorable Jim Mattis, Secretary of Defense, March 8, 2018. Similar arrangements were made in June 2014, when apprehensions of UAC reached an all-time high. ORR coordinated with DOD to temporarily allow UAC to be housed at Lackland Air Force Base in San Antonio, TX, and at Naval Base Ventura County in Oxnard, CA. Arrangements at both sites ended August 2014.

Statistics and Timeline on Family Separation

In FY2017, CBP apprehended 75,622 alien family units and separated 1,065 (1.4%) of them. Of those separations, 46 were due to fraud and 1,019 were due to medical and/or security concerns.

In the first five months of FY2018, prior to enactment of the zero tolerance policy, CBP apprehended 31,102 alien family units and separated 703 (2.2%), of which 191 resulted from fraud and 512 from medical and/or security concerns.[46]

Prior to Attorney General Session's announcement of the zero tolerance policy, the American Civil Liberties Union (ACLU) filed a lawsuit against ICE (referred to as "Ms. L. v. ICE") on behalf of two families separated at the Southwest border: a woman from the Democratic Republic of the Congo who was separated from her 6-year-old daughter at a port of entry for five months; and a woman from Brazil who had crossed into the United States illegally between ports of entry and was separated from her 14-year-old son for eight months.[47] The lawsuit, filed on February, was subsequently expanded in March 2018 to a class-action lawsuit filed by ACLU against ICE on behalf of all parents who were separated from their children by DHS.

In the early months of the policy, the Administration repeatedly revised the number of families that had been separated. According to CBP testimony in May 2018, 658 children were separated from 638 adults who were referred for prosecution between May 7 and May 21.[48] DHS subsequently reported that 1,995 children had been separated from their

---

[46] Email correspondence from CBP Legislative Affairs to CRS, June 8, 2018. Figures represent separated family units, not the number of separated children; the latter is likely higher given that some family units consist of more than one child.

[47] See *Ms. L v. ICE,* No. 18-cv-00428-DMS-MDD (S.D. Cal. Feb. 18, 2018).

[48] Testimony of Richard Hudson, Deputy Chief of the Operations Program, Law Enforcement Operations Directorate, U.S. Customs and Border Protection, in U.S. Congress, Senate Committee on the Judiciary, Subcommittee on Border Security and Immigration, *TVPRA and Exploited Loopholes Affecting Unaccompanied Alien Children*, 115th Cong., 2nd sess., May 23, 2018.

parents between April 19 and May 31.[49] DHS updated these figures in June 2018, reporting that 2,342 children were separated from their parents between May 5 and June 9.[50] DHS then reported that CBP had since reunited with their parents 538 children who were never sent to ORR shelters.[51] HHS Secretary Alex Azar then reported that "under 3,000" minor children (under age 18) had been separated from their families in total, including roughly 100 under age 5.[52] As of July 13, 2018, HHS reported that 2,551 children ages 5 to 17 remained separated.[53]

On June 20, 2018, following considerable and largely negative public attention to family separations stemming from the zero tolerance policy, President Trump issued an executive order (EO) mandating that DHS maintain custody of alien families "during the pendency of any criminal improper entry or immigration proceedings involving their member," to the extent permitted by law and appropriations.[54] The EO instructs DOD to provide and/or construct additional shelter facilities, upon request by ORR, and it instructs other executive branch agencies to assist with housing as appropriate to implement the EO.[55] The EO mandates that the Attorney General prioritize the adjudication of detained family cases, and it requires the Attorney General to ask the U.S. District Court for the Central District of California, which oversees the Flores Settlement Agreement, to modify the agreement to permit detained families to remain together.

---

[49] These figures were obtained from DHS by the Associated Press on June 15, 2018. See Colleen Long, "DHS reports about 2,000 minors separated from families," Associated Press, June 16, 2018.

[50] On June 18, Senator Dianne Feinstein reportedly released DHS statistics showing that 2,342 children were separated from their parents between May 5 and June 9. See Arit John and Jennifer Epstein, "All About the U.S. Separating Families at Its Border," Bloomberg, June 18, 2018.

[51] U.S. Department of Homeland Security, "Fact Sheet: Zero-Tolerance Prosecution and Family Reunification," June 23, 2018.

[52] Dan Diamond, "HHS says hundreds more migrant kids may have been separated than earlier count," *Politico*, July 5, 2018; and Caitlin Dickerson, "Trump Administration in Chaotic Scramble to Reunify Migrant Families," *New York Times*, July 5, 2018.

[53] Dan Diamond, "Trump administration expedites reunifications for 2,551 migrant children," *Politico*, July 13, 2018.

[54] The White House, *Affording Congress an Opportunity to Address Family Separation*, Executive Order, June 20, 2018.

[55] Thus far, only DOD has made arrangements with ORR to provide housing for alien families and children.

On June 25, 2018, CBP announced that, because of ICE's lack of family detention bed space, it had temporarily halted the policy of referring adults who cross the border illegally with children to DOJ for criminal prosecution.[56] According to a White House announcement, the zero tolerance policy may be reinstituted once additional family detention bed space becomes available.[57] Also on June 25, 2018, DOD announced plans to permit four of its military bases to be used by other federal agencies to shelter up to 20,000 UAC and family units.[58] DOD subsequently announced that 12,000 persons would be housed on its facilities,[59] before another report appeared suggesting the number was 32,000 UAC and family units.[60] Since these announcements, no efforts have been made to house apprehended UAC or family units on military installations.

On June 26, 2018, in response to the ACLU class action lawsuit, Judge Dana Sabraw of the U.S. District Court for the Southern District of California issued an injunction against the Administration's practice of separating families and ordered that all separated families be reunited within 30 days. The judge ruled that children under age 5 must be reunited with their parents within 14 days, all children must have phone contact with their parents within 10 days, children could be separated at the border only if accompanying adults presented an immediate danger to them, and parents were not to be removed unless they had been reunited with their separated children.[61]

In response to the June 26 injunction, the Trump Administration reportedly instructed DHS to provide all parents with final orders of

---

[56] Ron Nixon, Erica L. Green and Michael D. Shear, "Border Officials Suspend Handing Over Migrant Families to Prosecutors," *New York Times*, June 25, 2018.

[57] Ibid.

[58] Michael D. Shear, Helene Cooper and Katie Benner, "U.S. Prepares to House Up to 20,000 Migrants on Military Bases," *New York Times*, June 21, 2018. It was unclear what proportion of the DOD facilities would have been used for UAC shelters versus immigration detention for families.

[59] U.S. Department of Defense, "DHS Requests DoD House Up to 12,000 Migrants," *Defense.gov*, June 28, 2018.

[60] Lara Seligman, "Pentagon Says It Won't Pay for Housing of Immigrants," *Foreign Policy*, July 9, 2018.

[61] Michael D. Shear, Julie Hirschfeld Davis, Thomas Kaplan, and Robert Pear, "Federal Judge in California Halts Splitting of Migrant Families at Border," *New York Times*, June 26, 2018.

removal and whose children were separated from them with two options.[62] The first was to return to their countries of origin with their children. This option fulfilled the mandate from the June 26 court order to reunite families but also forced parents and children to abandon any claims for asylum. The second option was for parents to return alone to their country of origin. This option would leave the children in the United States to apply for asylum on their own. Parental decisions were to be recorded on a new ICE form.[63]

On July 9, 2018, Judge Dolly Gee of the U.S. District Court for the Central District of California, which oversees the Flores Settlement Agreement, ruled against a DOJ request to modify the agreement to permit children to remain with their parents in family detention. Judge Gee held that no basis existed for amending the court's original decision requiring the federal government to release alien minors in immigration detention after 20 days, regardless of any unlawful entry prosecution of the parents.[64]

On July 10, ICE officials reportedly indicated that parents reunited with their children would be enrolled in an alternative detention program, such as the use of ankle bracelets that permit electronic monitoring, and then released into the U.S. interior, essentially reverting to the prior policy that has been labeled by some as "catch and release."[65] DOJ continued to maintain that its zero tolerance policy was in effect.[66]

---

[62] Nick Valencia and Tal Kopan, "The options parents facing deportation have after they've been separated from their kids," *CNN*, July 3, 2018; Julia Ainsley and Jacob Soboroff, "New Trump admin order for separated parents: Leave U.S. with kids or without them," *nbcnews.com*, July 3, 2018; and Jeremy Raff, "ICE Is Pressuring Separated Parents to Choose Deportation," *The Atlantic*, July 6, 2018. Immigration advocates contend that the new form misleads parents who have outstanding asylum claims into thinking that they must leave the United States without their children, despite the fact that the forms indicate that they apply only to parents with final orders of removal. DHS responds that "it is 'long-standing policy' to offer parents facing deportation the option of leaving their [children] behind, noting it is 'not uncommon' for parents to elect to do so, historically. Any child who remains in the United States in the custody of the government or with a family member is allowed to pursue their own right to stay, and ICE 'does not interfere' in that decision."

[63] U.S. Immigration and Customs Enforcement, Enforcement and Removal Operations, Separated Parent's Removal Form, July 2018.

[64] Miriam Jordan and Manny Fernandez, "Federal Judge Rules that Trump Administration Cannot Hold Migrant Families in Long-Term Detention," *New York Times*, July 9, 2018.

[65] More recently, the sizable influx of migrants have overwhelmed the capacity of some ICE facilities, leading to the release of family units. See Nick Miroff, "Migrant families

On July 11, 2018, in response to the requirements of the ACLU lawsuit, ORR certified a list of 2,654 children that the agency stated were in its custody at the time of the June 26 injunction that it believed had been separated from their parents and whose parents met the lawsuit's class definition.[67] According to a subsequent HHS Office of Inspector General (OIG) report, one or more data sources showed that an additional 946 children may have been separated from family members at the time of apprehension, but their family members did not meet the criteria needed for inclusion in the lawsuit.[68]

On July 16, 2018, in response to concerns expressed by the ACLU about potential abrupt deportations following family reunification, Judge Sabraw temporarily halted, for one week, the deportations of parents who had been reunited with their children.[69] The judge issued the stay of deportations to provide parents slated for removal with a week's time to better understand their legal rights regarding asylum or other forms of immigration relief for themselves and their children.

On July 16, 2018, Jonathan White, Deputy Director for Children's Programs at the Office of Refugee Resettlement testified before Judge Sabraw that ORR had identified 2,551 separated children in its custody ages 5 to 17 and had matched 2,480 to their parents, while 71 children's parents remained unidentified.[70] ORR was undertaking intensive background checks to ensure that separated children were reunited with

---

overwhelm detention capacity in Arizona, prompting mass releases," *Washington Post*, October 9, 2018.

[66] Miriam Jordan, Katie Benner, Ron Nixon, and Caitlin Dickerson, "As Migrant Families Are Reunited, Some Children Don't Recognize Their Mothers," *New York Times*, July 10, 2018.

[67] The class was defined as "all adult parents who enter the United States at or between designated ports of entry who (1) have been, are, or will be detained in immigration custody by the [DHS], and (2) have a minor child who is or will be separated from them by DHS and detained in ORR custody, ORR foster care, or DHS custody absent a determination that the parent is unfit or presents a danger to the child." Parents are excluded from the class if they have a criminal history or communicable disease See *Ms. L v. ICE,* No. 18-cv-00428-DMS-MDD (S.D. Cal. June 26, 2018).

[68] U.S. Department of Health and Human Services, Office of Inspector General, "Separated Children Placed in Office of Refugee Resettlement Care," *HHS-OIG Issue Brief*, January 2019. OEI-BL-18-00511.

[69] Caitlin Dickerson, "Court Orders Temporary Halt to Migrant Family Deportations," *New York Times*, July 16, 2018 and Ted Hesson, "Judge will temporarily halt deportations of reunited families," *Politico*, July 16, 2018.

[70] Ibid.

their actual parents and did not face personal security risks such as child abuse.[71] According to White, 1,609 parents of separated children remained in ICE custody. White noted that ICE was also conducting its own security checks and at that point had cleared 918 parents, failed 51 parents, and had 348 parents with pending clearances. As of July 16, 2018, ICE had approved about 300 children for release to be reunited with their parents.[72]

On July 18, 2018, HHS submitted a "Tri-Department Plan" in coordination with DHS and DOJ explaining actions the agencies were taking to reunify Ms. L v. ICE class members with their children. These steps include conducting and reviewing background checks of parents, confirming parentage, assessing child safety, interviewing parents, and reuniting families.[73]

As of July 19, 2018, the Administration had reportedly reunified 364 of the 2,551 children ages 5 to 17. Apart from the parents of those children, 1,607 parents were eligible to be reunited with their children, 719 of whom had final orders of deportation. Another 908 parents were not expected to be eligible for reunification because they possessed criminal backgrounds or required "further evaluation."[74]

On September 6, 2018, DHS and HHS proposed new regulations that would effectively terminate the Flores Settlement Agreement and replace it with formal regulations governing the "apprehension, processing, care, custody, and release" of minor children.[75] The primary provision in these proposed regulations would be the authority to hold migrant children and their parents until their cases have been adjudicated. Whether federal

---

[71] Nick Miroff, Maria Sacchetti and Amy Goldstein, "In D.C. command center, officials work to reunite migrant children by court deadline," *Washington Post*, July 19, 2018.

[72] Ibid.

[73] Department of Health and Human Services, Department of Homeland Security, and Department of Justice, The TriDepartment Plan for Stage II of Family Reunification, July 18, 2018. Accessed at https://www.hhs.gov/sites/default/ files/UAC-Tri-Department-Process.pdf on November 18, 2018.

[74] Julia Ainsley and Jacob Soboroff, "Facing deadline, government reunified 364 of 2,500-plus migrant children," *nbcnews.com*, July 19, 2018.

[75] Department of Homeland Security and Department of Health and Human Services, "Apprehension, Processing, Care, and Custody of Alien Minors and Unaccompanied Alien Children," 83 *Federal Register* 45486-45534, September 7, 2018.

courts will impose injunctions on or rule against the regulations based on their inconsistency with the Flores Settlement Agreement is not yet known.

In October 2018, it was widely reported that the Administration was considering alternative immigration enforcement policies involving family separation to reduce the persistent and relatively high level of unauthorized migrants seeking asylum at the Southwest border. One of these approaches, a "binary choice" policy, would give detained parents the option of keeping their children with them in immigration detention during the pendency of their immigration cases or being separated from their children, who would be referred to ORR shelters, including possible foster care.[76] This option gained traction as a large and expanding migrant group originating from Honduras, referred to as the migrant "caravan," garnered extensive media attention as it made its way through Central America and Mexico. As of this writing, DHS has not taken any action with regard to this proposed policy.

Apart from the number of separated children who have been included in the Ms. L. v. ICE lawsuit, other figures emerged on the total number of family separations that have occurred more generally. For example, on October 12, 2018, Amnesty International (AI) published a report citing statistics provided to the organization by CBP indicating that 6,022 "family units" had been separated between April 19, 2018, and August 15, 2018.[77] These cases, combined with the 1,768 family separations reported by DHS between October 1, 2016, and February 28, 2018 (the 1,065 in FY2017 plus the 703 in the first five months of FY2018 noted separately above) indicates that CBP has reported a total of 7,790 family separations to either CRS or AI. This total excludes an unknown number of family separations

[76] See, for example, Nick Miroff, Josh Dawsey and Maria Sacchetti, "Trump administration weighs new family-separation effort at border," *Washington Post*, October 12, 2018; and Miriam Jordan, Caitlin Dickerson and Michael D. Shear, "Trump's Plans to Deter Migrants Could Mean New 'Voluntary' Family Separations," *New York Times*, October 22, 2018.

[77] Amnesty International, USA: 'You Don't Have Any Rights Here': Illegal Pushbacks, Arbitrary Detention, and Ill-Treatment of Asylum-Seekers in the United States, October 2018. It is not clear from this chapter (see Footnote 144) whether "family unit" refers to family or to individuals who arrive at the Southwest border as part of a family. The report authors suggest that in the context of family separations, "family unit" refers to a family, while in the context of alien apprehensions reported monthly by CBP, the term refers to individuals who arrive at the Southwest border as part of a family.

occurring between March 1 and April 18, 2018. According to AI, it also may exclude an unknown number of families that were separated after requesting asylum at U.S. ports of entry.

In January 2019, HHS's OIG issued a report on ORR's challenges identifying all separated children, ultimately concluding that "the total number of children separated from a parent or guardian by immigration authorities is unknown."[78] The chapter cited limitations with both its information technology system for tracking such children as well as the complexity of determining which children should be classified as separated. According to this chapter, ORR's review of new information acquired between July and December 2018 indicated that an additional 162 children had met the criteria to be included in the Ms. L. v. ICE lawsuit, and that 79 previously included children had not actually been separated from a parent, changing the total from 2,654 to 2,737 children in the lawsuit.[79]

On February 7, 2019, a representative from HHS's OIG testified before Congress that DHS was continuing to separate children from their parents, although at a lower rate than during the zero tolerance policy of May-June 2018. The testimony noted that while DHS routinely separates families if parents have a criminal history, DHS had not provided HHS with sufficient information to facilitate appropriate placement within the ORR shelter system.[80] The testimony also noted that "thousands more" children were likely separated prior to June 26, 2018, but, lacking any formal system for tracking such separations, the witness could not provide more precise figures.

---

78 U.S. Department of Health and Human Services, Office of Inspector General, "Separated Children Place in Office of Refugee Resettlement Care," HHS OIG Issue Brief, OEI-BL-18-00511, January 2019.

79 Problems described in this HHS-OIG report had been reported earlier by DHS's OIG in September 2018, although DHS did not quantify children who may have been separated or incorrectly classified. See DHS Office of Inspector General, "Special Review - Initial Observations Regarding Family Separation Issues Under the Zero Tolerance Policy," OIG-18-84, September 27, 2018.

80 U.S. Congress, House Committee on Energy and Commerce, Subcommittee on Oversight and Investigations, *Examining the Failures of the Trump Administration's Inhumane Family Separation Policy*, Testimony of Ann Maxwell, Office of Inspector General, HHS Office of Refugee Resettlement, 116th Cong., 1st sess., February 7.

On February 21, 2019, the Joint Status Report filed on the status of a revised total of 2,816 children (2,709 ages 5 and above and 107 under age 5)[81] included in the Ms. L. v. ICE lawsuit indicated that 2,735 had been reunited with their parents.[82] The status of the remaining children are described in the chapter largely as follows: being determined upon further review to have not been separated from their parents; not reunited because of potential safety issues with the parent; and not being reunited because deported parents confirmed they wanted to allow the child to remain in the United States.[83] In addition, the chapter also indicated that up to 249 additional children not part of the Ms. L. v. ICE lawsuit had been separated between June 27, 2018 (the day after the lawsuit was filed) and January 31, 2019. According to ICE, the basis for separation was largely "parent criminality, prosecution, gang affiliation, or other law enforcement purpose."

On February 21, 2019, Texas Civil Rights Project released a report describing the findings from interviews with 272 adults who had experienced family separation subsequent to the President's executive order. The interviewees, a subset of almost 10,000 screened immigrants who were prosecuted for immigration violations at the Southwest border, had indicated to screeners that they had been separated from their children.[84] The data, the first on family separation collected on a large scale by an organization outside the federal government, indicated that since the zero tolerance policy was terminated, a considerable number of family separations had occurred between minor children and relatives other than parents and legal guardians. As noted above, the INA defines an

---

[81] HHS's Office of Inspector General testified that ORR has repeatedly revised the number of children determined to be eligible for inclusion in the Ms. L. v. ICE case. See U.S. Congress, House Committee on Energy and Commerce, Subcommittee on Oversight and Investigations, *Examining the Failures of the Trump Administration's Inhumane Family Separation Policy*, Testimony of Ann Maxwell, Office of Inspector General, HHS Office of Refugee Resettlement, 116th Cong., 1st sess., February 7.

[82] Joint Status Report, Ms. L. v. U.S. Immigration and Customs Enforcement, Case 3:18-cv-428, Document 360 (S.D. Cal. February 20, 2019).

[83] Ibid.

[84] Laura Peña and Efrén C. Olivares, *The Real National Emergency: Zero Tolerance & the Continuing Horrors of Family Separation at the Border*, Texas Civil Rights Project, undated, release reported by Dara Lind, "Hundreds of families are still being separated at the border," *Vox*, February 21, 2019.

unaccompanied child as an unauthorized minor under age 18 who is not in the care and custody of a parent or legal guardian.[85] According to DHS, minor children apprehended at the border who are accompanied by older siblings, cousins, aunts, uncles, grandparents, and other relatives who are not parents or legal guardians must be treated as unaccompanied alien children, separated from their accompanying relatives, and turned over to the custody of ORR. DHS reportedly does not count such related pairs of individuals as family units in its statistics, raising concerns among advocates that current CBP statistics may not fully capture the extent of family separation among apprehended migrants.

POLICY PERSPECTIVES

Perspectives on the zero tolerance policy generally divide into two groups. Those who support greater immigration enforcement point to recent surges in family unit migration and a substantial backlog of asylum cases that are straining DHS and DOJ resources, potentially compromising the agencies' abilities to meet their outlined missions. Those who advocate on behalf of immigrants decry the Administration's treatment of migrants as unnecessarily harsh and counterproductive.

Enforcement Perspectives

DHS and DOJ contend that the policy enforces existing law and is needed to reduce illegal immigration.[86] DHS notes that foreign nationals attempting to enter the United States between ports of entry or "without inspection" are committing a crime punishable under the INA as a

[85] 6 U.S.C. §279(g)(2).

[86] Sari Horwitz and Maria Sacchetti, "Sessions vows to prosecute all illegal border crossers and separate children from their parents," *Washington Post*, May 7, 2018. Senior immigration and border officials had reportedly issued a confidential memo to DHS Secretary Nielsen supporting the policy as the "most effective" way to reduce illegal entry.

misdemeanor on the first occasion and a felony for every attempt thereafter.

DHS maintains that it has a long-standing policy of separating children from adults when children are at risk because of threats from human trafficking or because the familial relationship is suspect. DHS also maintains that it does not have a formal policy of separating parents from children for deterrence purposes, and it follows a standard policy of keeping families together "as long as operationally possible."[87] According to DHS, the agency has "a legal obligation to protect the best interests of the child whether that is from human smugglings, drug traffickers, or nefarious actors who knowingly break [U.S.] immigration laws and put minor children at risk."[88] Accordingly, DHS considers it appropriate to treat children of apprehended parents as UAC.[89]

DHS posits that while family separation is an unfortunate outcome of stricter enforcement of immigration laws and criminal prosecution of illegal entry and re-entry, it is no different than the family separation that occurs in the U.S. criminal justice system when parents of minor children commit a crime and are taken into criminal custody.[90] Attorney General Sessions has stated that parents who do not want to be separated from their children should simply not attempt to cross the U.S. border illegally.[91]

---

[87] Testimony of the Honorable Kirstjen Nielsen, Secretary of Homeland Security, in U.S. Congress, House Committee on Appropriations, Subcommittee on Homeland Security, *FY 2019 Budget Hearing - Department of Homeland Security*, 115th Cong., 2nd sess., April 11, 2018 (hereinafter, "Nielsen testimony, April 11, 2018"). Other observers contend that Attorney General Sessions explicitly justified the zero tolerance policy on the basis of deterring migrants from coming to the United States. See, for example, Christopher Ingraham, "Sessions says family separation is 'necessary' to keep the country from being 'overwhelmed.' Federal immigration data says otherwise," *Washington Post*, June 18, 2017; and U.S. Department of Justice, Office of Public Affairs, "Attorney General Sessions Delivers Remarks Discussing the Immigration Enforcement Actions of the Trump Administration," May 7, 2018.

[88] Maria Sacchetti, "Top Homeland Security officials urge criminal prosecution of parents crossing border with children," *Washington Post*, April 26, 2018.

[89] For more information on ORR processing of UAC, see CRS Report R43599, *Unaccompanied Alien Children: An Overview*.

[90] Nielsen testimony, April 11, 2018.

[91] U.S. Department of Justice, Office of Public Affairs, "Attorney General Sessions Delivers Remarks Discussing the Immigration Enforcement Actions of the Trump Administration," May 7, 2018.

DHS Secretary Nielsen justified the zero tolerance policy with statistics showing a 223% increase in illegal border crossings and inadmissible cases along the Southwest border between April 2017 and April 2018.[92] Similar increases in monthly apprehensions between years were cited for family units and unaccompanied alien children. Secretary Nielsen also stated that while the apprehension figures "are at times higher or lower than in years past, it makes little difference," characterizing them as unacceptable either way.[93] DHS officials cite results of policies imposed at the Border Patrol's El Paso sector (covering West Texas and New Mexico) for part of 2017, where a similar family separation policy reduced the number of illegal family border crossings by 64%.[94]

DHS notes that its policy reflects President Trump's January 2017 Executive Order 13767[95] on border security directing executive branch departments and agencies to "deploy all lawful means to secure the Nation's Southwest border, to prevent further illegal immigration into the United States, and to repatriate illegal aliens swiftly, consistently, and humanely."[96] DHS further contends that parents who attempt to cross illegally into the United States with their children not only put their children at grave risk but also enrich transnational criminal organizations to whom they pay smuggling fees. DHS argues that some parents, aware of

---

[92] Nielsen testimony, April 11, 2018. CBP apprehended 15,766 unauthorized migrants at the southern border in April 2017 and 50,923 in April 2018. See U.S. Customs and Border Protection, "Southwest Border Migration FY2018," website, updated July 5, 2018.

[93] Because monthly apprehensions can fluctuate substantially between years, average monthly apprehensions may provide a more accurate measure of illegal border crossing activity. Average monthly apprehensions of all border crossers in FY2016, FY2017, and the first eight months of FY2018 were 46,934, 34,599, and 42,503, respectively. See U.S. Customs and Border Protection, "Southwest Border Migration FY2018," website updated July 5, 2018.

[94] Maria Sacchetti, "Top Homeland Security officials urge criminal prosecution of parents crossing border with children," *Washington Post*, April 26, 2018. That statistic has been criticized as inaccurate and misleading by at least one news report; see Dara Lind, "Trump's DHS is using an extremely dubious statistic to justify splitting up families at the border," *Vox*, May 8, 2018. In addition, other reports suggest that family separation was occurring because of increased prosecution of illegal border crossing since the summer of 2017; see Jonathan Blitzer, "How the Trump Administration Got Comfortable Separating Immigrant Kids from Their Parents," *The New Yorker*, May 30, 2018.

[95] Executive Order 13767, "Border Security and Immigration Enforcement Improvements," 82 *Federal Register* 8793- 8797, January 25, 2017.

[96] Email communication to CRS from CBP Legislative Affairs, June 4, 2018.

the limited amount of family detention space, intentionally use their children as shields from detention and anticipate that they will be viewed, as they had been in prior years, as low security risks.[97] DHS points to unpublished intelligence reports describing cases where unrelated adults have used or trafficked children in order to avoid immigration detention.[98] DHS and other observers also note that asylum requests have increased considerably, a trend that raises concerns about possible fraudulent asylum claims and the misuse of asylum claims to enter and remain in the United States.[99] DHS notes that ICE and ORR both play a role in family reunification and characterizes the process as "well-coordinated."[100] DHS maintains that it has procedures in place to connect separated family members and ensure that parents know the location of minors and can regularly communicate with them. Mechanisms to facilitate such communication include posted information notices in ICE detention facilities, an HHS Adult Hotline and email inquiry address, and an ICE call center and email inquiry address.[101] DHS and ORR are using DNA testing to confirm familial ties between parents and children.[102]

Immigrant Advocacy Perspectives

Immigrant advocacy organizations argue that migrant families are fleeing a well-documented epidemic of gang violence from the Northern

---

[97] Ibid.

[98] Ariane de Vogue and Tal Kopa, "ACLU class action lawsuit seeks to block immigrant family separations," *CNN*, March 9, 2018.

[99] See, for example, U.S. Citizenship and Immigration Services, "USCIS to Take Action to Address Asylum Backlog," press release, January 31, 2018.

[100] U.S. Department of Homeland Security, "Fact Sheet: Zero-Tolerance Prosecution and Family Reunification," press release, June 23, 2018. In some cases, expedited DOJ hearings resulted in family reunification occurring in CBP holding facilities because children had not yet been transported to ORR custody. In such cases, family reunification occurs in CBP custody before the family unit is transported to an ICE immigration detention facility for family units.

[101] U.S. Department of Homeland Security, "Myth vs. Fact: DHS Zero-Tolerance Policy," press release, June 18, 2018.

[102] Email correspondence from ORR Legislative Affairs, July 11, 2018; and U.S. Department of Health and Human Services, "Unaccompanied Alien Children Frequently Asked Questions," website, July 9, 2018, accessed by CRS on July 12, 2018.

Triangle countries of El Salvador, Guatemala, and Honduras.[103] They have criticized the practice of family separation because it seemingly punishes people for fleeing dangerous circumstances and seeking asylum in the United States. They posit that requesting asylum is not an illegal act,[104] Congress created laws that require DHS to process and evaluate claims for humanitarian protection, DHS must honor congressional intent by humanely processing and evaluating such claims, and many who request asylum have valid claims and compelling circumstances that merit consideration.[105]

Immigrant advocates have also criticized the Administration for creating what they consider to be a debacle of its own making, characterized by frequently changing policies and justifications,[106] what some describe as an uncoordinated implementation process, and the absence of an effective plan to reunify separated families.[107] In some cases, records linking parents to children reportedly may have disappeared or been destroyed, hampering efforts to establish relationships between family members.[108] Media reports

---

[103] See CRS Report RL34112, *Gangs in Central America*.

[104] See, for example, American Immigration Council, "Asylum in the United States, Fact Sheet," May 14, 2018; and International Justice Resource Center, Asylum and the Rights of Refugees, accessed by CRS on July 12, 2018, at https://ijrcenter.org/refugee-law/.

[105] According to the 1951 Convention on the Status of Refugees, countries should not punish asylum-seekers who violate immigration laws if they present themselves to authorities. Although not a party to this convention, the United States is a party to a 1967 Protocol to the Convention, provisions of which are found in the 1980 Refugee Act. Under current U.S. policy, most aliens arriving in the United States without proper documentation who claim asylum are held until their "credible fear" hearing, but some asylum seekers are held until their asylum claims have been adjudicated. For background information, see archived CRS Report RL32369, *Immigration-Related Detention*.

[106] Maria Sacchetti, "DHS proposal would change rules for minors in immigration detention," *Washington Post*, May 9, 2018. This proposal was first publicly suggested by then DHS Secretary John Kelly in March, 2017. See Daniella Diaz, "Kelly: DHS is considering separating undocumented children from their parents at the border," *CNN*, March 7, 2017. Following the ensuing controversy over his interview, he subsequently stated that DHS would not implement such policies. See Tal Kopan, "Kelly says DHS won't separate families at the border," *CNN*, March 29, 2017.

[107] See, for example, Kevin Sieff, "The chaotic effort to reunite immigrant parents with their separated kids," *Washington Post*, June 21, 2018; Erik Hanshew, "Families will no longer be separated at the border. But where are my clients' kids?," *Washington Post*, June 20, 2018; and Jonathan Blitzer, "The Government has no plan for reuniting the immigrant families it is tearing apart," *The New Yorker*, June 18, 2018.

[108] Caitlin Dickerson, "Trump Administration in Chaotic Scramble to Reunify Migrant Families," *New York Times*, July 5, 2018.

have described obstacles to reuniting families after separation, including a lack of communication between federal agencies, the absence of information about accompanying children collected by CBP at the time of apprehension, the inability of ICE detainees to receive phone calls without special arrangements, and a cumbersome vetting process to ensure children's safe placement with parents.[109] Similar observations have since been made by government agencies.[110] In addition, while DOJ typically detains and prosecutes parents for illegal entry at federal detention centers and courthouses near the U.S.-Mexico border, ORR houses their children at shelters geographically dispersed in 17 states, in some cases thousands of miles away from the parents.

Child welfare professionals assert that family separation has the potential to cause lasting psychological harm for adults[111] and especially for children.[112] Some point to the findings of a DHS advisory panel as well as those of other organizations that discourage family detention as neither

---

[109] See, for example, Ian Lovett and Louise Radnofsky, "Amid Chaos at Border, Some Immigrant Families Reunite," *Wall Street Journal*, June 24, 2018; Jonathan Blitzer, "The Government has no plan for reuniting the immigrant families it is tearing apart," *The New Yorker*, June 18, 2018; Ted Hesson and Dan Diamond, "As deadline looms, Trump officials struggle to reunite migrant families," *Politico*, July 2, 2018; Ritu Prasad, "Undocumented migrant families embark on chaotic reunion process," *BBC*, June 25, 2018; and Caitlin Dickerson, "Trump Administration in Chaotic Scramble to Reunify Migrant Families," *New York Times*, July 5, 2018.

[110] DHS Office of Inspector General, "Special Review - Initial Observations Regarding Family Separation Issues Under the Zero Tolerance Policy," OIG-18-84, September 27, 2018; and U.S. Department of Health and Human Services, Office of Inspector General, "Separated Children Placed in Office of Refugee Resettlement Care," *HHS-OIG Issue Brief*, January 2019. OEI-BL-18-00511.

[111] See, for example, DHS Advisory Committee on Family Residential Centers, "Report of the DHS Advisory Committee on Family Residential Centers," September 30, 2016; and Alexander Miller, Julia Meredith Hess, Deborah Bybee, and Jessica R. Goodkind, "Understanding the mental health consequences of family separation for refugees: Implications for policy and practice," *American Journal of Orthopsychiatry*, vol. 88 (2018), pp. 26-37.

[112] See, for example, American Academy of Pediatrics, Letter from Colleen A. Kraft, President, to The Honorable Kirstjen M. Nielsen, U.S. Secretary of Homeland Security, March 1, 2018; Julie M. Linton, Marsha Griffin, Alan J. Shapiro, and Council on Community Pediatrics, "Detention of Immigrant Children," *Pediatrics*, vol. 139 (April 2017), pp. 1-13; and Kimberly Howard, Anne Martin, Lisa J. Berlin, and Jean Brooks-Gunn, "Early Mother-Child Separation, Parenting, and Child Well-Being in Early Head Start Families," *Attachment & Human Development*, vol. 13 (2011), pp. 5-26.

appropriate nor necessary for families and as not being in children's best interests.[113]

Some immigration observers question the Administration's ability to marshal resources required to prosecute all illegal border crossers given that Congress has not appropriated additional funding to support the zero tolerance policy. One news report, for example, noted that 3,769 foreign nationals were convicted of illegal entry in criminal courts during March 2018, a month in which 37,383 foreign nationals were apprehended for illegal entry.[114] Given the relative size of the task they face, observers question how DOJ and DHS can channel fiscal resources to meet this objective without compromising their other missions. They contend that the policy is counterproductive because it prevents CBP from using risk-based strategies to pursue the most egregious crimes, thereby making the Southwest border region less safe and more prone to criminal activity.[115] Some have suggested that the zero tolerance policy is diverting resources from, and thereby hindering, other DHS operations.[116]

Some in Congress have criticized the family separation policy because of its cost in light of alternative options, such as community-based detention programs. They cite, for example, the Family Case Management Program (FCMP), which monitored families seeking asylum and demonstrated reportedly high compliance rate with immigration requirements such as court hearings and immigration appointments.[117] The FCMP, which began in January 2016,[118] was terminated by the Trump Administration in April

---

[113] DHS Advisory Committee on Family Residential Centers, "Report of the DHS Advisory Committee on Family Residential Centers," September 30, 2016. This chapter cites similar findings by Government Accountability Office, the United Nations High Commissioner for Refugees, and the American Bar Association, among others.

[114] Alan Bersin, Nate Bruggeman and Ben Rohrbaugh, "Trump's 'zero tolerance' bluff on the border will hurt security, not help," *Washington Post*, May 31, 2018.

[115] Ibid.

[116] Nick Mirnoff, "Seeking a split from ICE, some agents say Trump's immigration crackdown hurts investigations and morale," *Washington Pos*t, June 28, 2018.

[117] DHS Office of Inspector General, "U.S. Immigration and Customs Enforcement's Award of the Family Case Management Program Contract (Redacted)," OIG-18-22, November 30, 2017.

[118] U.S. Immigration and Customs Enforcement, "Fact Sheet, Stakeholder Referrals to the ICE/ERO Family Case Management Program," January 6, 2016.

2017.[119] According to DHS, the FCMP average daily cost of $36 reportedly exceeded that of "intensive supervision" programs ($5-$7 daily),[120] although both programs are considerably lower than the average daily cost of family detention ($319).[121]

More broadly, immigration advocates contend that the Administration is engaged in a concerted effort to restrict access to asylum and reduce the number of asylum claims.[122] They caution that prosecuting persons who cross into the United States in order to present themselves before a CBP officer and request asylum raises concerns about whether the United States is abiding by human rights and refugee-related international protocols.[123] They note a considerable current backlog of pending defensive asylum cases, which numbered almost 325,000 (45%) of the roughly 720,000 total pending immigration cases in EOIR's docket as of June 11, 2018.[124] They also cite Attorney General Sessions's recent decision to substantially limit the extent to which immigration judges can consider gang or domestic violence as sufficient grounds for asylum.[125] Such efforts could have the unintended effect of sustaining illegal immigration flows of desperate

---

[119] Frank Bajak, "ICE Shutters Detention Alternative for Asylum-Seekers," *U.S. News and World Report*, June 9, 2017.

[120] Ibid. Intensive supervision programs monitor aliens in deportation proceedings who have been released from detention. They often involve electronic monitoring devices such as GPS ankle bracelets or voice recognition software for telephone-based reporting, and intensive case management.

[121] DHS currently oversees three family detention facilities. Berks Family Residential Center in Berks County, PA; Karnes Residential Center in Karnes City, TX; and South Texas Family Residential Center in Dilley, TX.

[122] Simon Romero and Miriam Jordan, "On the Border, a Discouraging New Message for Asylum Seekers: Wait," *New York Times*, June 12, 2018; and Jonathan Blitzer, "The Trump Administration Is Completely Unravelling the U.S. Asylum System," *The New Yorker*, June 11, 2018. For a contrary view on the weakening of the asylum system, see Dan Cadman, "Asylum in the United States," Center for Immigration Studies, March 26, 2014.

[123] Jonathan Blitzer, "The Trump Administration Is Completely Unravelling the U.S. Asylum System," *The New Yorker*, June 11, 2018.

[124] Email correspondence to CRS from DOJ Legislative Affairs, June 28, 2018.

[125] Matter of A-B-, Respondent, 27 I&N Dec. 316 (A.G. 2018), Interim Decisions #3929. The ruling vacated a 2016 decision by DOJ's Board of Immigration Appeals, the immigration appeals court for EOIR, granting asylum to a woman who experienced sexual, emotional, and physical abuse. See Ted Hesson and Josh Gerstein, "Sessions moves to block asylum for most victims of domestic, gang violence," *Politico*, June 11, 2018; and Katie Benner and Caitlin Dickerson, "Sessions Says Domestic and Gang Violence Are Not Grounds for Asylum," *New York Times*, June 11, 2018.

foreign nationals fleeing violent circumstances, particularly from Northern Triangle countries.

Congressional Activity

Given that this topic is developing rapidly, bills discussed below do not reflect all legislation or amendments introduced to date, or more recent developments. Instead, the bills presented here are intended to illustrate the range of legislative proposals to address family separation in the current context.

116th Congress

Bills introduced during the 116th Congress that are related to family separation are intended to prevent or limit the practice. These include H.R. 883/S. 271, the Families Belong Together Act, which would grant humanitarian parole and/or LPR status to separated parents and children upon request. Likewise, H.R. 541 S. 292, the Keep Families Together Act (similar to H.R. 6135/S. 3036 introduced in the 115th Congress) contains provisions to keep families together during all stages of processing following apprehension at a U.S. border, plus protections against the prosecution for illegal border crossing of asylum seekers and grantees. H.R. 1012, the REUNITE Act, includes provisions that would facilitate the expeditious reunification of separated families.

H.J.Res. 31, the Consolidated Appropriations Act, 2019, included additional funding to increase the number of participants in Alternatives to Detention (ATD) programs; additional ICE staffing dedicated to the management of ATD immigration cases, particularly those of asylum applicants; and the Family Case Management Program (FCMP), an alternative to family detention. The legislation directs ICE to prioritize both the use of ATD programs for families and the adjudication timeline for cases of individuals enrolled in ATD, particularly those of families and asylum seekers.

115th Congress

A number of bills were introduced in the 115th Congress in response to family separation resulting from the Administration's zero tolerance policy regarding the prosecution of illegal border crossing. With the exception of H.R. 6136, which failed to pass in the House by a vote of 121- 301, none of the bills introduced saw congressional action.

Bills that emphasized immigration enforcement included H.R. 6182, the Codifying President Trump's Affording Congress an Opportunity to Address Family Separation Executive Order Act, which would have provided statutory authority for President Trump's executive order within the INA; H.R. 6173, which would have clarified standards for family detention; and Section 3102 of H.R. 6136, the Border Security and Immigration Reform Act of 2018, which would have permitted children accompanied by parents to remain in DHS custody during the pendency of a parent's criminal prosecution, rather than being referred to ORR and treated as UAC. On July 11, 2018, similar amendment language was included in an appropriations bill to fund the Departments of Labor, Health and Human Services, and Education, that was approved by the House Appropriations Committee. H.R. 6204, the Families First Act of 2018, included similar provisions, asylum reforms, and provided increased funding for family unit facilities, personnel, and judges, among other provisions.

Bills that intended to prevent or limit family separation included H.R. 6135/S. 3036, the Keep Families Together Act, and H.R. 6236, the Family Unity Rights and Protection Act, both of which contained provisions to keep families together during all stages of processing following apprehension at a U.S. border; H.R. 6232, the Preventing Family Separation for Immigrants with Disabilities Act, which would have prohibited family separation for individuals with developmental disabilities; and H.R. 6172, the Reunite Children with Their Parents Act, which would have required DHS and DOJ to reunite minor children already separated from their parents.

Other bills, such as H.R. 6181/H.R. 6190 /S. 3093, the Keep Families Together and Enforce the Law Act, would have maintained family unity by making the Flores Settlement Agreement and related laws and regulations inapplicable to children who are accompanied by adults when they are apprehended at a U.S. border. H.R. 6195/S. 3091, the Protect Kids and Parents Act, would have limited the separation of families seeking asylum by mandating that they be housed together, and facilitated asylum processing (e.g., by adding additional immigration judges and DHS personnel and establishing asylum processing deadlines), among other provisions.

APPENDIX. TRENDS IN ALIEN APPREHENSIONS

Increasing numbers of apprehensions of Central American families and children are occurring within the context of relatively low historical levels of total alien apprehensions (*Figure A-1*).

Apprehensions at the Southwest border had peaked at 1.62 million in 1986, the year Congress enacted the Immigration Reform and Control Act (IRCA), which gave legal status to roughly 2.7 million unauthorized aliens residing in the United States.[126] After dropping for multiple years, apprehensions increased again, climbing from 0.85 million in FY1989 to an all-time high of 1.64 million in FY2000. Apprehensions generally fell after that (with the exception of FY2004- FY2006), reaching a 40-year low of 327,577 in FY2011. They have fluctuated since that point, declining

[126] For more information, see CRS Report R42138, Border Security: Immigration Enforcement Between Ports of Entry.

even further in some years. For the first four months of FY2019, apprehensions at the Southwest border reached 201,497.[127]

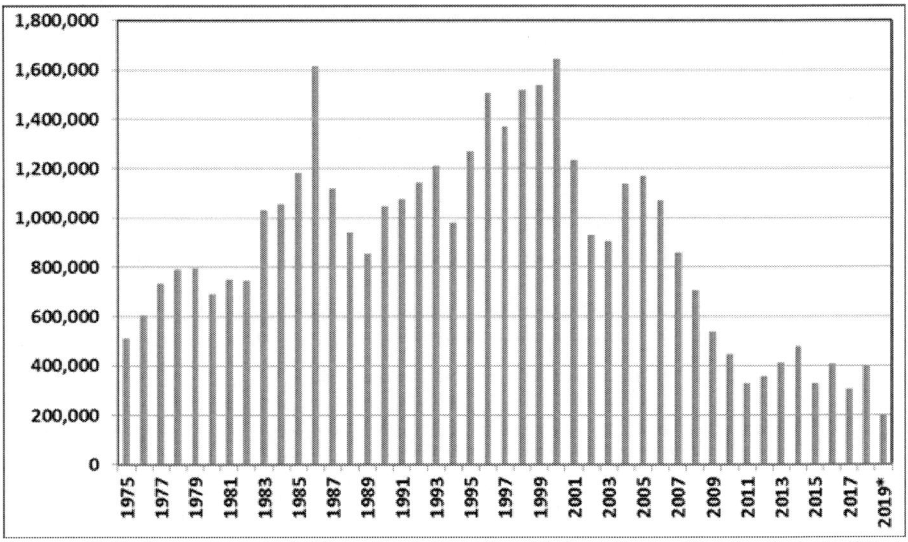

Source: U.S. Department of Homeland Security, United States Border Patrol, "Stats and Summaries," https://www.cbp.gov/newsroom/media-resources/stats.

Notes: *FY2019 includes October 2018 through January 2019, or one-third of the fiscal year.

Figure A-1. Total Alien Apprehensions at the Southwest Border, FY1975-FY2019.*

The national origins of apprehended aliens have shifted considerably during the past two decades (*Figure A-2*). In FY2000, for example, almost all aliens apprehended at the Southwest border (98%) were Mexican nationals. As recently as FY2011, Mexican nationals made up 84% of all apprehensions. However, beginning in FY2012, foreign nationals from countries other than Mexico made up a growing percentage of total apprehensions and for most years after FY2013, they made up the majority. In the first four months of FY2019, "other-than-Mexicans" comprised most (78%) of total alien apprehensions on the Southwest border.

---

[127] Border patrol apprehensions data count events rather than people. Thus, the same unauthorized alien caught trying to enter the country on three separate occasions during the same fiscal year counts as three apprehensions.

Among demographic categories, persons in family units and unaccompanied children currently make up the largest share of total alien apprehensions at the Southwest border (Figure A-3). According to CBP Commissioner Kevin McAleenan, single adult males made up over 90% of arriving aliens in the past.[128] However, in the first four months of FY2019, family units and unaccompanied children comprised roughly 60% of all apprehended aliens.

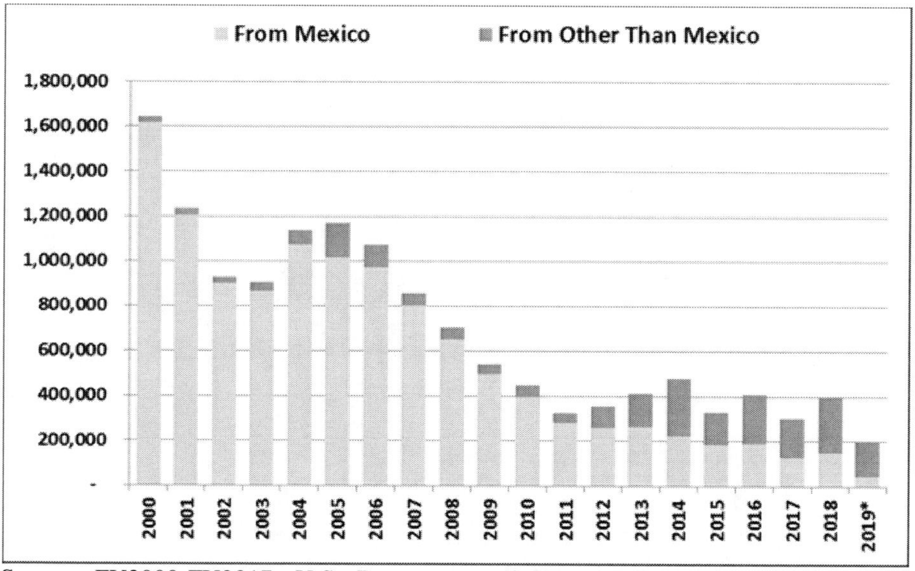

Source: FY2000-FY2017: U.S. Department of Homeland Security, United States Border Patrol, "Stats and Summaries," https://www.cbp.gov/newsroom/media-resources/stats; FY2018-FY2019: CRS presentation of unpublished data received from CBP Leg Affairs.

Notes: *FY2019 includes October 2018 through January 2019, or one-third of the fiscal year.

Figure A-2. Total Alien Apprehensions at the Southwest Border by Country of Origin, FY2000-FY2019. * (Country of origin is either Mexico or other-than-Mexico)

---

[128] Testimony of Kevin McAleenan, Commissioner, U.S. Customs and Border Patrol, in U.S. Congress, House Committee on Homeland Security, Subcommittee on Border and Maritime Security, *Border Security, Commerce and Travel: Commissioner McAleenan's Vision for the Future of CBP*, 115th Cong., 2nd sess., April 25, 2018. See also *Figure A-3*, which indicates that single adults made up 90% of all apprehensions as recently as FY2012.

CBP data on family unit apprehensions at the Southwest border are publicly available starting in FY2012, when they numbered just over 11,000. Since then, family unit apprehensions have increased considerably, reaching a peak of 107,212 in FY2018. In the first four months of FY2019, CBP apprehended 99,901 family units, which, if extrapolated to the remainder of FY2019, yields an projected estimate of almost 300,000 family unit apprehensions, exceeding the annual levels of all prior fiscal years.[129]

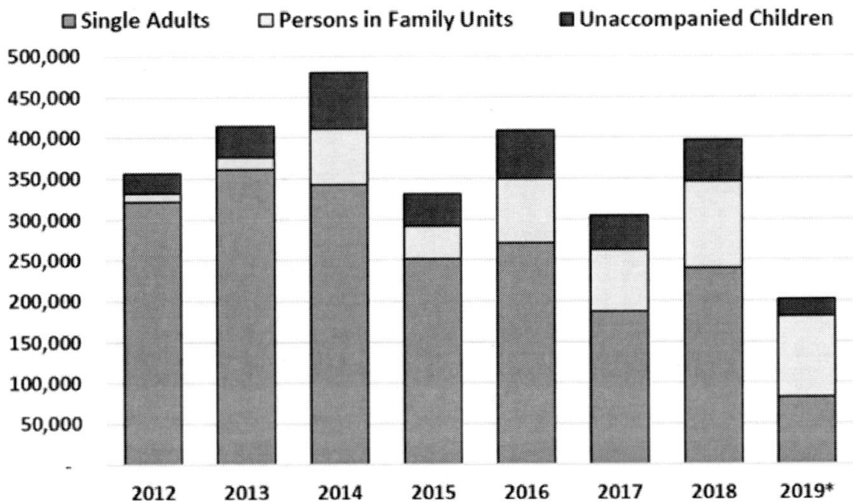

Source: For FY2008-FY2013: U.S. Department of Homeland Security, United States Border Patrol, "Juvenile and Adult Apprehensions—Fiscal Year 2013." For FY2014-FY2016, "Customs and Border Protection, Southwest Border Unaccompanied Alien Children." For FY2017-FY2019, "U.S. Border Patrol Southwest Border Apprehensions by Sector FY2017," https://www.cbp.gov/newsroom/stats/usbp-sw-border-apprehensions.

Notes: *FY2019 includes October 2018 through January 2019, or one-third of the fiscal year. Family unit apprehensions represent apprehended individuals in family units, not apprehended families.

Figure A-3. Total Alien Apprehensions at the Southwest Border, by Demographic Classification, FY2012-FY2019.*

---

[129] This projection is presented for illustrative purposes only, as the final total number of apprehended family units for FY2019 could diverge widely from the pattern that occurred during the first four months of the fiscal year.

CBP data on apprehensions of unaccompanied alien children at the Southwest border from FY2012 onward indicate a peak of 68,541 apprehensions in FY2014 and 20,123 apprehensions in the first four months of FY2019.

Since FY2012, the composition of family unit apprehensions by origin country has shifted from mostly Mexican (80%) to mostly El Salvadoran, Guatemalan, and Honduran (96%) (*Figure A-4*). Among these three Northern Triangle countries, the percentage of apprehensions from El Salvador, after increasing for several years, has recently declined, from 35% of all family unit apprehensions in FY2016 to 9% in the first four months of FY2019, while the percentage from Guatemala has increased steadily from 3% in FY2012 to 51% in FY2019.

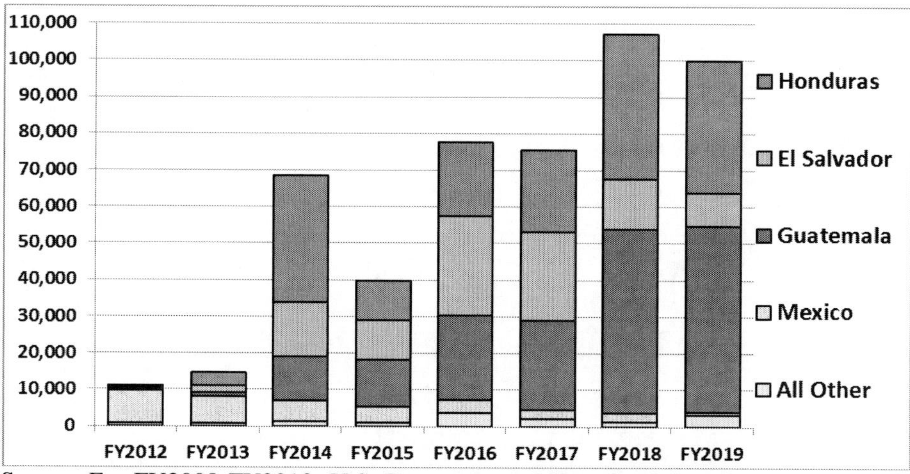

Source: For FY2008-FY2013: U.S. Department of Homeland Security, United States Border Patrol, "Juvenile and Adult Apprehensions—Fiscal Year 2013." For FY2014-FY2016, "Customs and Border Protection, Southwest Border Unaccompanied Alien Children." For FY2017-FY2019, "U.S. Border Patrol Southwest Border Apprehensions by Sector FY2017," https://www.cbp.gov/newsroom/stats/usbp-sw-border-apprehensions.

Notes: *FY2019 includes October 2018 through January 2019, or one-third of the fiscal year. Family unit apprehensions represent apprehended individuals in family units, not apprehended families.

Figure A-4. Total Alien Family Unit Apprehensions at the Southwest Border, FY2012-FY2019.*

Among unaccompanied alien children apprehended at the Southwest border, a similar country-of-origin compositional shift has also occurred. The percentage of apprehended unaccompanied children originating from Mexico declined from 57% in FY2012 to 15% in the first four months of FY2019, while the percentage of apprehended unaccompanied children from the Northern Triangle countries increased from 42% to 82% over the same period.[130]

---

130 For more information, see CRS Report R43599, *Unaccompanied Alien Children: An Overview*, Figure 1.

In: Immigration
Editor: Abel Thompson
ISBN: 978-1-53616-187-8

Chapter 6

IMMIGRATION CONSEQUENCES OF CRIMINAL ACTIVITY (UPDATED)*

Sarah Herman Peck and Hillel R. Smith

SUMMARY

Congress's power to create rules governing the admission of non-U.S. nationals (aliens) has long been viewed as plenary. In the Immigration and Nationality Act (INA), as amended, Congress has specified grounds for the exclusion or removal of aliens, including on account of criminal activity. Some criminal offenses, when committed by an alien who is present in the United States, may render that alien subject to removal from the country. And certain criminal offenses may preclude an alien outside the United States from being either admitted into the country or permitted to reenter following an initial departure. Further, criminal conduct may disqualify an alien from certain forms of relief from removal or prevent the alien from becoming a U.S. citizen. In some cases, the INA directly identifies particular offenses that carry immigration consequences; in other cases, federal immigration law provides that a general category of crimes, such as "crimes involving moral turpitude" or an offense defined by the INA as an "aggravated

* This is an edited, reformatted and augmented version of Congressional Research Service, Publication No. R45151, dated April 5, 2018.

felony," may render an alien ineligible for certain benefits and privileges under immigration law.

The INA distinguishes between the treatment of aliens who have been lawfully admitted into the United States and those who are either seeking admission into the country or are physically present in the country without having been lawfully admitted. Aliens who have been lawfully admitted into the country may be removed if they engage in conduct that renders them *deportable*, whereas aliens who have not been legally admitted into the United States—including both aliens seeking initial entry into the United States as well as those who are physically present in the country but were never lawfully admitted—may be excluded or removed from the country if they have engaged in conduct rendering them *inadmissible*. Although the INA designates certain criminal activities and categories of criminal activities as grounds for inadmissibility or deportation, the respective grounds are not identical. Moreover, a conviction for a designated crime is not always required for an alien to be disqualified on criminal grounds from admission into the United States. But for nearly all criminal grounds for deportation, a "conviction" (as defined by the INA) for the underlying offense is necessary. Additionally, although certain criminal conduct may disqualify an alien from various immigration-related benefits or forms of relief, the scope of disqualifying conduct varies depending on the particular benefit or form of relief at issue.

This chapter identifies the major criminal grounds that may bar an alien from being admitted into the United States or render an alien within the country removable. The chapter also discusses additional immigration consequences of criminal activity, including those that make an alien ineligible for certain relief from removal, including cancellation of removal, voluntary departure, withholding of removal, and asylum. The chapter also addresses the criminal grounds that render an alien ineligible to adjust to lawful permanent resident (LPR) status, as well as those grounds barring LPRs from naturalizing as U.S. citizens. The chapter also discusses the scope of several general criminal categories referenced by the INA, including "crimes involving moral turpitude," "aggravated felonies," and "crimes of violence."

Congress's power to establish rules for the admission of non-U.S. nationals (aliens[1]) has long been viewed as plenary.[2] In the Immigration

---

[1] The Immigration and Nationality Act (INA) uses the term "alien" to describe "any person not a citizen or national of the United States." 8 U.S.C. § 1101(a)(3).

[2] *See, e.g.*, Kleindienst v. Mandel, 408 U.S. 753, 769-70 (1972) ("[P]lenary congressional power to make policies and rules for exclusion of aliens has long been firmly established."); Boutilier v. INS, 387 U.S. 118, 123 (1967) ("It has long been held that the Congress has plenary power to make rules for the admission of aliens and to exclude those who possess

and Nationality Act (INA), as amended,[3] Congress has specified various grounds for the exclusion or removal of aliens, including grounds related to the commission of criminal conduct.[4] Some criminal offenses committed by an alien who is present in the United States may render that alien subject to removal from the country.[5] And certain offenses may preclude an alien outside the United States from either being admitted into the country or being permitted to reenter following an initial departure.[6] Further, committing certain crimes may disqualify an alien from many forms of relief from removal,[7] prevent an alien from adjusting to lawful permanent resident (LPR) status,[8] or bar an LPR from naturalizing as a U.S. citizen.[9]

This chapter provides an overview of the major immigration consequences of criminal activity. The chapter begins by briefly discussing the laws governing the immigration consequences of criminal conduct and the government entities charged with administering U.S. immigration laws. Next, the chapter enumerates specific crimes and categories of crimes that may render an alien inadmissible or deportable. Then, the chapter discusses the potential impact criminal activity may have for an alien's eligibility to obtain various forms of relief from removal or exclusion, including relief through a waiver of application of certain grounds for removal,

---

those characteristics which Congress has forbidden."). *But see* Zadvydas v. Davis, 533 U.S. 678, 695 (2001) (noting that Congress's plenary power in enacting immigration laws "is subject to important constitutional limitations"). *See generally* CRS Report R44969, *Overview of the Federal Government's Power to Exclude Aliens*, by Ben Harrington (discussing the scope of congressional authority over immigration).

[3] *See* 8 U.S.C. § 1101, *et seq.*

[4] *See id.* §§ 1182(a)(2), 1227(a)(2).

[5] *See, e.g., id.* § 1227(a)(2).

[6] *See, e.g., id.* § 1182(a)(2), (a)(9) (criminal grounds for inadmissibility, including for aliens previously removed on account of committing an aggravated felony); *see also id.* § 1101(a)(13)(C) (providing that an alien with lawful permanent resident status who departs from the United States and thereafter seeks to return shall not be considered an applicant for admission except in certain cases, including when the alien has committed conduct falling under the criminal grounds for inadmissibility or engaged in illegal activity after departing the United States).

[7] *See, e.g., id.* §§ 1158(b)(2), 1182(h)(2), 1229b(a), 1229c(b)(1).

[8] *See, e.g., id.* § 1255. An LPR is authorized to live permanently in the United States and may obtain many benefits unavailable to other categories of aliens. *See* Dep't of Homeland Security, *Lawful Permanent Residents (LPR)*, https://www.dhs.gov/immigration-statistics/lawful-permanent-residents (last visited Mar. 27, 2018).

[9] *See, e.g.*, 8 U.S.C. §§ 1101(f), 1427(a).

cancellation of removal, voluntary departure, asylum, or withholding of removal. Next, the chapter discusses criminal activity affecting an alien's ability to adjust to LPR status or naturalize as a U.S. citizen. Finally, the chapter examines select legal issues related to the intersection of criminal law and immigration, including the responsibilities of criminal defense attorneys representing alien defendants, as well as judicial interpretation of particular INA provisions that may render aliens who have been convicted of certain crimes removable.

ADMINISTRATION OF IMMIGRATION LAWS

The INA primarily governs the administration of U.S. immigration laws.[10] Originally enacted in 1952, the INA unified the country's immigration laws under one umbrella framework.[11] A number of federal agencies possess distinct responsibilities relating to the administration of the country's immigration laws, including the Department of Justice, the State Department, and, following the enactment of the Homeland Security Act of 2002, the Department of Homeland Security (DHS).

Before Congress enacted the Homeland Security Act most U.S. immigration laws—particularly as they related to enforcement activities and providing relief or services to aliens within the United States—were primarily administered by the Attorney General, who largely delegated his power to two agencies within the Department of Justice (DOJ): the Immigration and Naturalization Service (INS), which carried out enforcement and service activities, and the Executive Office for Immigration Review (EOIR), which carried out adjudication activities.[12]

---

[10] P.L. 107-296, 116 Stat. 2135 (2002).

[11] *See generally* USCIS History Office & Library (2012), *Overview of INS History,* at 9, *available for download at* https://www.uscis.gov/history-and-genealogy/our-history/agency-history/origins-federal-naturalization-service; USCIS, *Immigration & Nationality Act,* https://www.uscis.gov/laws/immigration-and-nationality-act (last visited Feb. 13, 2018).

[12] Immigration and Naturalization Act of 1952, Pub. L. No. 82-414, 66 Stat. 163, § 103 (June 27, 1952) (charging the Attorney General with administering and enforcing the INA and "all other laws relating to the immigration and naturalization of aliens, except insofar as this Act or such laws relate to the powers, functions, and duties conferred upon the President, the

The Homeland Security Act, as relevant here, dismantled the INS, created DHS, and transferred many of the Attorney General's immigration administration responsibilities to the DHS Secretary.[13] Thus, the DHS Secretary is now "charged with the administration and enforcement of [the INA] and all other laws relating to the immigration and naturalization of aliens, except insofar as this chapter or such laws relate to the powers, functions, and duties conferred upon the President, Attorney General" and other executive officers.[14]

Three components of DHS—Customs and Border Protection (CBP), Immigration and Customs Enforcement (ICE), and U.S. Citizenship and Immigration Services (USCIS)—carry out the major functions of the former INS.[15] In particular, ICE is the primary investigative arm of immigration enforcement within the United States.[16] When ICE determines that an alien located within the U.S. interior has violated the immigration laws—for example, by committing certain crimes—DHS typically apprehends the alien and initiates removal proceedings against him before an immigration judge (IJ) within DOJ's EOIR.[17] CBP, on the other hand, is authorized to enforce immigration laws at the border, which involves responsibilities including the inspection and admission of aliens seeking entry into the United States and the expedited removal of certain inadmissible aliens apprehended at or near the border while seeking entry to the United States.[18]

Secretary of State, the officers of the Department of State, or diplomatic or consular officers").

[13] USCIS History Office & Library, *supra* note 11, at 11. Other agencies in addition to the DHS, the DOJ, and the State Department play a role in immigration administration. For example, the Department of Health and Human Services is responsible for housing and caring for unaccompanied alien children, 8 U.S.C. § 1232(b)(1), and the Department of Labor provides labor certification to employers seeking to sponsor foreign nationals to work in the United States, *id.* § 1182(a)(5)(A); 20 C.F.R. § 656.

[14] 8 U.S.C. § 1103(a)(1); *see also* 8 C.F.R. § 2.1.

[15] GORDON & MAILMAN, ET AL., IMMIGRATION LAW & PROCEDURE, § 1.02, Scope, Agencies, and Sources.

[16] 8 C.F.R. § 100.1.

[17] 8 U.S.C. §§ 1229(a), 1229a(b)(4)(A).

[18] *See id.* § 1225(b)(1)(A) (authorizing expedited removal of certain aliens at or near the border); 8 C.F.R. § 235.3(b) (regulations implementing expedited removal procedures); 6 U.S.C. § 211(setting forth CBP's functions).

DHS, through USCIS, also plays a role in determining eligibility and approving applications for certain forms of relief and immigration benefits (e.g., granting asylum, adjusting status, or naturalizing).[19]

Despite the transfer of most enforcement functions to DHS, removal proceedings are primarily conducted by EOIR within DOJ.[20] During those proceedings, an IJ typically assesses an alien's removability and eligibility for relief from removal.[21] At the removal hearing—a civil proceeding[22]—aliens generally have a right to legal counsel at their own expense.[23]An IJ makes an initial removability determination, which may be appealed to the Board of Immigration Appeals (BIA), the highest administrative body charged with interpreting and applying federal immigration laws.[24] (The Attorney General is vested with discretion to review those appeals as well).[25] Additionally, as was the case before enactment of the Homeland Security Act, Attorney General rulings "with respect to all questions of law shall be controlling."[26]

Federal circuit courts of appeals have exclusive jurisdiction to adjudicate petitions for review of final removal orders issued in proceedings before EOIR.[27] However, the INA limits what issues the appellate courts may review. For instance, the INA limits federal courts' jurisdiction over cases involving an alien ordered removed based on certain criminal activity, unless the alien raises a constitutional claim or question

---

[19] *See* 6 U.S.C. § 271(b) (describing USCIS's adjudicatory functions); 8 C.F.R. § 100.1 (delegating authority to USCIS).

[20] P.L. 107-296, 116 Stat. 2135, § 1102; 8 C.F.R. § 1003.

[21] *See* 8 C.F.R. § 1003.9-1003.10.

[22] *See, e.g.,* Arizona v. United States, 567 U.S. 387, 396 (2012) ("Removal is a civil, not criminal matter").

[23] *See* 8 U.S.C. § 1229(a)(1)(E).

[24] 8 C.F.R. §§ 1003.1-1003.8.

[25] *Id.* § 1003.1(h).

[26] 8 U.S.C. § 1103(a)(1).

[27] *Id.* § 1252(a)(5). In addition, federal district courts have jurisdiction to review habeas corpus petitions by aliens challenging the legality of their detention pending their removal. *See* 28 U.S.C. § 2241 (authorizing federal courts to grant writs of habeas corpus to prisoners in federal custody); INS v. St. Cyr, 533 U.S. 289, 305 (2001) ("The writ of habeas corpus has always been available to review the legality of Executive detention."); Leonardo v. Crawford, 646 F.3d 1157, 1160 (9th Cir. 2011) (providing that aliens held in custody may file habeas corpus petitions in federal district court).

of law (e.g., whether particular conduct an alien allegedly committed is of the type of conduct covered by a particular removal ground in the INA).[28]

Another executive branch agency, the State Department, takes the lead role in processing the visas that aliens must generally obtain (with notable exceptions)[29] to travel to, and be admitted into, the United States.[30] Immigrant visas are granted to aliens seeking lawful permanent residency in the United States, whereas nonimmigrant visas are issued to aliens seeking temporary admission into the United States.[31] In both cases, the alien seeking a visa must submit supporting documentation to, and interview with, a consular official[32] who generally must be located in the country where the alien resides.[33] Eligibility for a particular visa depends

---

[28] 8 U.S.C. §§ 1252(a)(2)(C), (D); *see* Estrada-Ramos v. Holder, 611 F.3d 318, 321 (7th Cir. 2010) ("We lack jurisdiction to review removal orders of aliens removable under [INA] § 242(a)(2)(C) unless there is a valid constitutional claim or question of law.") (citing Zamora–Mallari v. Mukasey, 514 F.3d 679, 693–94 (7th Cir.2008)); James v. Mukasey, 522 F.3d 250, 253 (2d Cir. 2008) ("[W]e lack jurisdiction to review any final order of removal against an alien who is deportable because he or she was convicted of an aggravated felony, save for constitutional claims and questions of law.") (citing 8 U.S.C. § 1252(a)(2)(C)).

[29] *See id.* §§ 1181, 1184; *What is a U.S. Visa,* U.S. DEP'T OF STATE, BUREAU OF CONSULAR AFFAIRS, https://travel.state.gov/content/travel/en/us-visas.html (last visited Feb, 13, 2018). One notable exception to this general requirement is for persons travelling to the United States under the Visa Waiver Program. For more information on that program, under which citizens and nationals of 37 countries and Taiwan typically are not obligated to obtain a visa to visit the United States for business or tourism for 90 days or less, see *Visa Waiver Program,* U.S. DEP'T OF STATE, BUREAU OF CONSULAR AFFAIRS, https://travel.state.gov/content/travel/en/us-visas/tourism-visit/visa-waiverprogram.html (last visited Feb. 13, 2018); *see generally* CRS Report RL32221, *Visa Waiver Program*, by Jill H. Wilson. Another exception is for Canadian and Bermudan citizens, who do not need a visa for temporary travel to the United States for most purposes. *See* U.S. VISAS, *Citizens of Canada & Bermuda,* https://travel.state.gov/content/travel/ en/us-visas/tourism-visit/citizens-of-canada-and-bermuda.html (last visited Feb. 13, 2018).

[30] *See* 8 U.S.C. § 1104(c) (creating a Visa Office within the State Department).

[31] *See id.* § 1202; *Immigrant Visas vs. Nonimmigrant Visas,* U.S. CUSTOMS & BORDER PROT., https://help.cbp.gov/app/ answers/detail/a_id/72/~/immigrant-visas-vs.-nonimmigrant-visas (last visited Feb. 13, 2018). *See also supra* note 29 (describing some exceptions to visa requirements).

[32] A consular official is "any consular, diplomatic, or other officer or employee of the United States" who issues immigrant or nonimmigrant visas to aliens overseas or determines nationality of aliens. 8 U.S.C. § 1101(a)(9).

[33] *See id.* § 1202; *The Immigrant Visa Process,* U.S. DEP'T OF STATE, BUREAU OF CONSULAR AFFAIRS, http://travel.state.gov/content/visas/en/immigrate/immigrant-process.html (last visited Feb. 13, 2018); *Tourism & Visit,* U.S. DEP'T OF STATE, BUREAU OF CONSULAR AFFAIRS, https://travel.state.gov/content/travel/en/us-visas/ tourismvisit.html (last visited Feb. 13, 2018); *Business,* U.S. DEP'T OF STATE, BUREAU OF CONSULAR AFFAIRS, https://travel.state.gov/content/travel/en/us-visas/business.html

on specified criteria set forth in the INA.[34] And, as will be discussed in further detail below, certain criminal activity may render an alien ineligible to obtain a visa to enter the United States.

CRIMINAL GROUNDS FOR INADMISSIBILITY AND DEPORTATION

Aliens who commit certain crimes may be ineligible to enter or remain in the United States. The term "inadmissible" is used to describe aliens who are generally ineligible to receive visas or otherwise be lawfully admitted into the United States.[35] "Deportable" refers to aliens who have been lawfully admitted to the United States, but have engaged in proscribed activities that render them removable from the country.[36]

Criminal Grounds of Inadmissibility Under INA § 212(a)(2)

The criminal grounds for inadmissibility are primarily set forth in INA § 212(a)(2).[37] The criminal grounds are a mix of specific crimes and

---

(last visited Feb. 13, 2018); *Employment,* U.S. DEP'T OF STATE, BUREAU OF CONSULAR AFFAIRS, https://travel.state.gov/content/travel/en/us-visas/employment.html (last visited Feb. 13, 2018); *Study & Exchange,* U.S. DEP'T OF STATE, BUREAU OF CONSULAR AFFAIRS, https://travel.state.gov/ content/travel/en/us-visas/study.html (last visited Feb. 13, 2018). In some circumstances, however, an alien may submit a visa application in a country where he is not a resident if he is physically present there and the consular office has agreed to accept the alien's application. *See* 22 C.F.R. §§ 41.101(a)(1)(ii), 42.61(a).

[34] *See, e.g.,* 8 U.S.C. §§ 1101(a)(15), (a)(20), 1182.

[35] *Id.* § 1182(a).

[36] *Id.* § 1227(a). Additionally, an alien may be deportable on the ground that he was inadmissible at the time he entered the United States or adjusted status. *Id.* § 1227(a)(1)(A).

[37] *Id.* § 1182(a)(2). Other provisions of INA § 212 also address criminal conduct, but they are not listed within § 212(a)(2). For example, INA § 212(a)(3) covers "Security and Related Grounds" of inadmissibility, such as terrorist activities, genocide, and acts of torture, which would likely involve conduct that is criminal in nature. *Id.* § 1182(a)(3). In addition, INA § 212(a)(6) includes provisions relating to entering the United States without authorization and alien smuggling, which may be subject to separate criminal sanction. *See id.* §

categories of crimes with varying levels of proof required for the crime to render an alien inadmissible.[38]

Table 1. Criminal Grounds of Inadmissibility Under INA § 212(a)(2)

Ground of Inadmissibility	Covered Aliens	Exceptions
Crimes involving moral turpitude	An alien who has been convicted of, admitted to having committed, or admitted to committing acts that constitute the essential elements of a "crime involving moral turpitude," unless the crime was a purely political offense (or an attempt or conspiracy to commit such a crime)	Does not apply to an alien who committed only one crime if (1) the crime was committed when the alien was under 18 and the crime was committed (and the alien released from confinement) more than five years before applying for admission; or (2) the maximum penalty for the crime of conviction does not exceed imprisonment for more than one year and the alien was sentenced to no more than six months' imprisonment.
Controlled substance offenses	An alien who has been convicted of, admitted to having committed, or admitted to committing acts that constitute the essential elements of a violation of any federal, state, or foreign controlled substance law (or an attempt or conspiracy to commit such a crime)	None
Multiple criminal convictions	An alien who has been convicted of two or more offenses for which the aggregate sentences were five or more years of confinement	None
Drug trafficking	An alien who immigration authorities know, or have reason to believe, has been involved in drug trafficking (includes alien's spouse, son, or daughter if they have, within the previous five years, obtained any financial or other benefit from the drug trafficking activity and knew or reasonably should have known that the financial or other benefit resulted from such activity)	None
Prostitution and commercialized vice	An alien who is coming to the United States to engage in prostitution, has engaged in prostitution within 10 years of applying for admission or	None

1182(a)(6)(A)(i), (E)(i); *id.* §§ 1324 (crime of unlawful entry), 1325(a) (criminal offenses related to alien smuggling and harboring).

[38] *Id.* § 1182(a)(2).

Table 1. (Continued)

Ground of Inadmissibility	Covered Aliens	Exceptions
Prostitution and commercialized vice	adjustment of status, has procured or attempted to procure or import prostitutes or persons for the purpose of prostitution within that 10-year period, has received the proceeds of prostitution during that 10-year period, or is coming to the United States to engage in another unlawful commercialized vice	None
Serious criminal activity	An alien who has been involved in serious criminal activity[a] in the United States, gained immunity from prosecution, and, as a result, departed the United States	None
Human trafficking	An alien who has committed or conspired to commit a human trafficking offense in the United States or abroad, or who the U.S. government knows or has reason to believe has been involved in severe forms of human trafficking[b] (includes alien's spouse, son, or daughter if they have, within the previous five years, obtained any financial or other benefit from that activity, and knew or reasonably should have known that such benefit resulted from the activity)	Does not apply to a son or daughter of human trafficker who was a child at the time of receiving benefit from human trafficking activity
Money laundering	An alien who relevant immigration authorities know, or have reason to believe, has engaged in, is engaging in, or seeks to enter the United States to engage in money laundering[c] (including aiding or conspiring in money laundering)	None

Source: 8 U.S.C. §§ 1182(a)(2)(A), (a)(2)(B), (a)(2)(C), (a)(2)(D), (a)(2)(E), (a)(2)(H), (a)(2)(I). Notes:

a. The INA defines a "serious criminal offense" as any felony, a "crime of violence," or any crime of reckless driving or driving while under the influence of alcohol or a prohibited substance that results in personal injury to another person. 8 U.S.C. § 1101(h).

b. *See* 22 U.S.C. § 7102(9) (defining "severe forms of trafficking in persons").

c. *See* 18 U.S.C. §§ 1956-1957 (money laundering offenses).

Criminal Grounds of Deportability Under INA § 237(a)(2)

Criminal grounds for deportation are primarily listed in INA § 237(a)(2).[39] Like the inadmissibility grounds, criminal deportation grounds

[39] *Id.* § 1227(a)(2). Aliens who were inadmissible at the time of their entry to the United States because of the criminal grounds mentioned above (among other grounds) are also removable. *Id.* § 1227(a)(1)(A). Other provisions of INA § 237 also address criminal conduct, but they are not listed within § 237(a)(2). For example, INA § 237 covers alien

also consist of specific crimes and categories of crimes. One main difference between the criminal grounds for inadmissibility and deportability is that the deportability grounds largely require the alien to have been convicted of the listed offense, whereas the inadmissibility grounds for certain crimes may only require that the alien admitted committing the offense or that immigration authorities have "reason to believe" the alien committed the proscribed conduct.[40]

Table 2. Criminal Grounds of Deportation Under INA § 237(a)(2)

Ground of Deportability	Covered Aliens	Exceptions
Crimes involving moral turpitude	Aliens convicted of a crime involving moral turpitude (committed within 10 years of admission in the case of an LPR, or five years after admission for other categories of aliens) for which a sentence of imprisonment for one year or longer may be imposed	Does not apply if the alien is granted a full and unconditional pardon following the criminal conviction
Multiple criminal convictions	Aliens convicted of two or more crimes involving moral turpitude that did not arise out of a single scheme of criminal misconduct	Does not apply if the alien is granted a full and unconditional pardon following the criminal conviction
Aggravated felonies	Aliens who were convicted of an aggravated felony	Does not apply if the alien is granted a full and unconditional pardon following the criminal conviction
High speed flight	Aliens convicted of engaging in a high-speed flight from an immigration checkpoint[a]	Does not apply if the alien is granted a full and unconditional pardon following the criminal conviction
Failure to register as a sex offender	Aliens convicted for failing to register as a sex offender under the Sex Offender Registration and Notification Act (SORNA)[b]	None

smuggling, marriage fraud, falsification of documents, terrorist activities, genocide, and acts of torture, which may be subject to separate criminal sanction. *Id.* § 1227(a)(1)(E), (a)(1)(G), (a)(3)(B), (a)(4).

[40] *See e.g.,* Lopez-Molina v. Ashcroft, 368 F.3d 1206, 1209 (9th Cir. 2004) (observing that INA § 212(a)(2)(C)'s ground of inadmissibility for drug trafficking "does not require a conviction in order for the alien to be deemed removable," and only requires a "reason to believe" that the alien has been involved in drug trafficking).

Table 2. (Continued)

Ground of Deportability	Covered Aliens	Exceptions
Controlled substance offenses	Aliens convicted of violating any federal, state, or foreign controlled substance[c] law or regulation (including a conspiracy or attempt to violate such law or regulation)	Does not apply if conviction is for a single offense of possessing for personal use 30 grams or less of marijuana
Certain firearm offenses	Aliens convicted of unlawfully purchasing, selling, offering for sale, exchanging, using, owning, possessing, or carrying a firearm or destructive device[d] (including an attempt or conspiracy to engage in such activity)	None
Miscellaneous crimes	Aliens convicted of offenses related to espionage, sabotage, treason, or sedition for which a term of imprisonment of five or more years may be imposed; or offenses involving threats against the President, participation in a military operation against a United States ally, a violation of any provision of the Military Selective Service Act or the Trading with the Enemy Act, a violation of certain restrictions and prohibitions relating to United States entry and departure, or the importation of an alien into the United States for prostitution[e]	None
Domestic violence offenses	Aliens convicted of a crime of domestic violence, stalking, child abuse, child neglect, or child abandonment	None
Violators of protective orders	Aliens who have violated a protective order related to harassment or domestic violence	None
Human trafficking offenses	Aliens who have committed human trafficking offenses as described in 8 U.S.C. § 1182(a)(2)(H)	Does not apply to a son or daughter of human trafficker who was a child at the time of receiving benefit from human trafficking activity

Source: 8 U.S.C. §§ 1227(a)(2)(A)(i), (a)(2)(A)(ii), (a)(2)(A)(iii), (a)(2)(A)(iv), (a)(2)(A)(v), (a)(2)(B)(i), (a)(2)(C), (a)(2)(D), (a)(2)(E).

Notes:

a. See 18 U.S.C. § 758 (high speed flight offenses).

b. See id. § 2250.

c. See 21 U.S.C. § 802 (defining a "controlled substance").

d. See 18 U.S.C. § 921(a) (defining "firearm" and "destructive device").

e. See 8 U.S.C. § 1227(a)(2)(D) (describing offenses under 18 U.S.C. §§ 791-799, 2151-2157, 2381-2391; 8 U.S.C. §§ 1185 and 1328; 18 U.S.C. §§ 871 and 960; and 50 U.S.C. App. §§ 1 and 451).

CRIME INVOLVING MORAL TURPITUDE

Both the criminal grounds of inadmissibility and deportability under the INA reference a "crime of moral turpitude" as one of the bases for denying admission or deporting an alien from the United States. The federal courts and legal community have long grappled over the meaning of the term "crime involving moral turpitude" (alternatively referred to as "crime of moral turpitude").[41] Neither the INA nor any earlier immigration law defines the term.[42] Some federal appellate courts have opined that the term's legislative history, or lack thereof, "leaves no doubt ... that Congress left the term 'crime involving moral turpitude' to future administrative and judicial interpretation."[43] According to the BIA, moral turpitude "refers generally to conduct that shocks the public conscience as being inherently base, vile, or depraved, and contrary to accepted rules of morality and the duties owed between persons and to society in general."[44] In addition, moral turpitude, according to the BIA, involves "malicious intention" and actions "contrary to justice, honesty, principle, or good morals."[45]

---

[41] *See, e.g.,* In re Ajami, 22 I. & N. Dec. 949, 950 (BIA 1999) ("We have observed that the definition of a crime involving moral turpitude is nebulous."); De Leon v. Lynch, 808 F.3d 1224, 1228 (10th Cir. 2015) ("The phase 'crime involving moral turpitude' is not defined in the INA; instead, its contours have been shaped through interpretation and application by the Attorney General, the Board [of Immigration Appeals], and federal courts. It is perhaps the quintessential example of an ambiguous phrase.") (internal quotation marks and citation omitted); Brian C. Harms, *Redefining "Crimes of Moral Turpitude": A Proposal to Congress,* 15 GEO. IMMGR. L.J. 259, 259-60 (2001) ("No court has been able to define with clarity what 'crimes involving moral turpitude' means."); Christina LaBrie, *Lack of Uniformity in the Deportation of Criminal Aliens,* 25 N.Y.U. REV. L. & SOC. CHANGE 357, 362 (1999) ("Because the classification 'crimes of moral turpitude' is not clearly defined in the INA, courts have struggled to create a definition.") The term "moral turpitude" first appeared in federal immigration law in 1891. *See* Act of March 3, 1891, ch. 551, 26 Stat. 1084; *see also* Arias v. Lynch, 834 F.3d 823, 831 (7th Cir. 2016) (Posner, J., concurring); Harms, *supra* at 262.

[42] *See* Cabral v. INS, 15 F.3d 193, 194-95 (1st Cir. 1994).

[43] *See id.* at 195; *see also* Estrada-Rodriguez v. Lynch, 825 F.3d 397, 403 (8th Cir. 2016).

[44] Matter of Zaragoza-Vaquero, 26 I. & N. Dec. 814, 815 (BIA 2016); *see also Ajami*, 22 I. & N. Dec. at 950 (collecting BIA decisions containing definition of moral turpitude).

[45] Matter of Awaijane, 14 I. & N. Dec. 117, 118-19 (BIA 1972); *see also* Avendano v. Holder, 770 F.3d 731, 734 (8th Cir. 2014) (noting that the court applies the BIA's "'longstanding general definition' of a crime involving moral turpitude, which included 'acts accompanied by 'a vicious motive or a corrupt mind''").

The federal courts generally agree that a crime that is inherently fraudulent or involves an intent to defraud is a crime involving moral turpitude.[46] It is less settled, however, when other, nonfraudulent crimes constitute crimes involving moral turpitude. Indeed, before Attorney General Michael Mukasey's 2008 opinion in *Matter of Silva-Trevino* (*Silva-Trevino I*), which set forth a standard for assessing whether a crime involved moral turpitude, there had been an "absence of an authoritative administrative methodology for resolving moral turpitude inquiries [which had] resulted in different approaches across the country."[47] In *Silva-Trevino I,* the Attorney General ruled that a crime involving moral turpitude must involve both reprehensible conduct and a culpable mental state, such as specific intent, deliberateness, or recklessness.[48] Since then, the BIA has adopted this formulation as the standard for determining whether an offense constitutes a crime involving moral turpitude.[49]

---

[46] *See Zaragoza-Vaquero*, 26 I. & N. Dec. at 816; In re Kochilani, 24 I. & N. Dec. 128, 130-31 (BIA 2007) ("It is true that crimes that have a specific intent to defraud as an element have always been found to involve moral turpitude, but we have also found that certain crimes are inherently fraudulent and involve moral turpitude even though they can be committed without a specific intent to defraud."); Jordan v. De George, 341 U.S. 223, 229 (1951) ("[F]raud has consistently been regarded as such a contaminating component in any crime that American courts have, without exception, included such crimes within the scope of moral turpitude."); Palma-Martinez v. Lynch, 785 F.3d 1146, 1148 n.1 (7th Cir. 2015) ("Crimes involving fraud have always been considered crimes of moral turpitude.").

[47] Matter of Silva-Trevino [hereinafter *Silva-Trevino I*], 24 I. & N. Dec. 687, 693 (A.G. 2008). *See* 8 C.F.R. § 1003.1(h)(1)(i) (providing that the Attorney General may direct the BIA to refer cases to him "for review of [the BIA's] decision"); Matter of E-L-H-, 23 I. & N. Dec. 814, 825 (BIA 2005) (noting that "the Attorney General retains ultimate authority over the meaning of immigration laws and regulations"); Matter of D-J-, 23 I. & N. Dec. 572, 575 (BIA 2003) (stating that, when the Attorney General reviews BIA decisions, "the delegated authorities of the IJ and BIA are superseded and [the Attorney General] [is] authorized to make the determinations based on [his] own conclusions on the facts and the law.").

[48] *Silva-Trevino I*, 24 I. & N. Dec. at 706 (ruling that indecency with a child in violation of a Texas statute constituted a crime involving moral turpitude).

[49] Matter of Silva-Trevino, 26 I. & N. Dec. 826, 834 (BIA 2016) [hereinafter *Silva-Trevino III*] ("To involve moral turpitude, a crime requires two essential elements: reprehensible conduct and a culpable mental state"); *see* Bobadilla v. Holder, 679 F.3d 1052, 1054 (8th Cir. 2012) (observing that the BIA's "basic definition" of a crime involving moral turpitude "has generated little if any disagreement by reviewing circuit courts"). While the BIA in *Silva-Trevino III* adopted a definition for a "crime involving moral turpitude," the litigation in that case was centered on the extent to which an adjudicator may consider the factual evidence underlying a criminal conviction in order to assess whether an alien was convicted of a crime involving moral turpitude. *See Silva-Trevino III*, 26 I. & N. Dec. at 830; Matter of Silva-Trevino, 26 I. & N. Dec. 550, 550-51 (A.G. 2015) [hereinafter *Silva-Trevino II*]; *Silva-Trevino I*, 24 I. & N. Dec. at 688-90.

AGGRAVATED FELONY

INA § 101(a)(43) provides a list of crimes deemed to be aggravated felonies for immigration purposes; a list which Congress has repeatedly expanded over the years to cover additional crimes.[50] The list includes many specific offenses, as well as several broad categories of crimes.[51] Moreover, the "aggravated felony" definition is not limited to offenses that are punishable as felonies (i.e., offenses punishable by at least a year and a day imprisonment); certain misdemeanors are also defined as aggravated felonies for INA purposes.[52] INA § 101(a)(43) defines the term aggravated felony by designating certain crimes and categories of crimes as aggravated felonies.[53] Specific crimes include the following:

Table 3. Aggravated Felony Offenses Under INA § 10 1 (a)(43)(F)

Enumerated Offense	Enumerated Offense	Enumerated Offense
Murder	Theft or burglary offenses for which the term of imprisonment is at least one year	Tax evasion with a revenue loss to the government exceeding $10,000
Rape	Offenses related to demanding or receiving ransom	Alien smuggling (but not if it is a first offense and the alien has shown that the offense was committed to help the alien's spouse, child, or parent)
Sexual abuse of a minor	Child pornography offenses	Unlawful reentry into the United States by an alien previously removed on the basis of a conviction for an aggravated felony
Illicit trafficking in a controlled substance as defined in 21 U.S.C. § 802	Racketeering or gambling offenses for which a sentence of one year of imprisonment or	Falsely making, forging, counterfeiting, mutilating, or altering a passport or immigration

[50] 8 U.S.C. § 1101(a)(43).

[51] *Id.*

[52] *See Felony,* BLACK'S LAW DICTIONARY (defining "felony" as a "serious crime usu[ally] punishable by imprisonment for more than one year or by death") (10th ed. 2014); Lopez v. Gonzales, 549 U.S. 47, 52-60 (2006) (analyzing, for the purposes of determining whether a particular crime is an aggravated felony under the INA, "the proper understanding of conduct treated as a felony by the State that convicted a defendant of committing it, but as a misdemeanor under the [Controlled Substances Act]").

[53] 8 U.S.C. § 1101(a)(43).

Table 3. (Continued)

Enumerated Offense	Enumerated Offense	Enumerated Offense
(including a "drug trafficking crime," which is defined in 18 U.S.C. 944(c) as any felony punishable under the Controlled Substances Act)	more may be imposed	document for which the term of imprisonment is at least twelve months (but not if it is a first offense for the purpose of aiding or assisting the alien's spouse, child, or parent)
Illicit trafficking in firearms, destructive devices, or explosive materials	Offenses involving a prostitution business (including offenses involving the transportation of persons for the purpose of prostitution or unlawful sexual activity as described in 18 U.S.C. §§ 2421 to 2423, if committed for commercial advantage)	Failing to appear to serve a sentence if the underlying offense is punishable by imprisonment for five years or more
Money laundering or engaging in monetary transactions in property derived from specific unlawful activity, if the amount of funds exceeded $10,000	Offenses related to peonage, slavery, involuntary servitude, or human trafficking	Commercial bribery, counterfeiting, forgery, or trafficking in vehicles with altered identification numbers, if the term of imprisonment is at least one year
Offenses related to firearms or explosive materials	Gathering or transmitting national defense information, disclosing classified information, unlawfully identifying undercover agents, sabotage, or treason	Obstruction of justice, perjury, subornation of perjury, or bribery of a witness for which the term of imprisonment is at least one year
A crime of violence (as defined in 18 U.S.C. § 16) for which the term of imprisonment is at least one year	Fraud offenses in which the loss to the victim(s) exceeds $10,000	Failing to appear in court pursuant to a court order to answer or dispose of a felony charge for which a sentence of two years' imprisonment or more may be imposed

Source: 8 U.S.C. §§ 1101(a)(43)(A), (B), (C) (describing conduct in 18 U.S.C. §§ 921, 841(c)), (D) (describing conduct in 18 U.S.C. §§ 1956 to 1957), (E) (describing conduct in 18 U.S.C. §§ 842(h), (i), or 844(d) to (i), 922(g)(1) to (g)(5), 924(b), (h); 26 U.S.C. § 5861), (F), (G), (H) (describing conduct in 18 U.S.C. §§ 875 to 877, 1202), (I) (describing offenses in 18 U.S.C. §§ 2251, 2251A, 2252), (J) (describing offenses in 18 U.S.C. §§ 1962, 1084, 1955), (K)(i), (K)(ii), (K)(iii) (describing offenses in 18 U.S.C. §§ 1581 to 1585 or 1588 to 1591), (L) (describing offenses in 18 U.S.C. §§ 793, 798, 2153, 2381, 2382, 50 U.S.C. §3121), (M)(i), (M)(ii) (describing 26 U.S.C. § 7201), (N) (describing offenses in 8 U.S.C. §§ 1324(a)(1)(A), (a)(2)), (O) (describing conduct in 8 U.S.C. §§ 1325(a), 1326), (P) (describing offenses in 18 U.S.C. §§ 1543, 1546(a)), (Q), (R), (S), (T).

Note: When the INA references a "term of imprisonment," that means the term of imprisonment ordered by the court, not the time actually served by the defendant. 8 U.S.C. § 1101(a)(48)(B).

The offenses described above include violations of state or federal law, as well as violations of foreign law if the term of imprisonment was completed within the prior 15 years.[54] Additionally, an attempt or conspiracy to commit any of the above offenses qualifies as an aggravated felony.[55]

An alien convicted of a crime that falls within the scope of the aggravated felony definition may be subject to serious immigration consequences. A conviction for an aggravated felony is a ground for deportation.[56] Additionally, an alien who has committed an aggravated felony and is removed from the United States will become inadmissible indefinitely,[57] and may be ineligible for various forms of relief from removal.[58]

Crimes Affecting "Good Moral Character"

As discussed in detail below, aliens must demonstrate good moral character for a certain period to qualify for various forms of relief from removal[59] and for naturalization.[60] The INA specifies many criminal

---

[54] *Id.* § 1101(a)(43).

[55] *Id.* § 1101(a)(43)(U).

[56] *Id.* § 1227(a)(2)(A)(iii).

[57] *Id.* § 1182(a)(9)(A).

[58] *See id.* §§ 1158(b)(2) (barring aliens convicted of an aggravated felony from asylum), 1229b(a)(3) (barring LPRs convicted of an aggravated felony from cancellation of removal), 1229b(b)(1)(C) (barring non-LPRs from cancellation of removal if they have been convicted of certain enumerated offenses including aggravated felonies), 1229c(b)(1)(C) (barring aliens from voluntary departure if they have aggravated felony convictions), 1231(b)(3)(B) (providing that an alien who has been convicted of an aggravated felony for which the term of imprisonment is at least five years is statutorily ineligible for withholding of removal).

[59] *See id.* §§ 1229b(b)(1)(B) (requiring showing of good moral character for at least ten years to qualify for cancellation of removal and adjustment of status for nonpermanent residents), 1229b(b)(2)(A)(iii) (requiring showing of good moral character for at least three years to qualify for cancellation of removal and adjustment of status for aliens who have been battered or subjected to extreme cruelty); 1229c(b)(1)(B) (requiring good moral character for at least five years to be eligible for voluntary departure).

[60] *See id.* § 1427 (requiring showing of good moral character for at least five years preceding date of application for naturalization, but not precluding USCIS from considering applicant's conduct and acts at any time before that period).

activities that would preclude an adjudicator from finding that an alien has good moral character.[61] In most cases, the relevant criminal activity precludes a finding of good moral character only if it is committed within a particular statutory period; in some cases, however, criminal conduct may permanently bar a finding of good moral character. The table below lists major criminal bars to finding good moral character.

Table 4. Criminal Bars to Good Moral Character

If Occurring During Statutory Period	Occurring at Any Time
Acts related to prostitution and other commercialized vices	Conviction for an aggravated felony (for naturalization applications, the aggravated felony conviction must have occurred on or after November 29, 1990; but murder convictions will bar good moral character if they occurred at any time)
Crimes involving moral turpitude (other than a purely political offense), unless (1) the crime was committed before the alien turned 18 and more than five years before relief application; or (2) the maximum possible penalty for the crime did not exceed imprisonment for one year	Participation in genocide
Violations of any law or regulation relating to a controlled substance	Commission of acts of torture or extrajudicial killings
Engaging in, assisting in, or conspiring to commit a drug trafficking offense (except for simple possession of 30 grams or less of marijuana); Deriving income principally from illegal gambling activities; Convictions for two or more gambling offenses; Confinement for an aggregate period of 180 days or more in a corrections facility (regardless of whether offense was committed within statutory period)	

Source: 8 U.S.C. §§ 1101(43)(f)(3) (referencing conduct described in id. §1182(a)(2)(A)(i), (B), (C), (D)), (f)(4), (f)(5), (f)(7), (f)(8), (f)(9) (referencing conduct described in id. § 1182(a)(3)(E)(ii)-(iii)); 8 C.F.R. §§ 316.10(b)(1)(i)- (ii).

The list above is not exhaustive, and so an adjudicator may find that an alien lacks good moral character for other criminal activities not listed in the statute.[62]

---

[61] *Id.* § 1101(f).

[62] *Id.* § 1101(f) ("The fact that any person is not within any of the foregoing classes shall not preclude a finding that for other reasons such person is or was not of good moral character").

Relief from Removal and Obtaining Certain Immigration Benefits

If an alien commits conduct that falls under a ground for inadmissibility or deportability, it does not necessarily follow that the alien cannot enter or remain in the United States. The INA provides several grounds for relief—mandatory and discretionary—from exclusion or removal. These forms of relief include adjustment of status, waivers of certain grounds of inadmissibility by immigration authorities, cancellation of removal, voluntary departure, withholding of removal, and asylum, among others. However, certain criminal activity may bar an alien from being eligible for some types of relief. The Attorney General, with authority typically delegated to EOIR, adjudicates applications for relief from removal.[63] In addition, the DHS Secretary, with authority delegated to the agency's adjudicatory component, USCIS, has the authority to adjudicate applications for immigration benefits, including asylum, refugee admissions, and adjustment of status.[64] Some of these forms of relief and adjustment are discussed below.[65]

Waiver for Criminal Inadmissibility Grounds

The INA provides that immigration authorities have discretion to waive certain grounds of inadmissibility in qualifying circumstances. Concerning the criminal grounds for inadmissibility, the scope of this waiver authority differs depending on whether the alien is seeking admission as an LPR, or whether the alien is, instead, seeking admission into the country temporarily as a nonimmigrant.

---

[63] *Id.* § 1103(g); 8 C.F.R. § 1240.1(a)(1)(ii).

[64] 6 U.S.C. § 271(b); 8 U.S.C. § 1103(a)(1); 8 C.F.R. §§ 2.1, 103.2.

[65] While this chapter describes some of the principal avenues of relief for aliens who may be subject to removal, it does not provide an exhaustive list of all immigration-related relief.

Aliens Seeking Admission as LPRs

INA § 212(h) grants the Attorney General and the DHS Secretary[66] discretion to waive the application of specified criminal grounds for inadmissibility for aliens seeking admission as an LPR if certain conditions are met.[67] In particular, the Attorney General or DHS Secretary may waive the inadmissibility grounds relating to

- crimes involving moral turpitude;
- multiple criminal convictions;
- prostitution and other commercialized vices;
- involvement in serious criminal activity for which immunity from prosecution was granted; or
- drug crimes relating to a single offense of simple possession of 30 grams or less of marijuana.[68]

But for the Attorney General and the DHS Secretary to exercise their discretion, the alien must establish that (1) he is inadmissible solely on the basis of prostitution-related crimes, *or* the activities for which he is inadmissible took place more than 15 years before applying for admission; (2) his admission would not be contrary to the national welfare, safety, or security of the United States; and (3) he has been rehabilitated.[69]

For an alien who is the spouse, parent, son, or daughter of a U.S. citizen or LPR, the Attorney General and the DHS Secretary may also waive inadmissibility if the alien establishes that the denial of admission would result in "extreme hardship" to the qualifying family member.[70] Additionally, under the Violence Against Women Act of 1994, as amended (VAWA), the Attorney General and DHS may waive the criminal

---

[66] As discussed in the summary of this chapter, *supra* at 2, the Homeland Security Act dismantled the former INS, created DHS, and transferred many of the Attorney General's immigration administration responsibilities to the DHS Secretary; DHS, through USCIS, has the authority to adjudicate and approve applications for certain forms of relief such as adjustment of status. 6 U.S.C. § 271(b); 8 U.S.C. § 1103(a)(1); 8 C.F.R. §§ 2.1, 103.2.

[67] 8 U.S.C. § 1182(h).

[68] *Id.*

[69] *Id.* § 1182(h)(1)(A).

[70] *Id.* § 1182(h)(1)(B).

inadmissibility grounds if the alien is a battered spouse or child of a U.S. citizen or LPR.[71]

Notwithstanding the Attorney General's and DHS Secretary's discretion noted above, INA § 212(h) bars waivers for aliens convicted of murder or criminal acts involving torture, or an attempt or conspiracy to commit those crimes.[72] Additionally, a waiver may not be granted to an alien previously admitted as an LPR if, since the date of admission, the alien has been convicted of an aggravated felony, or has not lawfully resided continuously in the United States for at least seven years before removal proceedings have been initiated against the alien.[73]

Aliens Seeking Admission as Nonimmigrants

For an alien seeking admission as a nonimmigrant (e.g., students, athletes, temporary workers),[74] DHS may exercise its discretion to

---

[71] *Id.* § 1182(h)(1)(C); VAWA, P.L. 103-322. VAWA, as relevant here, allows an alien who is the spouse or child of a U.S. citizen or LPR, and who has been battered or subject to extreme cruelty by the U.S. citizen or LPR spouse or parent, to apply for LPR status without the involvement of the abusive relative. *See* 8 U.S.C. §§ 1154(a)(1)(A), 1186a(c)(4)(C), 1229b(b)(2).

[72] 8 U.S.C. § 1182(h). This bar also applies to aliens who admit committing acts that constitute murder or criminal acts involving torture (or an attempt or conspiracy to commit those offenses). *Id.*

[73] *Id.* Initially, the BIA interpreted this bar to apply to all LPRs who have been convicted of aggravated felonies (or otherwise failed to accrue the seven years of continuous residence), regardless of the manner in which they acquired their LPR status – in other words, the bar applied to both aliens who were initially admitted into the United States as LPRs and aliens who later adjusted their status to LPRs post-entry. Matter of Rodriguez, 25 I. & N. Dec. 784, 789 (BIA 2012); Matter of Koljenovic, 25 I. & N. Dec. 219, 224-25 (BIA 2010). The majority of the federal circuit courts of appeals disagreed with this interpretation and held that the bar applies only to aliens who were initially admitted as LPRs. Medina-Rosales v. Holder, 778 F.3d 1140, 1145 (10th Cir. 2015); Husic v. Holder, 776 F.3d 59, 66 (2d Cir. 2015); Stanovsek v. Holder, 768 F.3d 515, 517 (6th Cir. 2014); Negrete-Ramirez v. Holder, 741 F.3d 1047, 1053-54 (9th Cir. 2014); Papazoglou v. Holder, 725 F.3d 790, 794 (7th Cir. 2013); Hanif v. Att'y Gen. of the United States, 694 F.3d 479, 487 (3d Cir. 2012); Bracamontes v. Holder, 675 F.3d 380, 389 (4th Cir. 2012); Lanier v. United States Att'y Gen., 631 F.3d 1363, 1366-67 (11th Cir. 2011); Hing Sum v. Holder, 602 F.3d 1092, 1101 (9th Cir. 2010); Martinez v. Mukasey, 519 F.3d 532, 544 (5th Cir. 2008). *But see* Roberts v. Holder, 745 F.3d 928, 932-33 (8th Cir. 2014) (deferring to BIA's interpretation that § 212(h) bar applies to LPRs regardless of the manner in which they acquired LPR status). Ultimately, "[g]iven the overwhelming circuit court authority in disagreement" with its prior rulings, the BIA revisited the issue in *Matter of J-H-J-*, and held that the § 212(h) bar applies only to aliens who entered the United States as LPRs. Matter of J-H-J-, 26 I. & N. Dec. 563, 564-65 (BIA 2015).

[74] *See* 8 U.S.C. § 1101(a)(15) (listing classes of nonimmigrants).

authorize the nonimmigrant visa if the Secretary of State or consular officer recommends that the alien be temporarily admitted despite a criminal ground for inadmissibility.[75] This waiver, however, is not available if the alien is inadmissible because (1) he seeks to enter the United States to engage in espionage or sabotage; (2) he seeks to enter the United States to engage in any other unlawful activity; (3) he seeks to enter the United States to engage in activity with the purpose of opposing, controlling, or overthrowing the U.S. government through force or other unlawful means; (4) the Secretary of State has reasonable grounds to believe that the alien's entry "would have potentially serious adverse foreign policy consequences for the United States"; or (5) the alien has participated in Nazi persecution or genocide.[76]

Cancellation of Removal

INA § 240A authorizes cancellation of removal, another form of discretionary relief available to certain LPRs and nonimmigrants in removal proceedings.[77] For non-LPRs, this relief is available to up to 4,000 aliens each year.[78] Cancellation of removal allows the Attorney General to cancel the removal of qualifying LPRs and nonpermanent residents (including both those lawfully admitted as nonimmigrants and aliens who do not possess a lawful immigration status) who are inadmissible or

---

[75] *Id.* § 1182(d)(3)(A). The Seventh Circuit, however, has ruled that an alien could apply for a nonimmigrant visa waiver even after she was already in removal proceedings, on the grounds that the government's "ineffective screening methods" prevented the consular officer who had issued the alien's nonimmigrant visa from discovering that the alien was inadmissible and would need a waiver to overcome her inadmissibility, and the alien, who was detained upon arriving at Chicago O'Hare International Airport, was still seeking admission into United States at the time of her removal proceedings. Atunnise v. Mukasey, 523 F.3d 830, 838-39 (7th Cir. 2008).

[76] 8 U.S.C. § 1182(d)(3)(A). In addition, DHS, in consultation with the Attorney General and the State Department (or the State Department, in consultation with the Attorney General and DHS) may allow the admission of nonimmigrants who are inadmissible on the basis of terrorist activities in certain limited circumstances. *Id.* § 1182(d)(3)(B).

[77] *Id.* § 1229b(a), (b).

[78] *Id.* § 1229b(e)(1).

deportable.[79] But some criminal activity may bar the Attorney General from exercising that discretion.

Eligibility for cancellation of removal differs for LPRs and non-LPRs. For LPRs, the Attorney General may exercise discretion to cancel removal if the alien

1. has been an LPR for at least five years;
2. has resided in the United States continuously for seven years after having been admitted to the United States in any status; and
3. has not been convicted of an aggravated felony.[80]

For non-LPRs, the Attorney General may exercise discretion to cancel the removal of an alien who is inadmissible or deportable *and* adjust the alien's status to LPR if the alien

1. has been physically present in the United States for a continuous period of at least 10 years immediately preceding the application for relief;
2. has been a person of good moral character during that 10-year period;
3. has not been convicted of an offense described in INA § 212(a)(2) (criminal grounds of inadmissibility), § 237(a)(2) (criminal

---

[79] *Id.* § 1229b.

[80] *Id.* § 1229b(a). Previously, under former INA § 212(c), the Attorney General could grant discretionary relief to an LPR subject to deportation proceedings if he had "a lawful unrelinquished domicile of seven consecutive years." 8 U.S.C. § 1182(c) (1995). Notably, § 212(c) relief was available to an LPR even if he had been convicted of an aggravated felony, as long as he did not serve a term of imprisonment of at least five years. *Id.* Ultimately, § 212(c) was repealed by the Illegal Immigration Reform and Immigrant Responsibility Act of 1996 (IIRIRA) in favor of the new cancellation of removal provision (which categorically bars relief to aliens convicted of any aggravated felony). *See* IIRIRA, P.L. 104-208, § 304, 110 Stat. 3009 (1996). However, in *INS v. St. Cyr*, the Supreme Court ruled that § 212(c) relief remained available to aliens whose criminal convictions resulted from plea agreements and who would have been eligible for § 212(c) relief at the time of their plea. 533 U.S. 289, 326 (2001). Therefore, although § 212(c) relief has been superseded by statute, there is a small (and decreasing) category of aliens who may still be eligible for such relief.

grounds of deportability), or § 237(a)(3) (failure to register and falsification of documents); and

4. establishes that his removal would result in "exceptional and extremely unusual hardship" to a spouse, parent, or child who is a U.S. citizen or LPR.[81]

Thus, LPRs who have been convicted of an aggravated felony cannot receive cancellation of removal.[82] But this statutory bar does not preclude the Attorney General from canceling the removal of LPRs who have been convicted of other types of offenses. Conversely, non-LPRs may be rendered ineligible to obtain cancellation of removal by committing any offense described within the criminal grounds for inadmissibility or deportability.[83]

Additionally, an alien who is not an LPR cannot receive cancellation of removal if he has not been a person of good moral character for at least 10 years immediately preceding the date of the application.[84] As listed

[81] 8 U.S.C. § 1229b(b).

[82] *Id.* § 1229b(a). An LPR with an aggravated felony conviction will be barred from cancellation of removal even if he has not been charged and found removable based on the aggravated felony conviction. *See* Becker v. Gonzales, 473 F.3d 1000, 1002 (9th Cir. 2007) ("A conviction for an aggravated felony precludes eligibility even absent a charge and finding of removability on that ground.").

[83] 8 U.S.C. § 1229b(b). The BIA has held that this criminal bar applies to any offense *described* within INA §§ 212(a)(2), 237(a)(2), or 237(a)(3), regardless of whether the alien was charged with removal as an inadmissible alien (§ 212) or a deportable alien (§ 237). Matter of Almanza-Arenas, 24 I. & N. Dec. 771, 776 (BIA 2009); *see also* Coyomani-Cielo v. Holder, 758 F.3d 908, 915 (7th Cir. 2014) (upholding BIA's interpretation); Gonzalez-Gonzalez v. Ashcroft, 390 F.3d 649, 652 (9th Cir. 2004) ("The plain language of [8 U.S.C.] § 1229b indicates that it should be read to cross-reference a list of offenses in three statutes, rather than the statutes as a whole."). Further, a non-permanent resident seeking cancellation of removal cannot receive a waiver of the criminal conviction bar under INA § 212(h). *See* Matter of Bustamante, 25 I. & N. Dec. 564, 567 (BIA 2011) (explaining that § 212(h) waives grounds of inadmissibility only arising from a conviction and other actions involving criminal conduct but does not waive recognition of the fact of a conviction itself); Guerrero-Roque v. Lynch, 845 F.3d 940, 943 (9th Cir. 2017) (same); Barma v. Holder, 640 F.3d 749, 752-53 (7th Cir. 2011) (same).

[84] 8 U.S.C. § 1229b(b). The period for good moral character is calculated backward from the date on which the application is finally resolved before the immigration judge or the BIA. *See* Matter of Ortega-Cabrera, 23 I. & N. Dec. 793, 798 (BIA 2005) ("[W]e conclude that, in line with long-standing practice, an application for cancellation of removal remains a continuing one for purposes of evaluating an alien's moral character, and that the 10-year period during which good moral character must be established ends with the entry of a final administrative decision."); Rodriguez-Avalos v. Holder, 788 F.3d 444, 455 (5th Cir. 2015)

above, the INA provides many additional criminal activities—aside from convictions for crimes listed in INA §§ 212(a)(2) and 237(a)(2)—that would preclude a finding of good moral character.[85]

Voluntary Departure

INA § 240B authorizes relevant immigration authorities to allow an otherwise removable alien to voluntarily depart the United States at his own expense within 60 to 120 days of being granted that permission, instead of being formally removed by the government.[86] Voluntary departure is sometimes viewed as a quid pro quo: The government benefits by avoiding the costs of formal removal and, in exchange, the alien may depart to any country of his choosing at any time within the statutory period, while also avoiding bars to reentry that attach to a formal order of removal.[87]

There are two forms of voluntary departure. First, an alien may be granted voluntary departure instead of being subject to formal removal proceedings or before those proceedings are completed.[88] The INA bars voluntary departure for an alien deportable on account of being convicted

---

(deferring to the BIA's interpretation of the good moral character requirement); Duron-Ortiz v. Holder, 698 F.3d 523, 527-28 (7th Cir. 2012) (same).

[85] 8 U.S.C. § 1101(f). A non-LPR alien applying for cancellation of removal as a battered spouse or child has to show good moral character for at least three years immediately preceding the date of the application. *Id.* § 1229b(b)(2)(A)(iii). Notably, for a battered spouse or child seeking cancellation, an act or conviction that does not otherwise bar the alien from relief will not foreclose a finding of good moral character if the Attorney General determines that the act or conviction "was connected to the alien's having been battered or subjected to extreme cruelty" and that a waiver is otherwise warranted. *Id.* § 1229b(b)(2)(C).

[86] *Id.* § 1229c(a)(1), (a)(2)(A), (b)(1), (b)(2). If the alien fails to depart within the sixty-day period, the alien will be ineligible for certain forms of relief for ten years. *Id.* § 1229c(d)(1). An exception exists for aliens seeking to exercise their statutory right to file a motion to reopen the removal proceedings. *Id.* § 1229a(c)(7); Dada v. Mukasey, 554 U.S. 1, 5-6 (2008). In that case, the alien may withdraw the motion for voluntary departure within the sixty days to pursue the motion to reopen. *Dada,* 554 U.S. at 5-6.

[87] 8 U.S.C. § 1229c(a)(1), (a)(2); *see also* David S. Rubenstein, *Restoring the Quid Pro Quo of Voluntary Departure,* 44 HARV. J. ON LEGIS. 1, 1-2 (2007).

[88] 8 U.S.C. § 1229c(a)(1). An arriving alien seeking admission into the United States is not eligible for this form of voluntary departure. *Id.* § 1229c(a)(4).

of an aggravated felony or under the terror-related grounds of INA § 237(a)(4)(B).[89]

Alternatively, an alien may be granted voluntary departure at the conclusion of removal proceedings.[90] To qualify for this form of voluntary departure, the alien must, among other things, (1) have been a person of good moral character for at least five years immediately preceding the application for voluntary departure and (2) not have committed any aggravated felony.[91]

Withholding of Removal

INA § 241(b)(3) bars DHS from removing an alien to a country if the alien's life or freedom would be threatened because of the alien's race, religion, nationality, membership in a particular social group, or political opinion (i.e., a protected ground).[92] Unlike the forms of relief discussed above, withholding of removal is mandatory if an immigration judge[93] determines that the alien is eligible. To obtain this relief, the alien must establish a "clear probability that his life or freedom will be threatened upon return to his country" (i.e., that "it appears more likely than not that he will suffer persecution if removed").[94]

---

[89] *Id.* § 1229c(a)(1). EOIR regulations are somewhat more stringent, precluding the granting of voluntary departure to aliens described in any of the security-related grounds found in INA § 237(a)(4), not simply those concerning terrorism. 8 C.F.R. § 1240.36(b)(1)(i)(E).

[90] 8 U.S.C. § 1229c(b)(1).

[91] *Id. See also* Griffiths v. INS, 243 F.3d 45, 56 (1st Cir. 2001) (ruling that alien must show good moral character for 5 year period "immediately preceding" his *application* for voluntary departure, noting that it is "immaterial" whether the alien accrued five years of good moral character while his removal proceedings were pending).

[92] 8 U.S.C. § 1231(b)(3).

[93] Applications for withholding of removal are typically considered only in removal proceedings before an immigration judge. 8 C.F.R. §§ 208.16(a), 1208.16(a).

[94] Lozano-Zuniga v. Lynch, 832 F.3d 822, 826-27 (7th Cir. 2016); *see also* INS v. Stevic, 467 U.S. 407, 413 (1984) (analyzing the former INA § 243(h) governing withholding of removal); Cambara-Cambara v. Lynch, 837 F.3d 822, 824 (8th Cir. 2016); Hernandez-Lima v. Lynch, 836 F.3d 109, 113 (1st Cir. 2016); Gonzalez v. U.S. Attorney Gen., 820 F.3d 399, 403 (11th Cir. 2016); Htun v. Lynch, 818 F.3d 1111, 1121 (10th Cir. 2016); Zheng v. Lynch, 819 F.3d 287, 294 (6th Cir. 2016); Sesay v. Attorney Gen. of U.S., 787 F.3d 215, 219 (3d Cir. 2015); Hernandez-Avalos v. Lynch, 784 F.3d 944, 948 n.4 (4th Cir. 2015).

Certain conduct renders an alien ineligible to obtain withholding of removal. Proscribed conduct includes not only the commission of certain crimes, but also activity that, while not clearly identified as a criminal offense (e.g., the commission of genocide), is typically subject to criminal sanction. An alien is ineligible for withholding of removal, however, if, among other things, the alien

- participated in Nazi persecution, genocide, or the commission of any act of torture or extrajudicial killing;[95]
- ordered, incited, assisted, or otherwise participated in the persecution of an individual on account of a protected ground;[96]
- is "a danger to the community of the United States" as a result of having been convicted of "a particularly serious crime";[97]
- committed a serious nonpolitical crime outside the United States before arriving in the United States;[98]
- or is otherwise a danger to the security of the United States.[99]

An alien is considered to have committed a "particularly serious crime" if, among other things, the alien has been convicted of an aggravated felony (or felonies) for which the aggregate term of imprisonment is at least five years.[100] However, the Attorney General is authorized to determine, on a case-by-case basis, that an alien has been convicted of a particularly serious crime regardless of the length of sentence imposed for an offense.[101]

---

[95] 8 U.S.C. §§ 1231(b)(3)(B), 1227(a)(4)(D).

[96] *Id.* § 1231(b)(3)(B)(i).

[97] *Id.* § 1231(b)(3)(B)(ii).

[98] *Id.* § 1231(b)(3)(B)(iii).

[99] *Id.* § 1231(b)(3)(B)(iv). The Attorney General has reasonable grounds to believe an alien is a danger to the security of the United States if the alien has participated in terrorist activities or has been associated with a terrorist organization. 8 U.S.C. §§ 1182(a)(3)(B), 1182(a)(3)(F), 1227(a)(4)(B), 1231(b)(3)(B).

[100] *Id.* § 1231(b)(3)(B).

[101] *Id.* The BIA has held that, under this catch-all provision, the Attorney General is not limited to considering aggravated felony offenses, and may designate other offenses (including non-aggravated felonies) as particular serious crimes through case-by-case adjudication. Matter of N-A-M-, 24 I. & N. Dec. 336, 338-41 (BIA 2007). Several federal appellate courts have adopted this interpretation. *See* Flores v. Holder, 779 F.3d 159, 167 (2d Cir. 2015); Delgado

Convention against Torture

An alien who fears torture in the country of his removal may apply for protection under the Convention against Torture (CAT).[102] There are two forms of CAT protection: withholding of removal and deferral of removal.[103] To qualify for CAT-based relief, an alien must show that it is more likely than not that he would be tortured by the government or a person acting with the consent or acquiescence of that government in the country of removal.[104] If the Attorney General[105] determines that the alien has met that burden, the alien may not be removed to the country of removal, but DHS may still remove the alien to a different country where he would not more likely than not face torture.[106]

An alien who establishes eligibility for withholding of removal under CAT may not be afforded its protection if he falls within one of the criminal-related grounds that bar applications for withholding of removal under INA § 241(b)(3).[107] Nevertheless, deferral of removal under CAT is available to *all aliens* who would likely face torture if removed to a particular country, regardless of whether they have been convicted of a crime.[108] Unlike withholding of removal under CAT, deferral of removal is a more temporary form of protection that may be terminated if (1) DHS

---

v. Holder, 648 F.3d 1095, 1105 (9th Cir. 2011); Gao v. Holder, 595 F.3d 549, 555 (4th Cir. 2010); N-A-M v. Holder, 587 F.3d 1052, 1056 (10th Cir. 2009); Ali v. Achim, 468 F.3d 462, 470 (7th Cir. 2006). *But see* Alaka v. Att'y Gen. of the United States, 456 F.3d 88, 105 (3d Cir. 2006) (holding that an offense must be an aggravated felony in order to qualify as a "particularly serious crime"). In determining on a case-by-case basis whether an offense is a "particularly serious crime," the Attorney General considers "the nature of the conviction, the type of sentence imposed, and the circumstances and underlying facts of the conviction." *Matter of N-A-M-*, 24 I. & N. Dec. at 342.

102 *See* Foreign Affairs Reform and Restructuring Act of 1998, P.L. 105-277, § 2242, 112 Stat. 2681, 2681-821 (1998) (implementing the United Nations Convention Against Torture and Other Cruel, Inhuman or Degrading Treatment or Punishment).

103 8 C.F.R. §§ 1208.16(c), 1208.17(a).

104 *Id.* §§ 1208.16(c)(2), 1208.18(a)(1).

105 CAT protection claims are typically considered only in removal proceedings before an immigration judge. *Id.* §§ 208.16(a), 1208.16(a).

106 *Id.* §§ 1208.16(c)(4), (f). *See* Huang v. Ashcroft, 390 F.3d 1118, 1121 n. 2 (9th Cir. 2004) ("[N]either withholding nor deferral of removal prevents the government from removing an alien to a third country other than the country to which removal was withheld or deferred").

107 8 U.S.C. § 1231(b)(3)(B); 8 C.F.R. §§ 1208.16(c)(4), (d)(2).

108 8 C.F.R. §§ 1208.16(c)(4), 1208.17(a).

produces evidence that the alien might not be tortured, and, following a hearing, the alien fails to meet his burden of proving that he likely faces torture; or (2) U.S. authorities obtain adequate assurances from the government of the country of removal that the alien would not be tortured.[109]

Asylum

INA § 208 allows aliens to apply for asylum within one year of entering the United States, regardless of the alien's immigration status.[110] Once in the United States, an alien may affirmatively apply for asylum with USCIS, or, alternatively, the alien may defensively apply for asylum as a form of relief from removal after removal proceedings have been initiated.[111] An alien may be eligible for asylum if he is unable or unwilling to return to his country because of past persecution or a well-founded fear of future persecution on account of race, religion, nationality, political opinion, or membership in a particular social group.[112] In other words, the Attorney General or DHS has the discretion to grant an alien asylum if the alien can establish that he suffered past persecution in his home country or has a well-founded fear of future persecution in that country on account of belonging to a protected group.[113] The well-founded fear standard for asylum is less demanding than the clear probability standard for withholding of removal.[114]

---

[109] *Id.* §§ 1208.17(d), (f).

[110] 8 U.S.C. § 1158(a)(1), (a)(2)(B). An asylum applicant may file his application more than one year after arriving in the United States if he establishes (1) changed circumstances materially affecting his eligibility for asylum, or (2) extraordinary circumstances relating to the delay in timely filing the application. *Id.* § 1158(a)(2)(D); 8 C.F.R. § 208.4(a)(4), (5).

[111] *See* 8 C.F.R. § 208.2; Regina Germain, *Seeking Refuge: The U.S. Asylum Process,* 35-OCT COLO. LAW. 71, 74-75 (2006). Applying for asylum is different from applying for refugee status, which occurs *before* the alien arrives in the United States. For more information on the U.S. refugee program and policies, see CRS Report RL31269, *Refugee Admissions and Resettlement Policy*, by Andorra Bruno.

[112] 8 U.S.C. §§ 1101(a)(42)(A), 1158(b)(1).

[113] *Id.* § 1158(b)(1)(A); Legal v. Lynch, 838 F.3d 51, 54 (1st Cir. 2016).

[114] *See* Tang v. Lynch, 840 F.3d 176, 183 (4th Cir. 2016); Gaye v. Lynch, 788 F.3d 519, 533 (6th Cir. 2015); RodasOrellana v. Holder, 780 F.3d 982, 986-87 (10th Cir. 2015); Vanegas-Ramirez v. Holder, 768 F.3d 226, 237 (2d Cir. 2014).

Certain criminal activity may preclude an alien from receiving a grant of asylum. As in withholding of removal, asylum may not be granted to an alien who

1. is a danger to the United States community because of a conviction for a particularly serious crime;[115]
2. has committed a serious nonpolitical crime outside the United States before arriving in the country;[116]
3. has participated in the persecution of a person in a protected group;[117]
4. has engaged in or is associated with terrorist activities;[118]
5. is otherwise a danger to the security of the United States.[119]

Unlike withholding of removal, a conviction for *any* aggravated felony is considered a particularly serious crime in asylum determinations, regardless of the term of criminal incarceration.[120]

Refugee Status

Under INA § 207, an alien may apply for refugee status from outside the United States.[121] As with asylum, a person seeking refugee status must show that he suffered past persecution or has a well-founded fear of future persecution on account of his race, religion, nationality, membership in a

---

[115] 8 U.S.C. § 1158(b)(2)(A)(ii).
[116] *Id.* § 1158(b)(2)(A)(iii).
[117] *Id.* § 1158(b)(2)(A)(i).
[118] *Id.* § 1158(b)(2)(A)(v).
[119] *Id.* § 1158(b)(2)(A)(iv).
[120] *Id.* § 1158(b)(2)(B)(i). In addition, for purposes of asylum, additional crimes may be defined as "particularly serious crimes" or "serious nonpolitical crimes" by regulation. 8 U.S.C. § 1158(b)(2)(B)(ii). Further, courts have held that the Attorney General may designate a specific offense as a "particularly serious crime" through case-by-case adjudication. *See* Delgado v. Holder, 648 F.3d 1095, 11057 (9th Cir. 2011); Gao v. Holder, 595 F.3d 549, 556-57 (4th Cir. 2010); Nethagani v. Mukasey, 532 F.3d 150, 156 (2d Cir. 2008); Ali v. Achim, 468 F.3d 462, 469 (7th Cir. 2006).
[121] 8 U.S.C. § 1157(c)(1).

particular social group, or political opinion.[122] DHS has the discretion to admit a refugee if he (1) has not been firmly resettled in another country, (2) is determined to be "of special humanitarian concern to the United States," and (3) is generally admissible as an immigrant.[123] Certain inadmissibility grounds, however, do not apply to an alien seeking admission as a refugee, and DHS may waive most grounds of inadmissibility under INA § 212, including those related to criminal offenses (except for drug trafficking offenses) if the agency determines that a waiver is warranted "for humanitarian purposes, to assure family unity, or when it is otherwise in the public interest."[124]

An alien who has been admitted as a refugee may adjust to LPR status after being physically present in the United States for at least one year.[125] In adjudicating the adjustment application of a refugee, the relevant immigration authorities must determine whether, among other things, the alien is admissible for permanent residence.[126] At this stage, DHS has the authority to waive most criminal grounds of inadmissibility—other than drug trafficking—under the same standard that applies to the inadmissibility waivers for refugees seeking admission (humanitarian purposes, family unity, or public interest).[127]

---

[122] *Id.* § 1101(a)(42).

[123] *Id.* § 1157(c)(1).

[124] *Id.* § 1157(c)(3). In addition, waivers may not be granted to refugee applicants who are inadmissible on the basis of security and related grounds (e.g., seeking to enter the United States to engage in espionage or any other unlawful activity); terrorist activities; foreign policy concerns; or participation in Nazi persecution, genocide, or acts of torture or extrajudicial killings. *Id.* (referencing 8 U.S.C. § 1182(a)(2)(C), (a)(3)(A), (a)(3)(B), (a)(3)(C), (a)(3)(E)).

[125] *Id.* § 1159(a). Likewise, an alien who has been granted asylum in the United States may seek adjustment to LPR status one year after being granted asylum. *Id.* § 1159(b).

[126] *Id.* §§ 1159(a)(2), 1159(b)(5).

[127] *Id.* § 1159(c). As with refugee admissions under INA § 1157(c)(3), a waiver is also unavailable to aliens who are inadmissible on security and related grounds, terrorist grounds, foreign policy grounds, or on the basis of Nazi persecution, genocide, or the commission of any act of torture or extrajudicial killing. *Id.* (referencing 8 U.S.C. §§ 1182(a)(2)(C), (a)(3)(A), (a)(3)(B), (a)(3)(C), (a)(3)(E)).

Adjustment of Status

Both the DHS Secretary and the Attorney General have the discretion to adjust the status of certain nonimmigrants and other categories of aliens if certain criteria are met.[128] The primary statute governing adjustment of status is INA § 245. But nearly all inadmissibility grounds— including all of the criminal grounds listed in INA § 212(a)(2)—preclude an alien from adjusting status under that section.[129] However, as discussed previously, INA § 212(h) grants the Attorney General and the DHS Secretary discretion to waive the application of specified criminal inadmissibility grounds in certain circumstances.[130] Therefore, the presence of a criminal ground of inadmissibility does not always foreclose an alien from adjusting status.

Temporary Protected Status

Under INA § 244, the Attorney General or DHS may grant Temporary Protected Status (TPS) relief to certain aliens from designated countries that are (1) afflicted with ongoing armed conflict posing a serious threat to the nationals of those countries; (2) disrupted by natural disasters or an epidemic; or (3) otherwise experiencing "extraordinary and temporary

---

[128] INA §§ 245(a), 245(i); 8 U.S.C. §§ 1255(a), 1255(i).

[129] 8 U.S.C. §§ 1255(a), 1255(i); *see also id.* § 1182(a) (grounds of inadmissibility).

[130] *Id.* § 1182(h); *see also,* Palma-Martinez v. Lynch, 785 F.3d 1147, 1149 (7th Cir. 2015) ("Under INA § 212(h) the Attorney General may waive the ground of inadmissibility applicable to Palma–Martinez (the crime of moral turpitude) if the denial of admission would result in extreme hardship to a lawfully resident family member and he is applying or reapplying for a visa, admission, or an adjustment of status."); Roberts v. Holder, 745 F.3d 928, 931 (8th Cir. 2014) ("As the BIA noted, Roberts must receive a § 1182(h) waiver of his aggravated felony conviction before he may adjust his status."). But as previously discussed, no waiver is available for an alien convicted of murder or criminal acts involving torture, or an attempt or conspiracy to commit such crimes; nor is a waiver available for an alien who has previously been admitted as an LPR if, since the date of admission, the alien was convicted of an aggravated felony or the alien has not lawfully resided continuously in the United States for at least seven years immediately preceding the commencement of removal proceedings against the alien. 8 U.S.C. § 1182(h).

conditions in the foreign state that prevent aliens who are nationals of the state from returning to the state in safety."[131]

However, certain criminal activity can make an alien ineligible to receive TPS relief. Although the relevant immigration authorities have the discretion to waive most inadmissibility grounds in granting TPS relief,[132] they may not waive inadmissibility for aliens who have

- committed a crime involving moral turpitude other than a purely political offense (including an attempt or conspiracy to commit such a crime);[133]
- violated any federal, state, or foreign drug law (including an attempt or conspiracy to commit such a violation);
- engaged in drug trafficking (other than a single offense of simple possession of 30 grams or less of marijuana); or
- been convicted of two or more offenses (other than purely political offenses) for which the aggregate sentences were five or more years of imprisonment.[134]

In addition to those nonwaivable criminal inadmissibility grounds, the relevant immigration authorities may not grant TPS relief to an alien who (1) has been convicted of any felony or two or more misdemeanors

---

[131] 8 U.S.C. § 1254a(a), (b). For more information on TPS, including the designated countries from which aliens may receive TPS, see CRS Report RS20844, *Temporary Protected Status: Overview and Current Issues*, by Jill H. Wilson.

[132] 8 U.S.C. § 1254a(c)(2)(A)(ii). A waiver may be granted "for humanitarian purposes, to assure family unity, or when it is otherwise in the public interest." *Id.*

[133] Exceptions exist for an alien who committed only one crime if (1) the crime was committed before the alien turned eighteen and the crime was committed (and the alien released from confinement) more than five years before applying for admission; or (2) the maximum penalty possible for the crime committed did not exceed more than one year of imprisonment and, if convicted, the alien was not sentenced to a term of imprisonment of more than six months. *Id.* § 1182(a)(2)(A)(ii).

[134] *Id.* § 1254a(c)(2)(A)(iii). Further, a TPS relief applicant cannot receive a waiver of inadmissibility based on security and related grounds, terrorist activities, and adverse foreign policy reasons; or for participation in Nazi persecution, genocide, and acts of torture or extrajudicial killings. *Id.* § 1254a(c)(2)(A)(iii)(III).

committed in the United States; or (2) falls within the categories of aliens who are statutorily ineligible for asylum, as described above.[135]

NATURALIZATION: IMPACT OF CRIMINAL ACTIVITY

In general, LPRs may naturalize as U.S. citizens after residing continuously in the United States for five years and satisfying other qualifications.[136] But to be eligible to naturalize, an LPR (among other things) must have been a person of good moral character for at least five years preceding his application for naturalization.[137] As discussed above, the INA provides a nonexhaustive list of criminal activity that—if committed during the relevant period—would preclude a finding of good moral character and thus bar an LPR from naturalizing.[138] However, some types of criminal activity permanently bar an alien from showing good moral character if they were committed at any time, including a conviction for an aggravated felony.[139]

---

[135] *Id.* § 1254a(c)(2)(B).

[136] *Id.* § 1427(a).

[137] *Id.* Under DHS regulations, the agency may consider conduct and acts that occurred before the five-year period if the applicant's conduct during the statutory period "does not reflect that there has been reform of character from an earlier period or if the earlier conduct and acts appear relevant to a determination of the applicant's present moral character." 8 C.F.R. § 316.10(a)(2). Further, the statutory period for good moral character includes the period between the examination of the applicant and the administration of the oath of allegiance. *Id.* § 316.10(a)(1).

[138] *See supra* section, "Crimes Affecting Good Moral Character." In addition, the DHS regulations include a separate list of enumerated criminal activity that would preclude a showing of good moral character for naturalization applicants, some of which overlap the conduct referenced in INA § 1101(f). *See* 8 C.F.R. § 316.10(b).

[139] *See* 8 U.S.C. § 1101(f)(8) (aggravated felony), (f)(9) (Nazi persecution, genocide, acts of torture or extrajudicial killings, or severe violations of religious freedom); 8 C.F.R. § 316.10(b)(1)(i) (murder). For naturalization applicants, an aggravated felony will bar a good moral character finding if the conviction occurred on or after November 29, 1990. 8 C.F.R. § 316.10(b)(1)(ii). Reviewing courts have held that an aggravated felony conviction will preclude a showing of good moral character even if the crime was not considered an aggravated felony at the time of the conviction, or the alien had previously been granted discretionary relief from deportation. *See* Alocozy v. U.S. Citizenship and Immigration Servs., 704 F.3d 795, 797-98 (9th Cir. 2012) ("There is nothing in this record even remotely suggesting that when a removable alien is granted discretionary relief in the form of a waiver of deportation, the Government waives any objection based on the ground for which he was removable to his naturalization as a citizen"); Chan v. Gantner, 464 F.3d 289, 294

THE INTERSECTION OF CRIMINAL LAW AND IMMIGRATION: SELECT LEGAL ISSUES

Although immigration proceedings are civil matters, criminal proceedings are often linked to immigration proceedings because of the many immigration consequences of criminal activity. This section examines select legal issues related to criminal proceedings as they relate to immigration law, including the constitutional obligations of criminal attorneys representing alien defendants, what constitutes a "conviction" under the INA, and how adjudicatory bodies determine when a criminal conviction will trigger immigration consequences.

The Duty to Inform about Immigration Consequences from a Criminal Conviction

Criminal proceedings involving aliens may carry additional consequences for an alien defendant beyond criminal sanction, including potentially rendering the alien subject to removal from the country. Immigration proceedings are civil, not criminal, and so aliens facing removal charges have no Sixth Amendment right to counsel.[140] But aliens

(2d Cir. 2006) ("We agree with the District Court that no authority supports the proposition that the government is foreclosed by a waiver of deportation from considering a conviction when determining the unrelated question of fitness for naturalization."); Dar v. Olivares, 956 F. Supp. 2d 1287, 1293-99 (N.D. Okla. 2013) (retroactively applying good moral character bar to alien's 1994 attempted rape conviction even though rape was not added to the list of aggravated felonies until 1996, and rejecting claim that previous grant of relief under former INA § 212(c) barred USCIS from applying the good moral character bar). However, for naturalization applicants with aggravated felony and murder convictions, the good moral character bar does not apply if the alien "has received a full and unconditional pardon prior to the beginning of the statutory period," and the alien "demonstrates that reformation and rehabilitation occurred prior to the beginning of the statutory period." 8 C.F.R. § 316.10(c)(2)(i).

[140] *See* Zambrano-Reyes v. Holder, 725 F.3d 744, 750 (7th Cir. 2013); Contreras v. Attorney Gen. of U.S., 665 F.3d 578, 584 (3d Cir. 2012); Lara-Torres v. Ashcroft, 383 F.3d 968, 973 (9th Cir. 2004). The federal circuit courts are divided over whether the due process guarantees in the Fifth Amendment provide aliens with a right to effective assistance of counsel during their removal proceedings. *See Contreras,* 665 F.3d at 584 & n.3 (collecting cases). And though some courts have held that aliens have a Fifth Amendment right to effective

facing criminal charges in federal and state court *do* have a constitutional right to effective assistance of counsel.[141] This right applies throughout all "critical" stages of criminal proceedings, including pretrial stages when the defendant must make crucial decisions, like whether to plead guilty.[142] In *Padilla v. Kentucky,* the Supreme Court held that the Sixth Amendment guarantee to effective counsel requires a lawyer representing an alien in criminal proceedings to advise the alien client if the offense to which the alien is pleading guilty could result in removal from the United States.[143] The Court noted that under current immigration law, removal is "nearly an automatic result for a broad class of noncitizen offenders."[144] Thus, the Court reasoned, "[t]he importance of accurate legal advice for noncitizens accused of crimes has never been more important."[145] Recognizing that "[i]mmigration law can be complex, and ... some members of the bar who represent clients facing criminal charges ... may not be well versed in it," the Court added that "[w]hen the law is not succinct and straightforward ... a criminal defense attorney need do no more than advise a noncitizen client that pending criminal charges may carry a risk of adverse immigration consequences."[146] But when the INA is clear about the deportation

---

representation during their removal proceedings, there is no right to government *appointed* counsel in those proceedings. *See* United States v. Loaisiga, 104 F.3d 484, 485 (1st Cir. 1997) ("There is no constitutional right to appointed counsel in a deportation proceeding. But Congress has provided that a respondent may obtain his own counsel."); 8 U.S.C. § 1362 (providing that aliens in removal proceedings "shall have the privilege of being represented (at no expense to the Government) by such counsel, authorized to practice in such proceedings, as he shall choose").

141 U.S. CONST., amend. VI ("In all criminal prosecutions, the accused shall enjoy the right ... to have the assistance of counsel for his defense."); Gideon v. Wainwright, 372 U.S. 335, 342 (1963) ("[A] provision of the Bill of Rights which is fundamental and essential to a fair trial," like the Sixth Amendment, "is made obligatory upon the States by the Fourteenth Amendment") (internal quotation marks omitted).

142 *See* Lafler v. Cooper, 566 U.S. 156, 165 (2012); *see also* Padilla v. Kentucky, 559 U.S. 356, 364 (2010) ("Before deciding whether to plead guilty, a defendant is entitled to the effective assistance of competent counsel.") (internal quotation marks and citations omitted); Loden v. McCarty, 778 F.3d 484, 494 (5th Cir. 2015) ("The decision to plead guilty is a critical stage of criminal proceedings.").

143 *Padilla*, 559 U.S. at 360.

144 *Id.* at 366.

145 *Id.* at 364.

146 *Id.* at 369.

consequences of a particular crime, the Court admonished, "the duty to give correct advice is equally clear."[147]

What Constitutes a Conviction?

Numerous criminal grounds for inadmissibility and deportability require the rendering of a conviction for a particular crime to be applicable. INA § 101(a)(48)(A) provides two definitions for what constitutes a conviction for INA purposes. First, INA § 101(a)(48)(A) defines a conviction as a formal judgment of guilt entered by a court.[148] Generally, in federal cases, the final judgment ordered by the district judge contains the formal judgment of guilt.[149] A state court's written judgment and sentence would qualify as well.[150] If a conviction is vacated or set aside because of substantive or procedural defects in the criminal proceedings, the conviction no longer qualifies as a "conviction" under INA § 101(a)(48)(A).[151] However, a conviction that is vacated or set aside for rehabilitative purposes[152] (e.g., under state laws that permit a judge to

---

[147] *Id.* The Supreme Court later ruled in *Chaidez v. United States* that the rule announced in *Padilla* would not be applied retroactively, meaning that the holding would not apply to aliens whose criminal convictions became final before the *Padilla* opinion was published. 568 U.S. 342 (2013).

[148] INA § 101(a)(48)(A); 8 U.S.C. § 1101(a)(48)(A).

[149] *See e.g.,* FED. R. CRIM. P. 32(k)(1); Berman v. United States, 302 U.S. 211, 212 (1937) ("Final judgment in a criminal case means sentence. The sentence is the judgment."); Planes v. Holder, 652 F.3d 991, 995 (9th Cir. 2011) ("Under the first definition, a 'conviction' for purposes of § 1101(a)(48)(A), exists once the district court enters judgment, notwithstanding the availability of an appeal as of right.").

[150] *See* United States v. Saenz-Gomez, 472 F.3d 791, 794 (10th Cir. 2007). The INA's definition of "conviction" controls regardless of how a state designates a conviction. *See, e.g.,* Gonzalez v. O'Connell, 355 F.3d 1010, 1018 (7th Cir. 2004).

[151] *See, e.g.,* Estrada v. Holder, 611 F.3d 318, 321 (7th Cir. 2010); Alim v. Gonzales, 446 F.3d 1239, 1248 (11th Cir. 2006).

[152] For example, some state laws allow a judge to expunge certain convictions for rehabilitative purposes. *See e.g.,* ARIZ. REV. STAT. ANN. § 13-907 (authorizing a judge to set aside a criminal defendant's conviction following the completion of probation or sentence, except for convictions for certain serious criminal offenses); OR. REV. STAT. ANN. § 137.225 (permitting a person to request an order setting aside a conviction for certain crimes, such as unlawful possession of a controlled substance, if three years have elapsed since the date of the conviction, and the person has fully complied with the terms of his sentence). Such laws are similar to the provisions of the Federal First Offender Act (FFOA), which permit a

expunge convictions for simple drug possession) or solely for the purpose of avoiding immigration consequences, still qualifies as a conviction under the INA.[153] The same is true for expunged convictions: INA § 101(a)(48)(A) has been interpreted to exclude expunged convictions, unless the expungement was allowed solely for rehabilitative purposes.[154]

A second definition of conviction exists for situations in which adjudication of guilt has been withheld: There is also a "conviction" if (1) a judge or jury has found the alien guilty, or the alien pleaded guilty or nolo contendere,[155] or the alien has admitted sufficient facts to be found guilty, and (2) the judge has ordered some sort of punishment, penalty, or restraint on the alien's liberty.[156] Qualifying nonconfinement judicial

---

federal judge to order first-time simple drug possession offenders to probation without entering a judgment of conviction. 18 U.S.C. § 3607(a). If the defendant successfully completes the period of probation, the judge must dismiss the proceedings against the defendant. *Id.* Additionally, if the defendant committed the relevant offense before turning twenty-one, the court—at the defendant's request—shall expunge the criminal record. *Id.* § 3607(c). A disposition of a criminal offense under the FFOA "shall not be considered a conviction for the purpose of a disqualification or a disability imposed by law upon conviction of a crime, or for any other purpose." *Id.* § 3607(b).

[153] *See, e.g.,* Rodriguez v. Att'y Gen. United States, 844 F.3d 392, 396 (3d Cir. 2016) (distinguishing between convictions vacated on the basis of substantive or procedural defects and convictions vacated for reasons "such as for rehabilitation or to allow a petitioner to avoid the immigration effects of the conviction"); Nunez-Reyes v. Holder, 646 F.3d 684, 689-90 (9th Cir. 2011) (holding that "the constitutional guarantee of equal protection does not require treating, for immigration purposes, an expunged state conviction of a drug crime the same as a federal drug conviction that has been expunged under the FFOA," and assuming, without deciding, that a conviction under the INA includes expunged state convictions) (overruling Lujan-Armendariz v. INS, 222 F.3d 728 (9th Cir. 2000)); Wellington v. Holder, 623 F.3d 115, 120 (2d Cir. 2010) (adopting BIA's interpretation that relief from a state conviction for rehabilitative purposes still qualifies as a "conviction" under the INA); Pickering v. Gonzales, 465 F.3d 263, 266 (6th Cir. 2006) (collecting cases); In re Pickering, 231 I. & N. Dec. 621, 624-25 (BIA 2003), *rev'd on other grounds*, 465 F.3d 263 (6th Cir. 2006) ("[W]e find that there is a significant distinction between convictions vacated on the basis of a procedural or substantive defect in the underlying proceedings and those vacated because of post-conviction events, such as rehabilitation or immigration hardships").

[154] *See, e.g.,* Gradiz v. Gonzales, 490 F.3d 1206, 1208 (10th Cir. 2007); *Alim*, 446 F.3d at 1249.

[155]

[156] 8 U.S.C. § 1101(a)(48)(A). This includes suspended sentences. *Id.* § 1101(a)(48)(B); Dung Phan v. Holder, 667 F.3d 448, 452 (4th Cir. 2012) ("That Phan's prison sentence was suspended in favor of probation is irrelevant because the conditions of probation, backed by the specter of a suspended prison sentence, are most certainly a form of punishment or penalty and a restraint on one's liberty").

orders can include probation[157] and restitution.[158] Thus, even for crimes requiring a conviction for immigration consequences to attach, there need not be, necessarily, a formal judgment of guilt or a sentence of imprisonment imposed.[159]

Approaches to Determine Whether a Criminal Conviction Triggers Immigration Consequences

Although the INA, on some occasions, expressly identifies conduct referenced in a criminal statute that would render an alien removable or ineligible for certain relief, in many instances the INA simply refers to a general category of criminal behavior that carries immigration consequences.[160] Accordingly, reviewing courts and immigration authorities must sometimes determine whether the range of conduct covered by an alien's criminal conviction falls within the scope of criminal conduct proscribed by the INA.

The Supreme Court has instructed that, to make such a determination, reviewing courts should apply a "categorical approach," in which they compare the elements of the offense of conviction to the generic federal definition of the predicate crime.[161] Under this approach, reviewing courts

---

[157] *See* Reyes v. Lynch, 834 F.3d 1104, 1108 (9th Cir. 2016) (concluding that order of probation included a limitation on freedom to associate with certain categories of persons and thus restrains liberty); Jeff Joseph, *Immigration Consequences of Criminal Pleas & Convictions,* 35-OCT COLO. LAW. 55, 56 (2006).

[158] *See* De Vega v. Gonzalez, 503 F.3d 45, 49 (1st Cir. 2007).

[159] *See* Acosta v. Ashcroft, 341 F.3d 218, 222 (3d Cir. 2003) (recognizing that, in the absence of a formal judgment of guilt, an alien will be considered to have been convicted of an offense for purposes of the INA as long as the disposition of the criminal proceeding meets the two-part test set forth in INA § 1101(a)(48)(A)).

[160] *Compare, e.g.,* 8 U.S.C. § 1101(a)(43)(D) (defining an "aggravated felony" to include "an offense described in section 1956 of Title 18 (relating to laundering of monetary instruments) or section 1957 of that title (relating to engaging in monetary transactions in property derived from specific unlawful activity) if the amount of the funds exceeded $10,000)," *with* 8 U.S.C. § 1101(a)(43)(M)(i) (defining an "aggravated felony" as an offense that "involves fraud or deceit in which the loss to the victim or victims exceeds $10,000").

[161] Moncrieffe v. Holder, 569 U.S. 184, 190 (2013); Taylor v. United States, 495 U.S. 575, 599-600 (1990).

may look only to the statutory elements of the crime of conviction, rather than the particular facts of the case, in analyzing whether the crime "categorically fits" within the corresponding federal generic offense.[162] In doing so, the courts must presume that the conviction was based on the least culpable conduct under the criminal statute.[163] If the crime of conviction "sweeps more broadly" A nolo contendere plea is one in which the defendant does not admit guilt but submits to punishment, nonetheless. *See Nolo Contendere,* Black's Law Dictionary; *Plea,* Black's Law Dictionary; Julian A. Cook, III, *Crumbs from the Master's Table: The Supreme Court, Pro Se Defendants & the Federal Guilty Plea Process,* 81 NOTRE DAME L. REV. 1895, 1938 (2006); Mark Gurevich, *Justice Dep't's Policy of Opposing Nolo Contendere Pleas: A Justification,* 6 CAL. CRIM. L. REV. 2, 5 (2004).than the generic offense identified by the INA as grounds for an alien's removal, the criminal conviction cannot serve as a basis for removal.[164]

In some cases, however, the courts may look beyond the statutory definition of a criminal offense when the statute lists multiple, alternative elements of a crime, and only some of those alternatives correspond to the generic offense identified by the INA as carrying immigration consequences.[165] Under this "modified categorical approach," courts may examine the underlying conviction documents, such as the charging papers or plea agreement, to determine which statutory elements a defendant was convicted of, and compare those elements to the federal generic offense.[166] The Supreme Court has held, though, that a court may not apply this approach merely when a statute contains a "single, indivisible set of elements" that cover "a broader swath of conduct than the relevant generic offense."[167] Instead, "[a] court may use the modified approach only to

---

[162] *Moncrieffe*, 569 U.S. at 190 (citing Gonzales v. Duenas-Alvarez, 549 U.S. 183, 186 (2007)).

[163] *Id.* at 190-91 (citing Johnson v. United States, 559 U.S. 133, 137 (2010)).

[164] Descamps v. United States, 570 U.S. 254, 261 (2013); *see also* Mathis v. United States, 136 S. Ct. 2243, 2248 (2016) (noting that if the criminal statute "covers any more conduct than the generic offense," it does not meet the generic definition, "even if the defendant's actual conduct (*i.e.*, the facts of the crime) fits within the generic offense's boundaries").

[165] *Descamps*, 570 U.S. at 260-64 (citing *Taylor*, 495 U.S. at 602).

[166] *Id.*; Shepard v. United States, 544 U.S.13, 26 (2005).

[167] *Descamps*, 570 U.S. at 258.

determine which alternative element in a *divisible* statute formed the basis of the defendant's conviction."[168]

The strict limitations of the categorical and modified categorical approaches do not apply, however, when a comparison between the criminal statute and a generic offense requires an examination of the "particular circumstances in which an offender committed the crime on a particular occasion."[169] Applying this "circumstance-specific" exception, a number of reviewing courts have held that an adjudicator may consider evidence *outside* the conviction record to determine whether a criminal conviction involved factors specified in a generic offense that are not tied to the elements of a criminal statute. For example, the courts have considered evidence as to whether a fraud offense met a $10,000 loss threshold (a monetary threshold that must be exceeded for the offense to constitute an aggravated felony under the INA), or whether a drug conviction involved the personal use of 30 grams or less of marijuana (in which case the drug conviction would not be a deportable offense).[170]

In practice, the BIA employs the categorical and modified categorical approaches to determine whether a criminal conviction meets the definition of a predicate offense for immigration purposes.[171] Following the Supreme

---

[168] *Id.* at 278 (emphasis added). In addition, the Supreme Court has held that a court may not use the modified categorical approach where a statute lists different ways of committing a *single* element of a crime (as opposed to listing multiple alternative elements of a crime), and, in doing so, the statute covers more conduct than the relevant generic offense. *Mathis*, 136 S. Ct. at 2253-54 (reasoning that the modified categorical approach may only be used to identify the elements of a crime, but not the means by which a person committed the crime).

[169] Nijhawan v. Holder, 557 U.S. 29, 38 (2009).

[170] *See e.g., id.* (whether conviction is for an offense that "involves fraud or deceit in which the loss to the victim or victims exceeds $10,000"); Rojas v. Att'y Gen. of the U.S., 728 F.3d 203, 215-16 (3d Cir. 2013) (whether an offense is one "relating to a controlled substance"); Mellouli v. Holder, 719 F.3d 995, 1001 (8th Cir. 2013) (whether conviction is a "single offense involving possession for one's own use of 30 grams or less of marijuana"); Varughese v. Holder, 629 F.3d 272, 274-75 (2d Cir. 2010) (whether conviction is a money-laundering offense where the "amount of the funds exceeded $10,000"); Bianco v. Holder, 624 F.3d 265, 270-73 (5th Cir. 2010) (whether the victim of a crime of violence had a qualifying "domestic" relationship to the offender for purposes of the "crime of domestic violence" charge).

[171] *See e.g.,* Matter of Alvarado, 26 I. & N. Dec. 895, 897 (BIA 2016); Matter of Carachuri-Rosendo, 24 I. & N. Dec. 382, 389 (BIA 2007); Matter of Puente-Salazar, 22 I. & N. Dec. 1006, 1011 (BIA 1999); Matter of Pichardo, 21 I. & N. Dec. 330, 335 (BIA 1996); Matter of Madrigal, 21 I. & N. Dec. 323, 325 (1996); Matter of Short, 20 I. & N. Dec. 136, 137-38 (BIA 1989).

Court's guidance, the BIA generally limits its analysis of criminal convictions to the statutory elements of the crime, rather than the specific facts underlying the conviction. The BIA will turn to the record of conviction only in cases in which the statute has a divisible structure that lists alternative elements of an offense, only some of which categorically match the generic offense identified by the INA as carrying immigration consequences.[172]

Previously, however, in analyzing whether a criminal conviction is a crime involving moral turpitude, the BIA adopted a less restrictive form of the categorical approach that merely examines "whether there is a 'realistic probability,' as opposed to a 'theoretical possibility,' that the statute under which the alien was convicted would be applied to reach conduct that does not involve moral turpitude."[173] Under that analysis, if the criminal statute realistically could reach conduct not involving moral turpitude, an adjudicator could look to the record of conviction as well as "any additional evidence the adjudicator determines is necessary or appropriate to resolve accurately the moral turpitude question."[174]

---

[172] *See* Matter of J-G-D-F-, 27 I. & N. Dec. 82, 83-86 (BIA 2017); Silva-Trevino III, 26 I. & N. Dec. 826, 831-33 (BIA2016); Matter of Chairez-Castrejon, 26 I. & N. Dec. 819, 820 (BIA 2016). The BIA has also recognized the "circumstance-specific" exception to the categorical approach in cases where comparing the criminal statute to a generic offense in the INA necessarily involves considering factors beyond the elements of the offense. *See* Matter of Garza-Olivares, 26 I. & N. Dec. 736, 739-40 (BIA 2016); Matter of Dominguez-Rodriguez, 26 I. & N. Dec. 408, 412 13 (BIA 2014); Matter of Davey, 26 I. & N. Dec. 37, 39 (BIA 2012); Matter of Babaisakov, 24 I. & N. Dec. 306, 322 (2007); Matter of Gertsenshteyn, 24 I. & N. Dec. 111, 115-16 (BIA 2007). Matter of Louissaint, 24 I. & N. Dec. 754, 757 (BIA 2009) (quoting *Silva-Trevino I*, 24 I. & N. Dec. at 698) (internal quotations omitted). In *Silva-Trevino I*, Attorney General Michael Mukasey, who had directed the BIA to refer its decision to him for review pursuant to 8 C.F.R. § 1003.1(h)(1)(i), established this approach for analyzing whether a criminal conviction is a crime involving moral turpitude. *Silva-Trevino I*, 24 I. & N. Dec. at 698.

[173] Matter of Louissaint, 24 I. & N. Dec. 754, 757 (BIA 2009) (quoting *Silva-Trevino I*, 24 I. & N. Dec. at 698) (internal quotations omitted). In *Silva-Trevino I*, Attorney General Michael Mukasey, who had directed the BIA to refer its decision to him for review pursuant to 8 C.F.R. § 1003.1(h)(1)(i), established this approach for analyzing whether a criminal conviction is a crime involving moral turpitude. *Silva-Trevino I*, 24 I. & N. Dec. at 698.

[174] *Matter of Louissaint*, 24 I. & N. Dec. at 757 (citing *Silva-Trevino I*, 24 I. & N. Dec. 687, 698-704 (A.G. 2008)).

Ultimately, after several reviewing courts rejected this formulation,[175] the BIA ruled that the categorical and modified categorical approaches—as outlined by the Supreme Court—are the proper methods for determining whether an alien was convicted of a crime involving moral turpitude.[176] The BIA, however, stated that it would continue using the realistic probability test when applying the categorical approach analysis; but, noting the circuit disagreement as to its appropriateness, announced that it would apply the controlling law of circuits that have expressly disavowed that approach.[177] The BIA also held that application of the modified categorical approach was limited to circumstances in which the statute is divisible and lists offense elements in the alternative.[178] And using this approach, the BIA clarified, adjudicators may look to only the record of conviction to determine which element formed the basis for the alien's conviction.[179]

Interpreting the INA Predicate Offense

In many instances Congress did not incorporate a statutory definition when defining a predicate offense that carries immigration consequences, leaving it up to the courts to carve out a generic definition. For example, the INA includes as an aggravated felony "a theft offense (including receipt of stolen property)" for which the term of imprisonment is at least

---

[175] *See* Silva-Trevino v. Holder, 742 F.3d 197 (5th Cir. 2014); Olivas-Motta v. Holder, 746 F.3d 907 (9th Cir. 2013); Prudencio v. Holder, 669 F.3d 472 (4th Cir. 2012); Fajardo v. U.S. Att'y Gen., 659 F.3d 1303 (11th Cir. 2011); Jean-Louis v. Att'y Gen. of the U.S., 582 F.3d 462 (3d Cir. 2009). Two circuits, however, deferred to the Attorney General's instructions in *Silva-Trevino I*. *See* Bobadilla v. Holder, 679 F.3d 1052 (8th Cir. 2012); Mata-Guerrero v. Holder, 627 F.3d 256 (7th Cir. 2010). Given "the variance between Attorney General Mukasey's binding opinion and the contrary controlling precedent in some circuits," as well as "intervening Supreme Court decisions that cast doubt on the continued validity of the opinion," Attorney General Eric Holder in 2015 vacated *Silva-Trevino I* and directed the BIA to develop a new uniform standard to determine whether an alien has been convicted of a crime involving moral turpitude. *Silva-Trevino II*, 26 I. & N. Dec. 550, 552-530 (A.G. 2015).

[176] *Silva-Trevino III*, 26 I. & N. Dec. 826, 830 (BIA 2016).

[177] *Id.* at 832-33.

[178] *Id.* at 833.

[179] *Id.*

one year, but does not define that phrase.[180] To fill that gap, the appellate courts have generally eschewed the more restrictive, common law definitions of "theft" or "larceny"[181] for a broader and more modern construction: The "taking of property or an exercise of control over property without consent with the criminal intent to deprive the owner of rights and benefits of ownership, even if such deprivation is less than total or permanent."[182]

In defining the scope of other undefined predicate offenses, the courts have been less consistent. For example, the INA also includes as an aggravated felony "murder, rape, or sexual abuse of a minor."[183] Until the Supreme Court's decision in *Esquivel-Quintana v. Sessions*, there was some disagreement among reviewing courts and the BIA over the scope of offenses constituting "sexual abuse of a minor" under the INA, with the BIA broadly interpreting the phrase to cover any sexually explicit conduct with a person under 18.[184] In *Esquivel-Quintana*, however, the Supreme Court construed the phrase as having a more limited scope and held that, for statutory rape offenses based solely on the age of the participants, the

---

[180] 8 U.S.C. § 1101(a)(43)(G).

[181] For example, the crime of larceny was traditionally limited to the permanent taking of property that was in another person's possession (or deemed to be in his possession). Bell v. United States, 462 U.S. 356, 358-59 (1983); Almeida v. Holder, 588 F.3d 778, 783-84 (2d Cir. 2009).

[182] *See* United States v. Medina-Torres, 703 F.3d 770, 774 (5th Cir. 2012); United States v. Venzor-Granillo, 668 F.3d 1224, 1232 (10th Cir. 2012); Ramirez-Villalpando v. Holder, 645 F.3d 1035, 1039 (9th Cir. 2011); Jaggernauth v. U.S. Att'y Gen., 432 F.3d 1346, 1353 (11th Cir. 2005); Soliman v. Gonzales, 419 F.3d 276, 283 (4th Cir. 2005); Abimbola v. Ashcroft, 378 F.3d 173, 176 (2d Cir. 2004); Hernandez-Mancilla v. INS, 246 F.3d 1002, 1009 (7th Cir. 2001).

[183] 8 U.S.C. § 1101(a)(43)(A).

[184] Matter of Esquivel-Quintana, 26 I. & N. Dec. 469, 477 (BIA 2015); Matter of V-F-D-, 23 I. & N. Dec. 859, 862 (BIA 2006); Matter of Rodriguez-Rodriguez, 22 I. & N. Dec. 991, 995-96 (BIA 1999). The Second, Third, Sixth, and Seventh Circuits have upheld the BIA's broad interpretation of "sexual abuse of a minor." *See* Esquivel-Quintana v. Lynch, 810 F.3d 1019, 1025-27 (6th Cir. 2016); Velasco-Giron v. Holder, 773 F.3d 774, 776-77 (7th Cir. 2014); Restrepo v. Att'y Gen. of the United States, 617 F.3d 787, 796 (3d Cir. 2010); Mugalli v. Ashcroft, 258 F.3d 52, 60 (2d Cir. 2001). The Ninth Circuit has held, however, that for statutory rape crimes, "sexual abuse of a minor" requires a person to knowingly engage in a sexual act (defined to involve direct physical contact) with a child under sixteen, and who is at least four years younger than the perpetrator. United States v. Medina-Villa, 567 F.3d 507, 514 (9th Cir. 2009).

term "sexual abuse of a minor" requires the age of the victim to be less than 16.[185]

Even in cases that involve interpreting an INA provision in which Congress has expressly incorporated a federal statutory provision to define a predicate offense, the courts sometimes have struggled to interpret that definition consistently. As mentioned above, INA § 101(a)(43) includes as an aggravated felony a "crime of violence" as that term is defined in 18 U.S.C. § 16, and for which the term of imprisonment is at least one year.[186] 18 U.S.C. § 16 defines a crime of violence as either (1) "an offense that has an element the use, attempted use, or threatened use of physical force against the person or property of another"; or (2) "any other offense that is a felony and that, by its nature, involves a substantial risk that physical force against the person or property of another may be used in the course of committing the offense."[187]

Initially, a question raised was whether a "crime of violence," as defined in 18 U.S.C. § 16, requires a particular *mens rea*, or mental state. Lower courts had reached varying conclusions over the state of mind that a person must possess in order to commit a crime of violence. Some courts, for example, had ruled that grossly negligent behavior was sufficient to meet the definition, whereas other courts required a showing of recklessness or specific intent.[188] Eventually, in its 2004 ruling in *Leocal v. Ashcroft*, the Supreme Court held that a crime of violence requires an

---

[185] Esquivel-Quintana v. Sessions, 137 S. Ct. 1562, 1572-73 (2017). The Supreme Court based its decision on the legal dictionary definition of the term "age of consent," the structure of the INA, and the language of similar federal and state criminal statutes that set the age of consent at sixteen. *Id.* at 1569-72. The Court left unresolved whether sexual abuse of a minor requires a particular age differential between the victim and the perpetrator, or whether the offense includes sexual intercourse involving victims over the age of 16 that is abusive because of the nature of the relationship between the participants. *Id.* at 1572.

[186] 8 U.S.C. § 1101(a)(43)(F).

[187] 18 U.S.C. § 16.

[188] *Compare* Jobson v. Ashcroft, 326 F.3d 367, 373-74 (2d Cir. 2003) (requiring intentional use of force), *and* Bazan Reyes v. INS, 256 F.3d 600, 611 (7th Cir. 2001) (same), *with* Tapia Garcia v. INS, 237 F.3d 1216, 1222-23 (10th Cir. 2001) (gross negligence), *and* United States v. Ceron-Sanchez, 222 F.3d 1169, 1172-73 (9th Cir. 2000) (recklessness causing physical injury), *and* United States. v. Chapa-Garza, 243 F.3d 921, 926-27 (5th Cir. 2001) (requiring intentional use of force).

"active employment" of force with "a higher degree of intent than negligent or merely accidental conduct."[189]

More recently, in October 2017, the Supreme Court heard oral argument in *Sessions v. Dimaya* to address the circuit split about whether the second clause in the definition of a crime of violence— "any other offense that is a felony and that, by its nature, involves a substantial risk that physical force against the person of property of another may be used in the course of committing the offense"[190]—is unconstitutionally vague.[191]

ISSUES FOR CONGRESS

Congress has repeatedly amended the INA to expand, curtail, or otherwise modify the immigration consequences of criminal conduct, and legislative proposals to alter the current framework are regularly introduced. For instance, Congress may legislate to expand or constrict criminal grounds for inadmissibility and deportability. Congress also could add or subtract crimes from those listed as aggravated felonies and clarify what crimes involve moral turpitude. Additionally, Congress could modify

---

[189] Leocal v. Ashcroft, 543 U.S. 1, 9 (2004). The Court did not address whether the reckless use of force qualified as a crime of violence. *Id.* at 13.

[190] 18 U.S.C. § 16(b).

[191] Sessions v. Dimaya, No. 15-1498, 137 S. Ct. 31 (2016); Dimaya v. Lynch, 803 F.3d 1110 (9th Cir. 2015). In *Dimaya*, the Supreme Court is reviewing the Ninth Circuit's conclusion that the clause is unconstitutionally vague in violation of the Fifth Amendment's Due Process Clause. In so holding, the Ninth Circuit had relied on the Supreme Court's ruling in *Johnson v. United States* that the Armed Career Criminal Act's (ACCA) "residual clause" defining a "violent felony" is unconstitutionally vague. *Dimaya,* 803 F.3d at 1111 (citing Johnson v. United States, 135 S. Ct. 2551 (2015)). Under the ACCA, a defendant convicted of firearm offenses in violation of 18 U.S.C. § 922(g) will face harsher punishment if that defendant has three or more previous convictions for a violent felony, which is defined to include any felony that "involves conduct that presents a serious potential risk of physical injury to another." 18 U.S.C. §§ 924(e)(1), (2)(B)(ii). In *Dimaya,* the Ninth Circuit ruled that the INA's definition of crime of violence—bearing language similar to the ACCA's residual clause—likewise is unconstitutionally vague. *Dimaya*, 803 F.3d at 1111, 1115. The Sixth, Seventh, and Tenth Circuits, applying *Johnson,* had reached the same conclusion. The Fifth Circuit, however, reached the opposite conclusion in United States v. Gonzalez-Longoria, 831 F.3d 670, 676-77 (5th Cir. 2016). For more information on the ACCA and *Johnson*, see CRS Report R41449, *Armed Career Criminal Act (18 U.S.C. 924(e)): An Overview*, by Charles Doyle.

the number of crimes that would render an alien statutorily ineligible for relief from removal or those that preclude a finding of good moral character. Further, Congress could clarify certain terminology in the INA that some courts have deemed ambiguous, like crime of moral turpitude and crime of violence. In short, given the immigration consequences that may follow from criminal activity, Congress may consider various legislative options that would modify the standards employed by the courts and relevant immigration authorities to determine whether an alien may be excluded or deported from the United States due to criminal conduct.

INDEX

A

B

C

D

E

F

G

H

I

J

L

M

N

O

P

R

U

V

W

Related Nova Publications

Career Optimism and Self-Efficacy in Immigrants

Authors: Charles P. Chen and Tara K. Kennedy

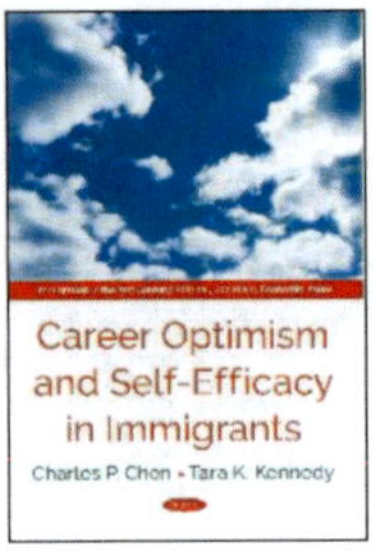

Series: Immigration in the 21st Century: Political, Social and Economic Issues

Book Description: The book presents a research study that examined the retraining and career development experiences of new and professional immigrants in Canada. The study intended to provide an in-depth perspective into the influence of immigrants' optimism and self-efficacy on their retraining and career development experiences.

Softcover ISBN: 978-1-63485-430-6
Retail Price: $82

Migrants: Public Attitudes, Challenges and Policy Implications

Editor: Stuart Rodriquez

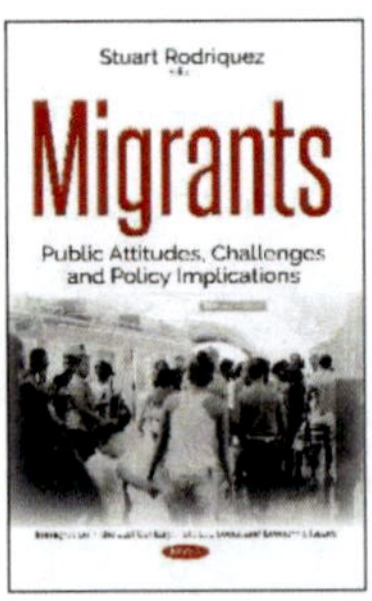

Series: Immigration in the 21st Century: Political, Social and Economic Issues

Book Description: Chapter One reviews the interplay between the phenomenon of migration and corresponding response from health care establishments, and analyzes the challenges posed by migrant crises and its implications for the future of public healthcare.

Hardcover ISBN: 978-1-53612-026-4
Retail Price: $195

To see a complete list of Nova publications, please visit our website at www.novapublishers.com